The Basic Treaty and the Evolution of East-West German Relations

Westview Special Studies

The concept of Westview Special Studies is a response to the continuing crisis in academic and informational publishing. Library budgets are being diverted from the purchase of books and used for data banks, computers, micromedia, and other methods of information retrieval. Interlibrary loan structures further reduce the edition sizes required to satisfy the needs of the scholarly community. Economic pressures on university presses and the few private scholarly publishing companies have greatly limited the capacity of the industry to properly serve the academic and research communities. As a result, many manuscripts dealing with important subjects, often representing the highest level of scholarship, are no longer economically viable publishing projects--or, if accepted for publication, are typically subject to lead times ranging from one to three years.

Westview Special Studies are our practical solution to the problem. As always, the selection criteria include the importance of the subject, the work's contribution to scholarship, and its insight, originality of thought, and excellence of exposition. We accept manuscripts in camera-ready form, typed, set, and word processed according to specifications laid out in our comprehensive manual, which contains straightforward instructions and sample pages. The responsibility for editing and proofreading lies with the author or sponsoring institution, but our editorial staff is always available to answer questions and provide guidance.

The result is a book printed on acid-free paper and bound in sturdy, library-quality soft covers. We manufacture these books ourselves using equipment that does not require a lengthy make-ready process and that allows us to publish first editions of 300 to 1000 copies and to reprint even smaller quantities as needed. Thus, we can produce Special Studies quickly and can keep even very specialized books in print as long as there is a demand for them.

About the Book and Author

The Basic Treaty between the Federal Republic of Germany (FRG) and the German Democratic Republic (GDR) for the first time provided a framework for the exchange of permanent missions and laid the foundation for expanded bilateral cooperation between the two German states. This book charts the progress of inner-German relations in the formative years of the 1970's and explains how the revival of the German question in the 1980's followed from striking changes in East and West German priorities and policies. Dr. Plock assesses the degree of practical cooperation in such areas as trade, travel, and the exchange of media representatives and also indentifies the impact of Soviet interests on the inner-German relationship.

Dr. Plock notes that despite a clear upgrading in FRG-GDR relations under Chancellors Willy Brandt and Helmut Schmidt, inner-German progress continues to be hostage to the overall East-West political and security climate. Yet the author sees a bipartisan West German commitment to partnership with the GDR as well as East Berlin's pragmatic approach to the relationship as stabilizing features of the European political landscape, even though the goals of future "Deutschlandpolitik" will continue to remain ill-defined.

Ernest D. Plock received his Ph.D. in international studies from The American University, Washington, D.C., where he was instructor of several world politics courses and a lecturer on West German domestic and foreign policy. Dr. Plock is currently employed by the International Trade Administration of the U.S. Department of Commerce.

The Basic Treaty
and the Evolution
of East-West German Relations

Ernest D. Plock

Foreword by Josef Joffe

Westview Press / Boulder and London

Westview Special Studies in International Relations

Copyright © 1986 by Westview Press, Inc.

Published in 1986 in the United States of America by Westview Press, Inc.;
Frederick A. Praeger, Publisher; 5500 Central Avenue, Boulder, Colorado 80301

Library of Congress Cataloging in Publication Data
Plock, Ernest D.
   The basic treaty and the evolution of East-West German
relations.

   (Westview special studies in international relations)
   Bibliography: p.
   Includes index.
   1. Germany (West)--Foreign relations--Germany (East)
2. Germany (East)--Foreign relations--Germany (West)
3. World politics--1945-   . I. Title. II. Series.
DD258.85.G35P56   1986   327.430431   85-31524
ISBN 0-8133-7142-2

Printed and bound in the United States of America

  The paper used in this publication meets the minimum requirements
        of the American National Standard for Permanence of Paper for
        Printed Library Materials Z39.48--1984.

10 9 8 7 6 5 4 3 2 1

Contents

Acknowledgments

Sustaining work on the following pages called for support and assistance at a variety of levels. I hope that I have fully acknowledged those who offered ideas, provided useful criticisms, and extended moral support for the undertaking.

Central to this examination of inner-German relations was William C. Cromwell, to whom I am indebted not only for stimulating the initial path of inquiry but for travelling the extra mile in reviewing the text and providing practical suggestions. Special thanks go to Josef Joffe, who devoted valuable time to critiquing the original manuscript and in his foreword placed the two German states' relations in their proper historical context. Steven I. Levine's solicitude and encouragement were also priceless ingredients over the long haul. My own interest in the subject was greatly sustained by discussions with Bruno F. Steinbruckner and his intuitive understanding of Germany past and present, while Margrit Krewson's readiness to talk was a beacon in difficult times.

Pursuing research on this side of the Atlantic would have been quite handicapped without the help of Dr. Gisela Ruess of the Ministry for Inner-German Relations in Bonn, who answered all requests completely and without delay. In addition, Tom Southall's eagerness to help in the preparation of the manuscript and retrieval of information was invaluable, as was the assistance of Robert L. Beckman. To Carmine D'Aloisio, M. Andre Dumont, Joe Keddell, Mohammed Kharabi, Juliette G. Tahar, and Thomas Alexander Vadakevetil, I am grateful for preventing my descent into total self-imposed isolation. Proper credit should go to Eugene V. and Ruth Plock, as well as Bill, Carl, Dwight, and Gary Plock; Bruce and Elaine Tasch were also welcome companions, while my good friend Brooke Beyerle stayed the course with detachment and irreverence.

Finally, this study was greatly aided by several others well acquainted with the complexities of German politics. Dr. Gerhard Wettig, in particular, faithfully critiqued the historical sections of the book and provided a wealth of factual information. Numerous useful comments by F. Gunther Eyck and Leroy Miller influenced my outlook on the subject. It was my especially good fortune to make the acquaintance of German Television Network ARD's Fritz Pleitgen, who kindly consented to several interviews that gave a human perspective to complex political developments.

Ernest D. Plock
Washington, D.C.

Foreword

Among the most important countries of Western Europe, postwar Germany is one of the most underresearched. For a long time after World War II, political science outside of Germany, notably in the United States, was heavily concentrated on the "pathology" of Germany. The premier object of investigation was the past--the phenomenon of Nazi totalitarianism, its structures, functions and causal antecedents. Thus we know a great deal about the course of German political philosophy and history and how both relate to the rise of Hitler. There is a rich literature about political and economic decay in the Weimar Republic. We enjoy an abundance of data and analyses on voting patterns and the political careers of Nazi leaders in the 1920's and 1930's. And we are familiar with the unique nature of German fascism and the cataclysmic effects of World War II.

Since political pathology is always more interesting than political health, postwar Germany came to attract far less academic interest than either the Weimar Republic or the "Third Reich." The Federal Republic quickly grew into a smoothly functioning democracy, buttressed by speedy integration into the Western community of nations and an astounding Wirtschaftswunder (economic miracle). Initial interest in the process of democratic reconstruction was soon replaced by relative neglect; the very solidity of West Germany's postwar development offered little that was fascinating or tantalizing. Nor did German foreign policy attract much scholarly attention in the Anglo-American world. Since Bonn's diplomacy was marked by a unique degree of dependence on its Western patrons, it was not so much an independent variable as virtually a function of the East-West conflict in Europe.

And what held true for the Federal Republic (FRG) was doubly true for the German Democratic Republic (GDR). Until the 1970's, the GDR was seen (and treated) as a mere province of the Soviet empire in Europe, hence hardly worthy of political or academic attention. What research there was accumulated mainly in West Germany--and then in a form that attracted only the most specialized of foreign experts. West German

writing on the GDR was either intensely factual or
intensely political. It amounted either to an inchoate
agglomeration of facts, figures and footnotes or to
reams and reams of normative/ideological ruminations on
the "State of the Nation" and the "German Question."
There was, in other words, little that resembled the
Anglo-American approach to comparative government and
foreign policy that was conceptual rather than
narrative, analytical rather than normative, rigorous
rather than discursive.

The 1970's, however, mark a twin watershed--first
in the political, then in the intellectual realm. With
the "New Ostpolitik" (1969-1972), the Federal Republic
shed a good deal of the dependence that had been the
hallmark of its postwar diplomacy. Thereafter, Bonn
moved to re-occupy Germany's traditional role in the
European center by adding an ever-more weighty Eastern
dimension to a foreign policy hitherto almost
exclusively devoted to <u>Westpolitik</u>. In the process,
the FRG changed not only its position in the European
system but the system itself. The most telling index
of transformation is the inner-German relationship, the
subject of this book.

Before the New Ostpolitik, the two Germanys were
not only the products but also the pillars of
bipolarity in Europe. They played a vanguard role in
the containment of each other and their respective
blocs. Their relationship was essentially one of
hostile competition for advantage and precedence. Each
tried to monopolize the nation's heritage, to deny
legitimacy to the other and to arrogate unto itself the
title of succession to the vanquished Reich. Indeed,
for more than twenty years after Nazi Germany's
unconditional surrender, the Federal Republic managed
to isolate the GDR in the community of nations by
holding its allies and much of the Third World to a
policy of non-recognition vis-a-vis what used to be
called the "Soviet Occupation Zone." The two Germanys
were the prime symbols and victims of "tight
bipolarity" in Europe.

That relationship would change drastically in the
wake of the New Ostpolitik. Though still tightly
integrated into their respective blocs, the two
Germanys moved fitfully and hesitantly toward a state
of benign coexistence, if not tacit partnership. The
process began with mutual quasi-diplomatic recognition
(i.e., the exchange of "permanent representatives"
rather than full-fledged ambassadors) in the early
1970's. It gathered speed as a network of
proliferating diplomatic and economic contacts was laid
down in the course of the "Detente Decade." And it
matured into the outlines of an implicit alliance in
the 1980's as the FRG and the GDR managed to shelter,
indeed accelerate, their rapprochement in spite of Cold

War II (circa 1979-1985), Pershing II and cruise
missiles, and Soviet and American attempts to
recentralize their alliances in the service of militant
counter-containment.

The process is still in flux but the mid-1980's
are a good vantage point for a searching look backward.
The keystone of the entire enterprise is the
Grundvertrag (Basic Treaty) between West and East
Germany. Initiating the process that led from
competitive to regulated and then to cooperative
coexistence, that treaty also constitutes the core
element of this book. Building on his doctoral
dissertation at The American University, Ernest D.
Plock presents a wealth of painstakingly assembled
detail, enveloped in a multi-dimensional framework of
explication that draws on the tools of legal,
diplomatic, economic and historical analysis.

The author limns the historical evolution
preceding the treaty (from 1949 onward) that provides
the necessary backdrop for an understanding of the
enormous transformation still to follow. He describes
the dramatic story of the transformation itself--the
four-year contest between the two Germanys over the
formalized terms of their future relationship as played
out in the arena of great-power detente politics. The
main weight of his effort falls on the legal
explication and the politico-economic consequences of
the Basic Treaty. And there is an almost as lengthy
analysis of the issues the Treaty did not solve, i.e.,
the abiding conundra of an ancient "German Problem"
whose present-day version comes under the label "two
states in one nation." Whatever the contemporary
nature of the beast, it is guaranteed to change under
our own eyes--as it did for centuries past.

Ernest D. Plock's analysis mirrors a profound
transformation of Central Europe in the space of only
one decade. Furthermore, his book reflects new
interest in a country--the German Democratic Republic--
that was once terra incognita of American academic
research. Finally, it exemplifies the effort of a new
generation of American scholars to fill in the many
white patches that still remain. There is no doubt
that Germany, diminished and fragmented as it is,
represents the key prop and the key prize of Europe's
postwar order, and in that respect the twentieth
century is no different from the nineteenth century
when the Bismarckian Reich shouldered its way into the
ranks of the great powers. And thus there is no doubt
that contemporary Germany--both East and West--deserves
at least as much attention as the Weimar Republic and
the Third Reich were accorded in the past.

Josef Joffe
Munich

Introduction: The German Problem and German Interests

"The German question" has posed different sets of
problems for both statesmen and scholars throughout
modern European history. One critical consequence of
World War II, the division of Germany into two states
adjoined to hostile military alliances, confirmed the
recognition that the fate of Germany was the pivotal
variable in future European peace. The internal German
political situation as well as German foreign policies
thus posed fundamental questions of security for the
Western powers and the states of the Warsaw Pact Treaty
Organization (WTO).   Successive US-Soviet   crises
centering on the divided city of Berlin in 1948,   1958,
and 1961 testified to the potential for conflict
existing at the European fault line represented by
Germany.

    To be sure, German disunity has been the norm
rather than the exception for most of the time since
the "official" inauguration of the nation-state system
with the Peace of Westphalia in 1648.   Students of
European history can readily point to breakdowns in the
European political order as a result of a consolidated
German   national   state   conducting   policies   of
territorial expansion.   Both the Second and Third
Reichs clearly fit this prototype.   Yet history also
suggests that the cause of European stability has been
poorly served by the excessive weakness of Germany.
Here it is worth noting that the existence of hundreds
of small German states and principalities after the
Peace of Westphalia corresponded with a succession of
major European conflicts, including Louis XIV's
attempts to extend French power,   Frederick the Great's
wars of Prussian consolidation and expansion, and the
Napoleonic Wars.

    In seeking an optimum political model of Germany
that is most identified with the security of its

1

neighbors, historians have pointed to the era beginning with the defeat of Napoleon and ending with the christening of the Imperial German Reich in 1871. The emergence of the German Confederation, 39 Germanic states among which Austria was most powerful, substantially removed German areas from the pivot of European military engagements. Such a political entity possessed sufficient cohesion to maintain internal equilibrium but, because of the diffusion of power within and outside regulation of German affairs, was unsuited as an instrument for projecting influence externally.

If, then, it is perceived that German ascendancy as well as German impotence are undesirable alternatives to be avoided, what are the consequences of the present division of Germany for the future of Europe? One need not look far to find competing voices. A.W. DePorte, to cite one, asserts that Europe's division has "provided a solution for... the problem of German power." This contention rests on the observation that "U.S. 'guardianship' of the FRG in the alliance has obviated concern in Europe about German military and economic strength so effectively as to make the very statement of fact seem irrelevant."[1] Former U.S. national security adviser Zbigniew Brzezinski, on the other hand, sees the division of Europe as "an inherently unstable and potentially dangerous situation. It is likely to produce new explosions in Eastern Europe and it could also generate a basic and destabilizing reorientation in Western Europe."[2]

There is, of course, no exact historical counterpart to the present German landscape, a situation on one hand more simplified and on the other more problematical than earlier periods. In terms of foreign policy alignment, the fealty of each German state is fairly sharply defined, certainly in contrast to prior centuries when alliances proved more transitory. However, new internal tensions are endemic to the Germans of today due to the fact that the power of the United States and Soviet Union prevents any near-term redrawing of German boundaries. Unlike in earlier times, the resort to war is not feasible. The result is a psychological condition described by Pierre Hassner in which Germany pursues "a national policy without national goals, a recipe for instability if ever there was one."[3]

The European dislocations that Brzezinski foresees and Hassner's identification of dangerous internal German disquiet, both of which are seen as the product of the division of Europe and Germany, rightly raise concerns which must be addressed in thinking about the German problem. One would furthermore be shortsighted to ignore the reality that the heavy concentration of nuclear and conventional forces in the two Germanies is a major source of insecurity from both a regional and global perspective. Yet there is equally no tangible evidence that a re-united Germany, even within Brzezinski's framework of a pan-European settlement, would ipso facto resolve the dilemmas posed by national rivalries. Here, DePorte's observation that U.S. supervision of West Germany's military development provided credible reassurances for Germany's former adversaries is a convincing counterargument, particularly when one considers the possibility that the leadership of a greater Germany might conceive of the nuclear option as a national necessity.

Hassner's noting of undeniable frustration at recent history's rigidification on the German question, however, suggests that inquiry be shifted away from the "legacy of Yalta" and in the direction of the two German states' own goals and interests. Such an investigation is demanded even though it is irrefutable that East and West Germany are primarily the objects of outside powers' policies regarding the fate of Germany and that only a massive collapse of Soviet and American power could alter this fact. The forging in 1972 of a basis for an East-West German understanding in which Bonn substantially, but not formally, extended recognition to the GDR offered the potential for new and greater inner-German links. Given the disappearance of reunification as an East-West agenda item over the last three decades, the problem of German objectives and their redefinition poses itself for policymakers as well as academicians. Specifically, in what way have the two German states moved closer together, what have been the immediate results of the modified relationship, and what are the implications for the future of Germany and of Europe?

Given the dominant political and military role of the US and USSR in the affairs of the newly-created East and West German states, it was hardly surprising that the external policies of the Federal Republic of Germany (FRG) and German Democratic Republic (GDR) were viewed as appendages to those conducted by their founding patrons. This conjunction was generally held to be valid even though historians have discovered several independent overtures by Konrad Adenauer to the Soviet leadership in the late 1950's and early 1960's exploring the possibility of an All-German solution. With the accession of Willy Brandt to the FRG Chancellorship in 1969, however, a blueprint for a new "Deutschlandpolitik" was articulated that questioned traditional U.S. and West German policy standards requiring non-recognition of the GDR.

The signing of the 1972 Basic Treaty by East and West German representatives was an unprecedented step in establishing official, direct lines of communication in divided Germany and set the relationship on an inter-state footing. In concluding the agreement, neither government imagined that the imperatives of military security had lessened in importance during the previous two decades, nor that this event would automatically lead to a reduction of political and military dependence on their preeminent alliance partners. Rather, it had now become possible to forge a new bilateral understanding based on treaty commitments but unfolding within the context of continued membership in NATO and the Warsaw Pact Treaty Organization (WTO).

The Basic Treaty is therefore the appropriate point of departure for investigating a considerably modified inner-German relationship after 1972. First, one can see in sharp relief the divergent goals and interests of each leadership respecting their mutual legal relationship and autonomy. Mutual behavior, as in the respecting of each state's territory during border incidents, can be explained against the backdrop of the treaty. Second, the document establishes a general standard for East and West German practical dealings such as the exchange of official representatives, trade, and political consultation among high-level officials. Third, and most importantly, the 1972 accord can serve as a barometer for evaluating each governing elite's successes and failures in vindicating its version of the German question. A key element of West German policy, for example, will be its ability to gain affirmation of its right to act on behalf of the German nation, as opposed to its earlier claim to be the only legitimate representative of East German inhabitants.

Consideration of these bilateral areas of inner-German relations has not received sufficient attention by American scholars, given their customary focus on the larger picture of "Ostpolitik" and the emphasis on the security, as opposed to the national, dimension of the German question. This book therefore aims at an evaluation of FRG-GDR relations through the "prism" of the Basic Treaty. An accompanying purpose of the study is to identify the scope and significance of actual changes in East and West German policies toward each other after 1972 in light of earlier positions.

THE TREATY'S BACKGROUND AND FORMULATION

While the willingness to deal with the East German state as an equally entitled partner departed from the practices of past West German governments, it was by no means clear to what degree implementation of the treaty would lead to Bonn's abandonment of actions such as treatment of East German visitors to the Federal

Republic that had long been denounced by the East German Socialist Unity Party (SED). Equally hypothetical was the question of whether the Federal Government would or could choose to extend a level of formal recognition to the East German state that would satisfy East Berlin's craving for recognition of GDR sovereignty. In order to better assess the resolution of such differences in the 1970's, one is well-advised to place them in their proper historical perspective. Prior to that decade, FRG and GDR governmental and judicial bodies issued constitutional decrees relating to the legal standing of each part of Germany, the question of succession to the German state that ceased to exist in 1945, and persisting German unity. In equal measure, both governments erected official standards (which were not always congruent with doctrinal precedents) governing the conditions for practical activities between the two and fixing in a policy context each leadership's position on mutual recognition.[4] Taken together, these two broad areas might be said to represent the "state image" which each leadership professed to uphold and nurture, denying to its German rival the legitimacy that the latter claimed for itself. By clarifying pre-1972 East and West German doctrines and policies, the task of identifying the unprecedented aspects of Basic Treaty-era practices will be much simplified.

The next section of the book will treat the formulation of the Basic Treaty, charting attempts by FRG and GDR leaders to define and attain their objectives prior to and during the treaty negotiations. Here it is important to bear in mind two realities of inner-German negotiation. East and West German preferences were at every stage of the dialogue substantially narrowed by the continued intervention and authority of the U.S., Great Britain, France, and the Soviet Union. In addition, little hope of a successful agreement could have been entertained if it did not sufficiently protect the symbolic and tangible interests of both governments, in however cryptic a form these might be safeguarded. An attempt will nevertheless be made to ascertain whether Bonn or East Berlin secured its aims in greater measure with the crafting of the final document. Toward this end, each of the treaty's articles will be discussed at length to determine their legally binding effect.

IMPLEMENTATION

In keeping with the intention expressed earlier of examining the two German states' affairs with a focus on mutual patterns of interaction, the analysis of the treaty's implementation will select those articles that have a bilateral application. The recent upsurge in interest in "the German problem," both within the two states and abroad,[5] suggests that immediate attention be paid to positions concerning the unity of the German nation. On paper, the Basic Treaty's preamble specified only that there existed a "national question"; in practice, the inauguration of a number of closer inner-German popular contacts compelled the GDR elite to refine its notion of ideological and political delimitation (Abgrenzung). For their part, the Brandt and Schmidt Governments were at pains to preserve at least the fiction of continuing national unity through measures such as a unique passport treatment of East Germans visiting the Federal Republic. In pursuance of such objectives, however, Bonn was simultaneously moved to recognize the potential for collision with a GDR leadership that it had acknowledged to be the effective authority in East Germany.

A bilateral issue that possessed no less potential for controversy was the regulation of sovereign jurisdiction, which is provided for in Article 4 of the Basic Treaty. SED consciousness of the larger and economically more prosperous West German state, memories of the mass exodus of Germans from the GDR in 1960-61, and the access of the East German public to West German television broadcasts all served to underline the relative vulnerability of the GDR in competition with the Federal Republic. In addition, the East German leadership's less than successful drives to implant an authentic "GDR consciousness" in the minds of the population as well as Bonn's commitment to eventual reunification necessitated that the former keep strict accounting of the West German treaty commitment to respect mutual independence and autonomy. West German treatment of East Germans escaping to the Federal Republic, FRG legislation regarding the application of laws to the GDR, and reactions to periodic border incidents provide clues as to the content each government lent to the term sovereign jurisdiction.

The East German program to secure international recognition accompanied attempts to secure Bonn's recognition of the status of the GDR as a sovereign state. In spite of the treaty's stipulation that neither German state might "speak for or act on behalf of" the other, one could easily predict that differences arising from Bonn's claim to speak "on behalf of the German nation" would not thereby be eliminated. This was especially true with regard to FRG consular and legal assistance for East German inhabitants in third countries as well as foreign recognition of GDR citizenship. Inner-German normalization can be assessed in part by examining the degree of resolution of these contended items.

A fundamental and, arguably, the most concrete component of East-West German affairs was the development of cooperation in a wide range of practical areas-- the desideratum of so many of Bonn's diplomatic exertions with East Berlin and Moscow. Of these areas, inner-German trade and travel and the exchange of media journalists loom the largest as prospective realms of accommodation and of friction. By noting the annual development of these activities and the outcomes of negotiations, one can draw a balance of progress measured against the original West German expectations and the records of earlier West German governments. Just as important, however, will be identification of the intrusion of political interests into these "functional" areas. Such an approach invites a discussion of the possibility of political "linkage" so often undertaken in studies of East-West economic relations. In exploring the connection between political and economic variables, this study will be sensitive to FRG and GDR status and doctrinal differences that further complicate the interplay of economics and politics.

Two final areas of activity will also be objects of analysis in the discussion of the treaty's implementation. In Article 8, East and West German agreement to exchange "Permanent Missions" formalized the mutual acknowledgment of the separate statehood of each; it also stopped short of legitimizing East Berlin's earlier demand that the two states adopt international relations, since embassies were not exchanged.' Not surprisingly, however, both the FRG and GDR took steps to implement this provision according to their separate notions of German unity. The accreditations of the two Missions will be addressed in the implementation chapter, but judgments will also be formed on the practical role and future use of the bodies by each government. The question of the practical status of the Missions, which the East German Government has sought to have transformed into embassies, is seen by many as a litmus test of West German commitment to national unity which the leadership of the FRG ignores only at great risk.

The second area, political consultation, is an important yardstick of intergovernmental cooperation. This is true in part because the 1972 arrangement opened up a new line of communication for Bonn which could presumably generate movement on the German question. East Berlin achieved some advantages as well, especially in terms of possible future payoffs. The cumulative impact of expanded consultations with the Federal Government was seen by the SED leadership as an instrument to facilitate an eventual upgrading of relations at the diplomatic level; deepened contacts with West German officials might also offer hitherto unknown economic and technological opportunities. An additional impulse for devoting attention to FRG-GDR high-level talks follows from the observation that they may permit the drawing of inferences as to the insulation of East-West German dealings from the vagaries of East-West, particularly US-Soviet, conflict and cooperation.

THE CHANGING AMBIENCE AND STRUCTURE OF INNER-GERMAN RELATIONS

At this point, the reader may be tempted to ask what implementation of the treaty can reveal about the long-term evolution of East-West German relations. This study will assume that any evaluation of the reorientation of policies should pursue three central questions. First, to what degree was the East German state destabilized by popular inner-German contacts, one possible outcome of closer links in the minds of SED leaders? Transportation between the two German states as well as West German media activity in the GDR particularly heightened the West German presence and influence in East Germany. In recognition of the inherent subjectivity of the word "destabilization," the following chapter on FRG-GDR problems will comment on GDR stability as perceived by the East German and Soviet leaderships and provide an alternative judgment.

A second problem area that analysis of the treaty's implementation will clarify relates to the relative importance of status differences in the day-to-day business of the two German governments. The incompatibility of East and West German positions was strikingly reflected in the thorny problems of German citizenship and official contacts in the 1950's and 1960's, when Bonn feared that dealings with the "Pankow regime" might be read as official blessing of Germany's division. The question of official recognition also led to entanglements in the international sphere, since diplomatic credit was expended on both sides to secure a validation of each state's representational claims. Examination of the role of such controversies in the post-1972 relationship will once again clarify the nature of recent "normalization" in view of the clash of policies in earlier periods.

The third and most multi-faceted object of inquiry concerns the evolution of the relationship within the larger framework of East-West political and security developments. Here there were several potential dangers to a calculable, stable inner-German understanding. While the West German Social-Liberal coalition expanded communication links with East Berlin, it could not hope to erode the dominant position of the Soviet Union as the ultimate arbiter of the pace and scope of liberal GDR policies and the relations between the two German states. Perennial Soviet incantations of the "Brezhnev Doctrine" had reemphasized the Kremlin's postwar precept of the security interdependence of the Socialist community, a principle born of past political upheavals in the GDR, Hungary and Czechoslovakia. Realization that the SED leadership would be no less vigilant than Moscow in shielding East Germany from disruptive external influences, whether emanating from the West or Eastern Europe, was reason to maintain Bonn's modest optimism. Moreover, it was inevitable that FRG-GDR relations would continue to be influenced by developments touching on divided Berlin, an area that was not only outside the purview of the Basic Treaty but which was the predominant concern of the four former wartime allies. This study will examine these problems of the FRG-GDR relationship during the Brandt and Schmidt chancellorships but will also evaluate the degree of West German adherence to or departure from the inner-German "business basis" after the accession of a Christian Democratic-Free Democratic government to office in October 1982.

The above considerations testify to the inability to detach the prospects for an FRG-GDR "modus vivendi" from the competition between the superpowers, for whom the stakes in Germany remain substantial. However, such observations also demand that some explanation be made of the growth of bilateral relations as they have been affected by outside developments, such as the rise of "Solidarity" in Poland, in order to determine instances when Bonn or East Berlin, for different reasons, sought or succeeded in FRG-GDR "damage limitation." The basic dynamics of bilateral relations in the aftermath of the Basic Treaty might be thereby defined by assessing the significance of bilateral disputes relative to problems that were external in their origin.[7]

---

[1]A.W. DePorte, "The Uses of Perspective," in Robert W. Tucker and Linda Wrigley, ed., The Atlantic Alliance and Its Critics (New York: Praeger, 1983), p. 47. Italian Foreign Minister Giulio Andreotti commented that the two German states should remain divided in the future for the sake of European stability. Washington Post, 3 February 1985.

[2]Zbigniew Brzezinski, "The Future of Yalta," Foreign Affairs 63 (Winter 1984-85): 294-295.

[3]Pierre Hassner, Change and Security in Europe, Part I: The Background, Adelphi Papers No. 45 (London:

Institute for Strategic Studies, February 1968). p. 13.

[4]For example, the West German "Hallstein Doctrine," a precept which affirmed the FRG as the only legitimate German political entity, usually resulted in Bonn's severance of diplomatic relations with states that recognized the GDR.

[5]To cite only a few examples, popular protests against U.S. and Soviet missile deployments in the FRG and GDR through the early 1980's inevitably prompted anew the consideration of "German interests," a campaign theme for the Social Democratic standard-bearer in the 1983 Federal elections. Even more noteworthy was SED General Secretary Erich Honecker's decision to allow articles to be published in the East German press which defended the promotion of economic contacts with Western states even in the face of Soviet recriminations against such undertakings. The GDR's intimate trade and credit arrangements with West Germany thus received hitherto unexpressed support. Washington Post, 15 February 1983; Neues Deutschland, 30 July 1984, 4 August 1984.

[6]Nor are the words "international" or "diplomatic" used to describe FRG-GDR relations anywhere in the treaty.

[7]All translations are the author's own, unless otherwise indicated. Interested readers are referred to footnotes from key or extended passages for quotations in the original German.

1
The Background to the Basic Treaty, 1949–1969

Most of the articles of the Basic Treaty focus on the questions of East and West German state sovereignty, mutual inner-German recognition, and representation of Germans (Articles 1-4, 6, and 8). The preamble also makes a brief reference to "different conceptions" on "the national question" which only by implication touches on the question of reunification. The treaty does not regulate the matter of citizenship, and the remainder of the document deals largely with practical and humanitarian affairs.[1]

Prior to the Brandt-Scheel Ostpolitik, the two governments maintained quite different positions on the doctrinal questions of the succession to or continuation of the German Reich, the unity of the nation, and the nature of FRG-GDR relations. Equally distinctive were the East and West German competing policies relating to state sovereignty, inner-German recognition, and the representation of all Germans. This chapter will explore both these doctrinal and policy facets of inner-German relations from 1949 to 1969. However, it should be emphasized that due to the complex nature of the relationship, involving, for example, legal non-recognition but frequent contacts in several technical areas, determining the status accorded by the two governments to one another can sometimes only be achieved by viewing the doctrinal positions of each. This is especially true when one examines the "legalistic" German policy of the Adenauer Government in the late 1950's and early 1960's. A third section will treat the inner-German regulation of practical and humanitarian affairs.

With regard to the doctrinal positions, they are most often to be discovered in the GDR Constitution and FRG Basic Law, court rulings, government declarations on German unity and the continuation of the Reich, and

11

resolutions of the GDR Volkskammer (People's
Chamber)and FRG Bundestag (Federal Diet).   The state
sovereignty,   inner-German   recognition,   and
representation of German issues,   on the other hand,
find their expression in the measures undertaken by the
two governments to: 1) domestically define one's part
of Germany as a state,   with or without All-German
claims,   and 2)   secure   acceptance   for this policy
internationally,   as   in   the   Federal Government's
pursuance of the so-called "Hallstein Doctrine" in the
1950s and 1960s.

FRG DOCTRINAL AND CONSTITUTIONAL CONCEPTIONS OF GERMANY

     The constitutional cornerstone of the Federal
Republic's position on German reunification is to be
found in the preamble to the Basic Law, which entered
into force on May 23,   1949 upon the signatures of
representatives of the United Kingdom, France, and the
United States.   After specifying the eleven German
Laender that were to form the Federal Republic of
Germany,   the preamble states: "The entire German
people is   called on   to achieve   in free   self-
determination the unity and freedom of Germany." [2] This,
then,   is   the   reunification   imperative
(Wiedervereinigungsgebot) of the Basic Law.   The
imperative,   together with   the   preamble's   prior
reference to the Laender's "desiring to give a new
order to political life for a transitional period" [3] was
so constructed as to   underline the   provisional
character of the Federal Republic and the normative
concept of German unity.
     Although the   reunification   imperative   was
expressly binding on the German people,   an August 16,
1956 ruling by the Federal Constitutional Court on the
illegality of the German Communist Party (KPD) endowed
this principle with a more fully legal character.
While the primary effect of   this ruling was to
proscribe the activities of the KPD and its fraternal
organizations in the FRG,   the decision also emphasized
that the imperative possessed not simply programmatic
but also legal content.   The court stated that the
Basic Law's preamble:

     is not   limited to   certain   legally enactable
     decisions and legal objections   which must be
     respected in interpreting the Basic Law.   Rather,
     what is to be derived from this claim for all
     political state organs of the Federal Republic of
     Germany is the legal obligation of striving for the
     unity of Germany with all power,   adjusting their
     measures to this goal,   and,   on the other hand,
     admitting the correctness of   this goal as a

standard for their political actions. . . On the
negative side, the reunification imperative means
that the state organs are to abstain from all
measures which legally hinder reunification or make
it factually impossible. However, that leads to
the conclusion that the measures of the political
organs can also be constitutionally examined as to
whether they are compatible with the reunification
imperative.[4]

The reunification imperative was thereby elevated
to a higher level of political commitment, reinforced
the Basic Law's command that the entire German people
"achieve the unity and freedom of Germany" and
established a policy obligation for the Bonn government
that legally prevented it from undertaking measures
impairing the recreation of German unity. The Court
was also now empowered to decide on cases brought
before it regarding the government's constitutional
observance of this obligation, as it did in 1973 on the
occasion of the Bavarian Government's contesting of the
Basic Treaty.

West German policies towards East Germany were
often described as being legalistic in nature in the
1950s and continuing into the 1960s essentially because
of their direct reliance on the reunification
imperative and the strict legal obligation, seen in the
KPD decision, to avoid undertaking steps judged
injurious to the reunification principle. Recognition
of the Ulbricht regime, in particular, would have made
irrelevant Bonn's All-German claims by legally
sanctioning the division of Germany in the form of the
FRG and a state governed by those whom West German and
Western policymakers repeatedly stressed were Soviet
dependents. The formal importance of reunification as
a policy priority could be discerned in countless West
German statements, decisions, and resolutions, as in
that of Dr. Wilhelm Grewe, Director of the Foreign
Office's Political Department, in December 1955. Asked
about the Federal Republic's simultaneous policies of
diplomatic recognition of the Soviet Union and non-
recognition of East European states such as Poland,
Grewe replied that relations with the Soviet Union

are to be a means on the way to the overcoming of
the splitting and towards the recreation of the
unity of Germany. Towards that end, however,
diplomatic relations with Poland, Hungary, Romania,
and other Communist states cannot help. That is
the great difference.[5]

While West German doctrine supported this goal of
a reunified German state, the preamble to the Basic Law
lays out no precise territorial definition of Germany,

as opposed to the FRG, in accordance with the Potsdam Agreement's provision that "the final delimitation of the western frontier of Poland should await the peace settlement."[6] By extension, however, the Federal Republic is equated with the German Reich of 1937; in the enumeration of constitutional rights in Articles 8, 9, 11, and 12, for example, the Basic Law stresses that these laws apply to "all Germans," and Article 116 states that "a German within the meaning of this Basic Law is a person who possesses German citizenship or who has been admitted to the territory of the German Reich, as it existed on 31 December 1937, as a refugee or expellee of German stock (Volkszugehoerigkeit) or as the spouse or descendant of such a person."[7] Furthermore, Article 38 declared that the deputies to the German Bundestag "shall be representatives of the whole Volk,"[8] confirming the Federal Republic's legitimacy for representing all Germans within the former Reich area. The West German right of sole representation, which became a fundamental foreign policy directive in the 1950's and 1960's, was thus foreshadowed in the above articles. A second connection between the GDR and the Reich is advanced in Articles 89, 90, and 134, in which the Federal Republic inherits the hitherto existing Reich waterways, highways, streets, and, in principle, property. Although continued Four Power rights and responsibilities in Germany and the incipient de facto division of its two parts precluded an unequivocal declaration of the continuation of the Reich, the founders of the Basic Law did affirm this for some purposes in Article 123: "the state treaties for the German Reich concerning matters for which ... Land legislation is competent, shall remain in force, if they are and continue to be valid in accordance with general principles of law."[9]

By establishing FRG ownership of the former Reich possessions and continuing to apply Reich law where it had not been invalidated, the Basic Law asserts a historical legitimacy of the Federal Republic and a qualified, but nevertheless clear, legal continuation of the Reich. The diplomatic legitimacy of the West German state as the representative of all Germans was given marked emphasis in Chancellor Konrad Adenauer's declaration to the Bundestag of October 21, 1949, a speech designed to address the problem posed by the founding of the GDR on October 7. In focusing on the differences between East and West German election methods employed in the previous months, Adenauer declared:

I must emphasize the following. In the Soviet Zone there is no free will of the German population. What has happened there is not supported by the population and therefore not legitimated.

On the other hand, the Federal Republic of Germany is founded on recognition through the freely expressed will of approximately 23 million eligible voters. Thus the Federal Republic of Germany is the only legitimate state organization of the German people until the attaining of German unity altogether... The Federal Republic of Germany also feels responsible for the fate of the 18 million Germans that live in the Soviet Zone... The FRG alone is authorized to speak for the German people... It does not recognize declarations of the Soviet Zone as binding for the German people... That applies especially to the declarations which have been delivered in the Soviet Zone concerning the Oder-Neisse Line.[10]

Adenauer's address thus established two doctrinal positions of the West German Government that continued to be maintained throughout the 1949-1969 period: FRG legitimacy to represent all Germans by virtue of free elections, with a corresponding illegitimacy of the GDR, and non-recognition of any German borders not fixed in a final peace settlement. The bestowing of legitimacy on the Federal Republic was not, of course, a West German invention but followed in agreement with the U.S. Government's October 12, 1949 statement on the illegality of the SED regime and was reaffirmed in a September 19, 1950 communique of American, British, and French foreign ministers in New York.[11]

In spite of the seeming unanimity of the FRG and Western states' position on German legitimacy, it must be pointed out that neither of these "Three Power" statements declared that the Federal Republic maintained the legal identity of a still-existing German Reich, although subsequent West German declarations represented variants of this claim. Nevertheless, a March 26, 1954 declaration of the Soviet Government, which declared the GDR to be a sovereign state "free to decide on internal and external affairs,"[12] compelled the Federal Republic and Bundestag to issue a joint declaration regarding "the non-recognition of the 'sovereignty' of the Soviet Zone Government." This document testified that "it is solely the organs of the Federal Republic of Germany which today represent this never-extinguished German state."[13] The FRG was thereby considered to contain the political identity of the pre-1945 German state and the Basic Law's more limited references to the Reich's continuation are thereby exceeded. However, the Allied High Commission in rejecting the notion of East German sovereignty made no mention of the continuation of the German state, confirming once more the Western powers'

interest in preserving their legal rights and
responsibilities in a divided Germany.[14]

It was the Federal Government's recognition of
this Four Power priority that prevented the theory of
the continued existence of the German Reich
(Fortbestand des deutschen Reiches) from being
elaborated as a unified position by a West German
government. Yet it was this doctrine which provided
the rationale for West German claims that the GDR and
FRG were not foreign lands vis-a-vis one another. In
its formulation by legal scholars, the theory
emphasized the maintenance of the "state personality"
of the German state even through Allied occupation and
the restoration of the state's "ability to act" with
the formation of German (e.g., West German) state
organs.[15] Since the state essence (Staatskern) remained
intact, one could observe the continued existence of
Germany from its emergence as the Reich in 1871 through
the Weimar Republic, the National Socialist state, and
the Federal Republic, an interpretation compatible with
the April 1954 Bundestag resolution. Whereas the
reunification imperative was the quite explicit legal
obligation of West German Deutschlandpolitik, belief in
the "Fortbestand" interpretation also mitigated against
recognizing the GDR or acquiescing in the 1950 East
German recognition of the Oder-Neisse Line. This
theory additionally provided the basis for Minister
Heinrich von Brentano's assertion that "the German
Reich in its 1937 borders continues to exist."[16] Yet
neither its full elaboration nor an alternative to the
Oder-Neisse Line could be advanced publicly.

Support for the concept of the continuation of the
Reich and the equating of the Federal Republic with the
identity of Germany also emerged in rulings of the West
German judiciary. One of the earliest decisions of the
Federal Constitutional Court declared that "the Soviet
Occupation Zone belongs to Germany and cannot be
essentially viewed as a foreign land in relation to the
Federal Republic."[17] As to the existence of the Reich,
a Federal Court of Justice in the Land of Schleswig-
Holstein offered a parallel example of the
"Fortbestand" thesis: although the Reich became
incapable of acting with respect to public law in 1945,
it did not perish as a public-legal nor private-legal
entity. The Constitutional Court nevertheless took
care to distinguish between "the legal relationships of
the public service" in the Hitler state and those of
the FRG,[18] since these first could only be said to
exist in a one-party state. The clearest expression of
the Reich's continuation and FRG identity with the
Reich, however, was presented in the Court's 1956
"Concordat" decision, which affirmed the 1954 Bundestag
resolution:

The German Reich, which had not ceased to exist after the collapse, continued to exist even after 1945. Even if the organization created through the Basic Law is temporarily restricted to a part of the Reich area, the Federal Republic of Germany is nevertheless identical with the German Reich.[19]

GDR DOCTRINAL AND CONSTITUTIONAL CONCEPTIONS OF GERMANY

The doctrinal and constitutional conceptions of the East German Government differed fron those of the Federal Republic in two important respects. First, the SED relied on the theme of the extinction of the German Reich (Untergangstheorie des deutschen Reiches), in contrast to the West German "Fortbestand" position, for most of this period. Second, while the GDR Constitution continued to contain the phrase "Germany is an indivisible democratic Republic"[20] until 1968, the Ulbricht leadership never departed from its support for the thesis of "two states in Germany" from 1955 onward. The East and West German conceptions were fundamentally similar, however, in claiming legitimacy as the representative of all Germans on the basis of the "democratic" nature of the political system and the counterpart's domination by foreign interests.

As it was promulgated by the "Third Congress of the German People" on May 30, 1949, the Constitution of the GDR included a number of references to the unity of Germany. In addition to the "indivisible" quality cited above, the GDR "decides on all matters essential for the continued existence and development of the German people as a whole," and deputies of the Volkskammer "are representatives of the entire Volk." All-German law is given primacy over Laender law, only one German citizenship is recognized, and "Germany constitutes a uniform customs and trade territory bounded by a common customs frontier."[21] Yet there is no attempt to establish a connection between this newly-created state and the former Reich, nor is there a "reunification imperative" or reference to the splitting of Germany. For the latter assertions, one must consult the October 14, 1949 "National Front of Democratic Germany" Decision of the SED, an "anti-fascist" and "anti-imperialist" account of postwar events. This decision calls for "the restoration of the political and economic unity of Germany" and "implacable active struggle against the betrayers of the German nation, the German agents of American imperialism, the criminal accomplices of the splitting of Germany and the enslavement of its Western parts."[22] The characterization of the West German Government as illegitimate due to its dependence on "American imperialism" was the mirror image of Bonn's recognition of the GDR as nothing more than the Soviet Zone.

East German positions concerning the continuation of the Reich, on the other hand, found their earliest expression in judicial decisions. In a September 1950 ruling of the GDR Supreme Court, it was determined that in the passage from a Reich rural district (Landkreis) to an East German district, "no relationship of legal succession has been created, rather, the identity has remained."[23] This fixing of an "identity theory" was rather short-lived, as a June 1951 decision of the Schwerin Supreme National Court emphasized that "through the unconditional surrender of May 8, 1945, the former German Reich forfeited its legal personality." The assumption by the Four Powers of supreme authority within Germany, inscribed in the Potsdam Agreement's "Principles to Govern the Treatment of Germany," was quoted as evidence of the Reich's permanent disappearance.[24] The Schwerin verdict also contended that the basic difference in the class structures of the Third Reich and the GDR was the second decisive factor in rejecting any legal association. This ideological principle was much amplified in an October 1951 Supreme Court (Oberstes Gericht) ruling which reaffirmed the "Untergangs-theorie" and described the GDR as "the new state of the anti-fascist, democratic order."[25] The theory continues to be adhered to by the SED leadership and East German judiciary today, although it should be noted that in the absence of a practice of judicial review, these decisions did not carry the same legally binding effect for GDR governmental institutions.

In denying the affirmation of East Germany as a "partial successor" to the Reich, the Ulbricht Government did not acknowledge that the legal de-coupling of the new state from the last territorially unified German state lessened the GDR's All-German legitimacy. To the contrary, since the West German "separatist state" was constantly equated with the Hitler state by the SED throughout the 1950's, both being synonymous with "monopoly capital," "militarism," and anti-labor tendencies,[26] GDR All-German legitimacy could be and was asserted on the basis of the superiority and equity of the social system. On this point, it was recognized at the Second SED Party Congress of July 1952 that "this building of socialism promotes the unity of Germany,"[27] even though the effect of East German economic restructuring decided on at the conference was to place East and West Germany on radically different economic courses, with implications for German reunification. The East German reluctance to abandon doctrinal support for German unity was also evident in a May 1957 article by Herbert Kroeger, a member of the Volkskammer and of the Editorial

Committee of the SED theoretical organ <u>Einheit</u>.
Kroeger attacked the Adenauer Government's adherence to
the "Fortbestand" notion as fostering the goal of West
German military expansion into former Reich areas, but
stated that despite the extinction of the German state,
"the unconditional and inalienable right of the German
people to an independent and democratic national
state... remained unchanged and became more than ever
of the greatest importance."[28]

In the face of this SED recognition that the East
German population was not immune to national loyalties
and a Soviet desire to keep the German question open
prior to the rearmament of West Germany, the "two
states" concept of the GDR leadership emerged only
gradually if one is to examine its public statements.
Official references to the FRG in the first half of the
1950's consisted of phrases such as "the Western part
of our Fatherland" or "West Germany; when Germany as a
whole was the subject, "Germany," "both parts of
Germany," or, as a National Front document read, "our
great and noble nation" were generally the
characterizations.[29] Although there were several
occasions upon which the authorities acknowledged the
existence of two German states prior to 1955, these
pronouncements must be regarded as exceptions to the
rule. The consistent use of the term "both parts of
Germany" by Walter Ulbricht, Wilhelm Pieck, Otto
Grotewohl, and Volkskammer President Johannes Dieckmann
is testimony to the preferred SED version of the state
of German unity.

It was only after the September 26, 1955
declaration of East German statehood and All-German
legitimacy, a direct counter to Adenauer's "Hallstein"
speech, that the "two states" notion became a permanent
feature of the East German vocabulary. Declaring the
GDR to be "the lawful German state," First Assistant
Prime Minister Ulbricht summarized the four foundations
of its legitimacy: the Soviet-East German Treaty of
Friendship, which announced GDR sovereignty, East
German implementation of Allied decisions regarding
"the elimination of militarism" and "land reform,"
retention of state power in the hands of the
population, and the GDR "example of peaceful and
friendly relations with other peoples."[30] On August 29,
1956, Foreign Minister Lothar Bolz announced that both
German states were successors to the Reich, neither
containing its identity.[31]

With "Germany" so defined, it only remained for
the principle to be enshrined constitutionally, but
this measure was not enacted until the April 1968
constitution was published. Here it was stated that
"<u>the people of the German Democratic Republic</u>," instead
of the German Volk, "have given themselves this
socialist constitution." Earlier constitutional

references to the German customs area and All-German
law are also deleted, and the GDR is described as a
"socialist state of the German nation."[32] Given the
necessity to defend the "two states" concept, it was
also not surprising that "the nation" was increasingly
characterized as a social, as opposed to an ethnic,
entity. An <u>Einheit</u> article by Albert Norden in April
1966 emphasized that "socialism guarantees the
continuity of the nation. For that reason, the founding of the GDR, the building of socialism, was the
highest national deed of the working class."[33] Nor was
self-determination to be necessarily understood as a
right of the German Volk. As J. Peck explained in
March 1964, the legal principle of self-determination
"can have national as well as social, historical,
religious, or other bases." Recent history, he
continued, "confirms that in practice the social side
of self-determination is increasingly becoming the
dominant factor."[34]

FRG-GDR POLICY REGARDING STATEHOOD AND INNER-GERMAN RECOGNITION

Each German government moved to implement its
doctrinal position on the German question during this
period: the West German conception of a legal
continuation of a German state unity represented by the
FRG, and, after 1955, the East German "two states"
notion which demarcated the two on the basis of the
Reich's 1945 extinction and the ideological legitimacy
of socialism. This section will explore the policy
measures attempted, both domestically and
internationally, to promote the FRG and GDR "state
images" in order to ascertain the correspondence of
stated goals with actual practice. East and West German actions will be discussed together, so that one may
obtain an idea of the special sensitivity of both
leaderships to one another as well as to outside events
and actors.

From 1949 to 1952 both the Adenauer Government and
the SED publicly stressed fealty to reunification but
also took steps toward divergent alignments in foreign
policy. The first tendency, as was shown earlier, was
prominent in the two constitutions and, given East-West
probings on German reunification, there were also some
inner-German exchanges on the matter. A letter
exchange between East and West German Presidents
Wilhelm Pieck and Theodor Heuss in November 1951, which
simply recorded the irreconcilable positions of both
governments, was in fact the first communication
between high-level officials in both. Government
officials in both states did frequently respond to
reunification suggestions issued in the rival capital,

as in the remarks by Adenauer and Grotewohl in
September 1951, but the expressed opinions largely
mirrored those of Western and Soviet policy. East
Berlin's preconditions for All-German elections,
including prior consultations between the GDR and the
Federal Republic, were fully unacceptable to Bonn.
Adenauer described Grotewohl, on the other hand, as not
receptive to the West German Government's September 27,
1951 election proposals "because he would then also
have to speak on the question of genuinely free
elections."[35] A January 9, 1952 "Draft Election Law of
the Volkskammer" was similarly rejected by the West
German Ministry for All-German Affairs on the grounds
that the proposal was doomed to failure because of the
centrality of SED election committees in the plan. The
"Law" also preceded the Bundestag's own election law of
February 6, 1952.[36] In spite of these impasses, the
East and West German leaderships did "recognize" one
another as "currency areas" for the purpose of conducting trade in the October 1949 Frankfurt Agreement and
the landmark 1951 Berlin Agreement.

Probably the most accurate harbingers of future
FRG and GDR positions in these years were the signing
of the Goerlitz Agreement by the East German Government
on June 6, 1950 and Konrad Adenauer's March 1951
"Assurance by the Federal Chancellor on German External
Debts." The former recognized the Oder-Neisse Line as
"the state frontier between Germany and Poland"[37] and
thereby lent weight to the later GDR judicial
assertions that the Reich no longer existed. Rejected
by the Bundestag in a July 6 "Protest," the agreement
was justified by Grotewohl in his claim that "the Yalta
and Potsdam Agreements...settled the frontier question
between Germany and Poland,"[38] but did little to
enhance the SED's All-German pretensions. Adenauer's
"Assurance," on the other hand, strove to strengthen
the connection between the FRG and the German Reich:
"The Federal Republic hereby confirms that it is liable
for the pre-war external debt of the German Reich,
including those debts of other corporate bodies
subsequently declared to be liabilities of the
Reich."[39]

In 1952 the SED leadership attempted to effect
fundamental economic and social changes internally.
The Second SED Party Congress on July 12, 1952
announced the "beginning of the planned building of
socialism,"[40] and the remaining weeks of the month saw
the continued expansion of the East German People's
Police, curbs on travel within the GDR as well as to
the FRG, a heightened program of nationalization of
agriculture, and the penetration of the state apparatus
into the Laender. A May 26 "Order Concerning Measures
on the Demarcation Line" for the first time introduced
the so-called "control sections" (Kontrollstreifen) and

prohibited zones (Sperrzonen), the first step toward a physical demarcation of Germany in the postwar period. It is significant that these last restrictive measures were enacted on the very day of the signing of the "Convention on the Settlement of Matters Arising out of the War and the Occupation" by the three Western powers. This document provided for the Federal Republic's receiving "the full authority of a sovereign state over its internal and external affairs" upon the formation of the European Defense Community. The official East German rationale for the border actions, namely, to "prevent a further incursion of undesirables, spies, terrorists, and wreckers,"[41] conveyed convincingly Soviet concerns about the prospect of West German rearmament and indicated that countermeasures could be taken against a further integration of the Federal Republic into the Western alliance.

In the next three years and especially after the June 1953 East German uprising, the Ulbricht regime took its first, if halting, steps toward declaring a state sovereignty for the GDR independent of West Germany. The First Secretary's initial references to two German states appeared in September and November of 1953; two advocates of German unity, State Security Minister Wilhelm Zaisser and the chief editor of the official East German newspaper Neues Deutschland, Rudolf Herrnstadt, were removed from the SED Central Committee by January 1954; the March 25, 1954 "Statement of the Soviet Government" established "sovereign state" relations between the Soviet Union and East Germany, leaving the latter "free to decide on internal and external affairs"[42] and making it unlikely that the former would now "abandon" the GDR; and the GDR President promulgated a "Passport Law of the German Democratic Republic" on September 15, 1954, although this regulation continued to recognize only one German citizenship. That the SED regime failed to take stronger measures of demarcation must be attributed to the Soviet interest in hindering a West German rearmament, a priority which had been momentarily fulfilled with the defeat of the European Defense Community in the French Parliament in August of 1954. Closely corresponding with the October 1954-January 1955 suggestions of the Soviet Government, the Ulbricht leadership soon began to sanction the holding of free, All-German elections in return for the Federal Republic's renunciation of the military participation foreseen in the October 1954 Paris Treaties. An SED Central Committee declaration on January 18, 1955 called for an understanding between the two parts of Germany and Four Power negotiations on the execution of All-German, free elections in the case of FRG rejection of the treaties. Yet Grotewohl's May suggestions, emphasizing that annulment of the just-ratified treaties and West German neutralization on the Austrian model would facilitate elections, were removed on June 3 in favor of new reunification preconditions, none of which mentioned free elections.[43]

It was thus clear that the developing East-West stalemate on the German question made 1955 the pivotal year in the official splitting of the two Germanys, regardless of the Adenauer Government's doctrinal adherence to a still-unified German state and East German use of the vocabulary of reunification. The membership of the FRG and the GDR in opposing military alliances in May of 1955 and the failure of the Geneva Conference to achieve visible progress on the German problem in July necessitated that both German governments take actions to more permanently operationalize their state conceptions. The Adenauer Government's immediate response was to elevate the West German right to speak for all Germans to a foreign policy directive, although the Chancellor at the same time adopted full diplomatic relations with the Soviet Union. FRG policy regarding East German recognition was made explicit in Adenauer's September 22, 1955 address to the Bundestag: "I must unequivocally emphasize that the Federal Government will in the future view the adoption of diplomatic relations with the GDR by third states with which it maintains official relations as an unfriendly act."[44] What came to be called the "Hallstein Doctrine" thus left the choice of reprisals against recognition of the Ulbricht regime in Bonn's hands. The chancellor also denied that simultaneous Soviet recognition of East and West Germany weakened the Federal Republic's exclusive claim of German recognition and legitimacy; this statement was defended by citing Adenauer's letter to Soviet Prime Minister Bulganin, which affirmed that FRG-Soviet recognition "does not represent a recognition of the mutual territorial ownership existing at this time" and "does not mean a change in the legal position of the Federal Government in relation to its authority to speak for the German people."[45] These declarations did not, however, gain the written acceptance of the Soviet Government.

Four days later, Ulbricht declared that the GDR "possesses full sovereignty as the only German state," yet such exhortations differed from the claims of the West German Government in not creating a policy corrolary such as the Hallstein Doctrine. Recognition of the FRG did not necessarily exclude diplomatic relations with the SED regime in the East German "two states" design. Potentially more troublesome to Bonn was a Soviet cession of authority to the GDR in a September 20, 1955 "Treaty Concerning the Relations between the GDR and USSR," specifically that contained

in an accompanying exchange of letters between Soviet
Assistant Foreign Minister Sorin and East German
Foreign Minister Bolz. "In connection with the
carrying out of protection and control" on the access
routes between the FRG and Berlin, it was declared that
East Berlin "will ensure the settlement with the
appropriate authorities of the German Federal Republic
of all questions pertaining to the transit of rail,
road, and water traffic of the German Federal Republic
or Western Berlin." This statement was issued in line
with the treaty's provisions for East Germany's
"sovereignty" and freedom "in solving questions of its
home and foreign policies." The transit access of
Western military hardware and personnel was explicitly
exempted from this new East German authority, however,
as the "command of the group of Soviet forces in
Germany" assumed "temporary" control of the above "on
the basis of the existing Four Power agreements."[46]
    Both the Kremlin and the SED thereby registered
the position that the civilian travel of West Germans
and West Berliners along the access routes was a
subject for inner-German discussion. Nevertheless,
this dual authority was never accepted by the Western
powers, nor was the distinction repeated by Soviet
representatives during and after the 1958 Berlin
crisis. Khrushchev's threat to turn access
responsibility over to the GDR clearly implied Soviet
control over the routes at that time. In addition,
with the exception of a January 1963 Ulbricht
statement,[47] one cannot find evidence to suggest that
the access of West Germans became a subject of serious
inner-German negotiation. This possibility only arose
with the FRG-GDR implementation of the 1971
Quadripartite Agreement on Berlin, which was based on a
direct Four Power authorization.
    Thereafter the East and West German versions of
"Deutschlandpolitik" did not resemble mirror images,
but developed unevenly and according to the different
needs and dangers perceived by each government. For
the Ulbricht regime, the period from 1955 to 1961 was
one of intensive party penetration of the state,
increasing collectivization, and attempts to upgrade
the status of the GDR vis-a-vis the Federal Republic.
On January 26 and 27, 1956, the newly created National
People's Army (Volksarmee) was accepted as the East
German contingent to the Warsaw Pact Organization along
with the armed forces of five East European states and
the Soviet Union. The emergence of political factions
around SED functionaries Karl Schirdewan, Ernst
Wollweber, and Gerhart Ziller lent some impetus to
slowing the pace of Ulbricht's orthodox collectivism,
proposing an inner-German detente, and implementing de-
Stalinization in an East German context in 1956.[48] The
Soviet crushing of the Hungarian Revolution, however,

was followed by Khrushchev's withdrawal of support for Schirdewan and the isolation of Ulbricht's opponents by the time of the February 1957 Thirtieth Meeting of the SED Central Committee. A series of laws passed in 1957 and 1958 sought to translate the principle of "democratic centralism" into administrative reality by making obligatory the decisions of the Volkskammer, the Council of Ministers, and the fifteen District Councils.[49] The effect of the SED's "two states policy" on inner-German relations cannot be overemphasized, as it was the 1960 collectivization of agriculture, for example, which contributed significantly to the mass outflow of East Germans from the GDR prior to the 1961 building of the Berlin Wall. Additionally. a GDR state flag and coat-of-arms were approved by the Ulbricht leadership in September 1959.

East German "confederation" proposals, on the other hand, generally entailed the precondition of parity-based inner-German contacts,[50] and since consultations would have amounted to recognition of a sort, they were the logical extension of internal measures to upgrade the GDR's statehood. The November 27, 1958 Khrushchev proposal for a "free city" status in Berlin[51] also indicated what was of central importance: the Soviet leadership was also interested in upgrading this East German status.

The SED proposals for inner-German contacts were issued during the era of Bonn's most formalistic adherence to the Hallstein Doctrine and non-recognition of the "Soviet Occupation Zone." In practice, FRG diplomatic relations with any government that established relations with East Berlin would be terminated, the sole exception being the Soviet Union; this policy was first given effect in the case of Yugoslavia on October 19, 1957.[52] The Adenauer Government also countered the Ulbricht regime's assertion that reunification was "a matter for Germans" by directing its own reunification suggestions to the Soviet Union and either ignoring or rejecting those issued by the SED. There were, however, several exceptions to the rule of no dealings with the East German Government. Trade, of course, was an ongoing activity which could be legalistically justified on the grounds that the Inter-zonal Trade Trusteeship was not technically a representative of the government but of German industry. The West German Minister of Justice, Fritz Schaeffer, took part in discussions in East Berlin with the Soviet ambassador in October 1956; these talks reportedly concerned reunification and took place "in the presence of" Volksarmee General Vincenz Mueller. Moreover, the Federal Government dispatched an official of the Economics Ministry to East Berlin during the crisis negotiations over trade and travel in late 1960.[53]

Nevertheless, the West German Government pursued

its policy of representation through aid programs and also secured recognition of its All-German claims in the Rome Treaty. The latter regarded trade between the FRG and "the German territories in which the Basic Law does not apply" as "German internal trade," requiring no special amendment and allowing East German products to obtain tariff-free entry into EEC member states.[54]

The years 1961 to 1963 saw the economic and ideological stabilization of the GDR with the construction of the Berlin Wall as well as further SED action to claim the attributes of a state. This program actually began in the midst of the erection of the Wall; the East German Government now began to use the expression "citizens of the German Democratic Republic," in directives issued to the population. General military conscription was established by the Volkskammer as a result of a September 20, 1961 law and although the Ulbricht leadership continued to make known proposals for inner-German cooperation, these now called for equal representation of both German states in the United Nations.[55] but the increase in physical demarcation and ideological education in the GDR after the building of the Wall was testimony to the renewed Soviet resolve. Henceforth the East German leadership intensified its efforts toward securing international recognition of the GDR as a sovereign state.

Meanwhile, the increasing frequency of East German diplomatic inroads into Third World countries compelled the Federal Government to consider the possibility that breaking off relations with offenders of the Hallstein Doctrine would enhance the GDR's official status by default. The Adenauer Government's termination of relations with Cuba after the latter's January 12, 1963 recognition of the SED regime rewarded such East German efforts that had also resulted in the dispatching of special missions to five other countries. As a result of growing dissatisfaction with the strict observance of the Doctrine, the Erhard Government began to publicly interpret it as a flexible device to serve West German interests, a practice that was not inconsistent with the original, rather vague formulation of it by Adenauer. After Ulbricht's visit to the United Arab Republic in early 1965, an FRG declararion announced that any further upgrading of the GDR would be "answered with measures suitable for each individual case."[56]

This softening of the punitive character of the Federal Republic's right of sole representration was not intended to and did not signify a change in Bonn's policy of non-recognition of the GDR. The countries of Eastern Europe, rather than the Ulbricht regime, were to be the target of Bonn's "small steps" diplomacy. Inner-German Minister Erich Mende acknowledged in April 1966 that his March 1965 suggestion of parity-based negotiations between East and West German technical commissions based on "mandates" authorized by the Four Powers "would presently find no majority in Bonn."[57] Additionally, the March 25, 1966 "Peace Note" of the Erhard Government sought an opening to the East European Communist regimes but ignored the East German leadership. SED demands for formal recognition of the GDR and acknowledgment of West Berlin's "independent" status now appeared as repetitive aspects of East German policy, and West German attempts to link trade concessions with East German facilitation of the travel situation inside divided Berlin were rejected by Ulbricht as an "immoral business."[58] If any more proof of this were needed after the breakdown in trade talks in early 1965, it was supplied by several Soviet and East German interdictions of air, water, and land travel to West Berlin in April and June of 1965.

It was in the presence of some notable East German successes in acquiring recognition of a GDR sovereignty, including the signing of the 1963 Test Ban Treaty, that the CDU/CSU-SPD "Grand Coalition" assumed power in December 1966. The new West German Government to an even greater extent than its predecessor aimed at the more practical goal of easing living conditions for the East German population rather than favoring an exclusive emphasis on reunification. The Grand Coalition did not depart from the past precedents of no legal recognition of the GDR and FRG representation of all Germans,[59] but it did undertake steps toward a dialogue and practical cooperation with the Ulbricht leadership and no longer foreswore relations with East European countries that recognized the GDR. It became apparent, however, that the expanded links with Eastern Europe antagonized the SED leadership, which perceived a new threat in the modified right of sole representation and, through "Treaties of Friendship, Cooperation, and Mutual Assistance" with four Warsaw Pact countries in 1967, received their practical assent not to recognize the Federal Republic until the latter had recognized East Germany.

In terms of the inner-German picture, West German recognition of Romania in January of 1967 was the occasion of a new East German counteroffensive. Consequently, Inner-German Minister Herbert Wehner's suggestion that Ulbricht's January 1 proposal for a discussion of the Potsdam Treaty "become the subject of current consideration and possibly of proposals for eventually necessary measures" was followed by an SED rebuke.[60] Wehner's raising the possibility of East-West German ministerial talks on February 3 led to what was possibly the most extended East German criticism of the right of sole representation ten days later.[61] On the domestic front, the Council of State's issuance of a "Law on the Citizenship of the German Democratic

Republic" was the first such law in the GDR and formally annulled the Reich and State Citizenship Law of 1913, upon which the FRG notion of German citizenship was partially based. The East German "State Secretariat for All-German Questions" was renamed the "State Secretariat for West German Questions." Two exchanges of letters between Willi Stoph, Chairman of the East German Council of Ministers, and Chancellor Kiesinger did, however, mark the first such public exchange between the two governments since the November 1951 Pieck-Heuss communications; they essentially repeated familiar positions regarding German representation and self-determination.

The remainder of the Grand Coalition's tenure witnessed significant inner-German trade agreements and West German recognition of Yugoslavia, which invalidated past Government explanations that FRG relations with some European states were permissible since those states had recognized the GDR prior to the inception of the Hallstein Doctrine.[62] Equally, the public exchanges between East and West German leaders served to strengthen the image of the SED as the de facto leadership in East Germany with which the Federal Republic might have official dealings. The Ulbricht regime for its part enshrined the principle of a GDR citizenry in its April 1968 constitution, which defined the state according to socialist criteria, and pressed the West German Government further in its demands for the conclusion of "sovereign state treaties" between the two.[63] This program was the center of a heightened crisis in May-June 1968 when the demand was accompanied by new traffic and visa requirements hindering Western travellers' access to West Berlin; Soviet anxiety over the Czechoslovakian liberalization at this time neatly coincided with the SED's demarcation towards Bonn. The paradox of the Grand Coalition's Deutschlandpolitik persisted up to the formation of the SPD-FDP coalition in October 1969. The East German establishment of diplomatic relations with Cambodia, Iraq and the Sudan in the spring of that year again benefitted the East German counter-policy to the revised policy of the Federal Republic. The West German recall of the FRG ambassador to Cambodia, the only one of the above three countries with whom relations were maintained, seemed to call for new approaches with which to neutralize or adapt to the growing impression of two German states.

INNER-GERMAN REGULATION OF PRACTICAL
AND HUMANITARIAN AREAS: TRADE

Inter-zonal trade had been entirely eliminated by the June 1948 Berlin Blockade and was only resumed through Soviet abandonment of the blockade on May 12, 1949 and the Jessup-Malik Agreement, which also provided for the lifting of the Western counterblockade against the Soviet Zone. The October 8, 1949 Frankfurt Agreement, signed one day after the founding of the GDR, included for the first time East and West German negotiations over future inner-German trade activities. The agreement was not especially noteworthy for the level of trade achieved, which fell short of expectations, but for the precedents established for later trade. These practices consisted of the creation of a special unit of account (VE) for transactions corresponding to the value of a West German mark, a prototype of the so-called "swing" or overdraw credit, amounting to 15 million and 1 million VE for the two quota-applicable and quota-free accounts. The agreement included the eastern and western sectors of Berlin in exchanges on the side of, respectively, the GDR and the FRG.[64]

Both governments concurred in treating trade as a "special" undertaking, especially in view of the Adenauer Government's stated refusal to recognize and tolerate official dealings with the SED regime. For this reason, the West German organization responsible for negotiating with its Eastern counterpart, the Inter-zonal Trade Trustee, maintained its formal staus as an organ of German industry and trade. Overall authority for trade in the GDR was vested in the Ministry of Foreign and Intra-German Trade. East-West German trade continued to be regarded as "inter-zonal," the two trading partners were designated in the agreement as "Currency Area- DM West" and "Currency Area- DM East," a useful device that made possible Berlin's inclusion. Moreover, the intentional use of the terms "deliveries" and "payments," rather than "exports" amd "imports," proved compatible with the All-German notions adhered to at this time by both governments.[65] The stringent controls on inner-German trade, which were almost entirely of West German origin, constituted another permanent feature first introduced here: a cumbersome licensing process for the exchange of goods was introduced some months later and was accompanied by a proviso list requiring Bonn's special permission for exporting certain items, mainly chemical and metal products, to the GDR.[66]

Lagging deliveries of East German goods, a steel embargo of the GDR by the Adenauer Government in February 1950, and the Cold War tensions of the 1950's contributed to the inter-zonal trade's worst stagnation of these two decades from 1950 to 1954. The total volume of goods exchanged declined to less than half its 1950 level in 1951 and 1952 and did not attain this amount again until 1954.[67] With the signing of the September 20, 1951 Berlin Agreement, however, the only

contractual basis for East-West German trade did come
into being; the document was consistently renewed each
year until 1960, when Bonn retaliated against East
German obstruction of the Berlin traffic. Trade
increased continuously, if modestly, during this
period. The Berlin Agreement left unchanged most of
the practices of the Frankfurt Agreement but added a
series of separate accords for 340 million VE of trade
in either direction, continuation of trade in coal,
payments transactions for services, deliveries of
electricity, listing exchangeable goods, and a system
of numbered account and sub-accounts for exchanging
specific categories of goods. This last measure was to
be supervised by the German Federal Bank and the (East)
German Central Bank and subjected this barter trade to
tight controls by West Germany: goods exchanged within
each account had to be balanced four times annually,
with no cash transactions allowed.[68]

The Federal Republic's much circumscribed
political and military sovereignty in the 1950's left
trade as one of the few levers it might independently
wield to influence East German behavior. The belief
that the Adenauer Government could do so was
strengthened by the reality that the inter-zonal trade
was relatively far more important to the GDR, stabilizing at approximately eleven percent of its total
foreign trade after 1955.[69] From 1955 to 1960 East and
West Germany experienced a seventy-five percent
increase in their mutual transactions, and agreements
reached from 1957 to 1959 allowed for East German cash
purchases of non-embargoed goods, a "special account"
for additional trade, and special exchanges of coal and
wheat.[70] Yet the absolute amount of trade continued to
be calibrated according to the Federal Republic's
political, as opposed to economic, purposes: the
desire to express solicitude for Germans in the East
and appear as the champion of German unity, the need to
prevent an excessive integration of the GDR into the
Soviet economy, and the desire to discourage possible
East German interference with transportation access to
West Berlin.

While the Adenauer Government offered important
concessions on the "swing" and lengthening of the time
period for planned trade, inner-German trade lapsed
into its second prolonged stagnation after 1960 because
of the East German demand that West Germans and West
Berliners acquire special "day passes" for visiting
East Berlin. The Inter-zonal Trade Agreement was
thereupon terminated by the "Representative for the
Currency Area DM-West," in keeping with the "inter-
zonal" symbolism, "including all additional
agreements." The FRG stated intention to "clarify
whether possibilities for a continuation" of the trade
could materialize was revealed only after East Berlin's

specification that it would in the future deal
separately with the Federal Republic and West Berlin in
trade negotiations. The West German Finance Ministry
did not heed this demand in its resoration of the trade
agreement on December 30. Bonn continued to represent
West Berlin in subsequent trade negotiations, but it
was reported that the pass restrictions remained in
effect.[71]

The announcement of an East-West German "Special
Protocol on Technical and Procedural Questions" did not
put an end to frictions as the Federal Government
imposed a "revocation clause" in the Berlin Agreement
on January 26. This action made it possible for the
FRG to suspend the delivery of "strategic" goods to the
GDR while shifting the onus of provocation to East
Berlin. East German enforcement of the pass
requirements did not disappear but gradually assumed a
more perfunctory character, however, it was clear that
neither the cancellation of the trade agreement nor the
threat of the revocation clause represented sufficient
pressure to dissuade the SED from its efforts at
demarcation during these days of East German flight to
the West. It was therefore not wholly unexpected when
after promising "necessary measures" in response to the
sealing off of East Berlin in August 1961,[72] Chancellor
Adenauer declined to invoke trade sanctions against the
GDR.

The East German resolution to de-couple inner-
German trade from other matters of interest to Bonn was
no less demonstrable in years to come. The 1961-1963
stagnation after the building of the Wall was not
devoid of attempts to expand trade; East Berlin showed
itself to be keenly interested in securing long-term
credits in 1962, putatively a five-year credit
equalling 1.2 billion marks. Nevertheless, the
collapse of trade talks in January 1963 was attributed
by the Federal Government to the East German position
that the Trade Trustee "only treat economic questions
in the future," while Ulbricht described the West
German drive for further Berlin agreements in
hyperbolic terms.[73] In addition, East German delays of
border traffic at a number of control points in
September of 1964, were followed by warnings that the
SED leadership could establish its own "linkage"--
between the "Wall Pass" agreement and the West German
rate fixed for the acquisition of East German marks.[74]

Although inner-German trade showed a substantial
increase by 1964,[75] West German decisionmakers
increasingly had to contend with East Berlin's linkage
of trade with its program to "normalize" relations with
the Federal Republic. SED declarations repeatedly
called for an East-West German exchange of trade
missions and the forming of parity-based commissions to
discuss trade as well as other areas of cooperation.

Given the intensified East German campaign against the Hallstein Doctrine and the Federal Government's linkage of trade to West Berlin, the breakdown of trade talks in late 1964 was not surprising. It should not go unnoticed, however, that even in the face of East German interference with inner-German travel in 1964 and April-June 1965, Bonn failed to resort to termination of the Berlin Agreement as in 1960, nor was the more selective revocation clause or curtailment of the "swing" utilized. In retrospect, the West German leadership preferred the more moderate option of withholding the extension of the lucrative credit arrangement that East Berlin had sought: the "swing's" level of 200 million DM-West was not increased until 1967 despite East German demands that it be raised to 500 million DM and that the strategic goods account be doubled.[76]

More fundamentally, although the Schroeder policy attempted to isolate the GDR diplomatically, West German policymakers now found it less useful to punish the East German leadership via trade reprisals. The experience of the 1963 trade negotiations had revealed not simply SED exasperation with Bonn's requirement that accounts be balanced and with the onerous system of licensing, but also the Ulbricht leadership's pointed refusal to extend political concessions in return for West German trade credits. As other OECD states began to show interest in trade with the GDR, the Erhard Government was forced to recognize that if East Berlin so chose, it might utilize more fully other Western trading partners.[77]

A March 1966 cabinet decision even went so far as to rule out any West German trade sanctions unless the Berlin access routes were interrupted.[78] Nor did the Erhard Government abide by the letter of the "special nature" of inter-zonal trade in the same way as the previous leadership; the Inter-zonal Trade Trustee was not the negotiating body for the 1963 "Wall Pass" discussions, having been superseded in this activity by the Federal Government and the Berlin Senate. Similarly, the replacement of Kurt Leopold, who had been considered suitable to head the trusteeship in his unofficial capacity as a representative of industry, was followed with the appointment of an official of the Economics Ministry.[79]

Bonn's less punitive trade policy occurred in a period that contrasted with the earlier stagnation, as the largest absolute increase yet achieved in inner-German trade was recorded in 1966.[80] The Grand Coalition then followed up Chancellor Kiesinger's April 1967 credit suggestions with the extension of five-year Federal export credits amounting to up to ninety percent of the value of the goods exchanged; hitherto the "swing" credit had only been made available through

West German private finance. Major concessions consisted of Bonn's willingness to allow East Berlin to trade "soft" goods against "hard" strategic goods for the first time, FRG rescinding of the revocation clause, the exemption of inter-zonal trade from value-added tax, and the raising of the "swing" to 300 million DM, all in 1967. Yet these trade-enhancing measures did little to stimulate the sale of East German goods; the sizeable GDR deficit in 1966 was thus followed by a lower trade volume in 1967 and 1968.[81]

This temporary downturn was to a great extent relieved by the December 6, 1968 "Agreement on Special Aspects of Trade" between the West German Inter-zonal Trade Trustee and the GDR Ministry of Foreign Trade. The most important innovations included were the provisions for long-term inner-German trade, the abandonment of the requirement that the net debit in trade be paid off by June 30, and the elevation of the "swing" amount to twenty-five percent of East German deliveries to the Federal Republic in the previous year. (The first foresaw mainly major increases in the sale of machinery on both sides until 1975).[82] The last step was particularly necessary in view of the constantly increasing East German debt that was a major factor in the 1967-1968 trade stagnation: the results were quite significant in bringing about the largest annual absolute increase ever.[83]

TRAFFIC AND TRANSPORTATION

The first actual meeting between East and West German transportation officials took place in May 1949 as a direct follow-up to the Jessup-Malik Agreement. The Helmstedt Agreement, signed on May 11 between the High Authority of the later German Federal Railway and the General Directorate of the Berlin Reich Railway, signalled the resumption of inter-zonal rail transportation after the Berlin Blockade. An additional agreement concluded on September 3, 1949, the Offenbach Agreement, opened up new rail routes to the cities of Ludwigstadt and Bebra, regulated certain transportation payments, and contained instructions for the sale of tickets. Both parts of Berlin were allowed to sell tickets for the inter-zonal travel, thus laying the groundwork for future inclusion of Berlin in inner-German travel arrangements. This railway accord was followed on October 4 by a settlement on autobus traffic between Eastern and Western zonal authorities. Of particular importance in this agreement was the equalization of rail and street tariffs for the traffic and, secondarily, specification of the lines to be used as well as of the amount of cross-border traffic. As was the case in East-West German trade agreements, a

mutually acceptable nomenclature was employed. The
East German designation of "German Reich Railway," a
phrase still used to this day, implied a still-existing
German state unity and the Offenbach Agreement's term
for the FRG, "the Unified Economic Zones," proved
unobjectionable to the SED leadership.[84]

From the year 1950 onward, in fact, regular
consultations on railroad scheduling have taken place
between the officials of these two organizations,
although they have not been responsible for tourist
travel and the transportation of goods. In comparison,
there was an almost complete absence of written regulations for inner-German motor vehicle traffic, a
shortcoming that proved to be of great concern to the
FRG. On September 1, 1951 the Ulbricht Government
imposed a toll for West German motorists entering the
GDR. Even more deleterious were the events of May
1952, as the East German Ministry for State Security
reduced the number of border crossing routes from
twelve to four in line with the declared goal of
preventing the "incursion of undesirables."[85] Inner-
German travel could be no more insulated from the
Federal Republic's inclusion in the Western treaties
and SED demarcation than could trade, for it was a
component part of the total East-West German
relationship; more importantly, Soviet policy, directed
toward preventing West German rearmament, could exert
pressure on Bonn quite handily via East Berlin in this
manner.

The overall travel situation, however, experienced
a period of relative calm and even some improvement
after these early setbacks. The SED regime continued
to require permits for West German visitors to the GDR,
formally issued by the local East German district to be
visited, and East German fortifications along the
border were continued. Yet the year 1954 saw two
notable agreements facilitating travel: one between the
German Reich Railway and the West Berlin Travel Agency
and a second expanding rail transportation. The first
undertaking allowed the Travel Agency to sell passes
and tickets for travel to Berlin in West Berlin in the
volume permitted by the Reich Railway, and the second
opened additional rail crossing points.[86] East Berlin's
April 1, 1955 doubling of the street tolls for West
German motorists appeared perplexing in view of the
impending Bundestag vote on the Paris Treaties, but
negotiations later led to the partial cancellation of
this increase.[87] Agreement was also reached in 1958 on
motor vehicle accident settlement between the German
Insurance Company Berlin (East) and the United
Insurance Company of Greater Berlin (East), on one
hand, and the West German Association of Liability,
Accident, and Traffic Insurance Corporations on the
other.[88]

Although the November 1958 Khrushchev ultimatum on
Berlin threatened to place responsibility for access to
the western sectors permanently in East German hands,
it was not until 1960 that the Federal Government
judged the actual travel hindrances to be severe enough
to merit reprisals against East Berlin. This response,
of course, took the form of cancellation of the Berlin
Agreement. The tense state of inner-German travel was
broken only briefly by the East German opening of a new
border crossing in Luebeck in April. The initial
August 20 East German requirement of day passes for
West Germans visiting East Berlin was justified in an
SED declaration the next day as a counter-measure to
the "revanchist event" of the "Berlin Day of the Home"
and the "Day of Union of Returned Soldiers, War
Prisoners, and Missing Members," a West German
commemoration.[89] (The former gathering had been held
nine previous times in Berlin). The resulting searches
and delays for West German travellers were executed
throughout the entire period up until late January,
when the Economics Ministry announced the trade
"revocation clause"; in the following weeks, the
severity of the travel checks was alternately tightened
and loosened but the requirements still remained in
effect.
     In the midst of the rising numbers of Germans
fleeing from East Germany in 1961 (Federal Minister
Lemmer reported a total of 66,000 from January to
April),[90] the intensity of SED measures to physically
obstruct or delay West German visits to East Berlin
fluctuated, with the day pass requirements still
remaining in effect. They were, however, increasingly
treated as a formality in contrast to the lengthy
searches of the previous fall; this was the case even
during the building of the Berlin Wall. West German
visits to the GDR in general, however, remained at a
minimal level, since the East German authorities as a
rule only permitted these for visiting close relatives
once a year for a maximum period of four weeks. Except
for day-visits to East Berlin, travel to the GDR was
restricted to business trips, attendance of the Leipzig
Fair, and acceptance of invitations from East German
government agencies or officials. The August 1961
measures cut the flow of visitation from West Berlin to
East Berlin and forebade East German visits to the FRG,
just as West Berliners had been for the most part
denied travel access to the GDR since 1952. At the
same time, the GDR authorities refused to continue the
Federal Railway's right to use sections of East German
track along the Hersfeld/Eisenach route. The only
visible progress in traffic cooperation at this time
was the March 1961 negotiated abolition of a waterway
toll imposed by East German authorities after FRG
construction of a dam in the Elbe River.[91]

With the sharp disruption in East-West Berlin travel after the building of the Wall, much of the initiative for further progress passed to the Senate of West Berlin and its mayor, Willy Brandt. Nevertheless, a new offer of trade credits to the GDR by Minister Erich Mende on November 30, 1963 was followed only five days later by a letter from East German Assistant Prime Minister Abusch to Brandt announcing the possibility of a Berlin pass agreement for the Christmas and New Year holidays; the pass agreement was in fact concluded on December 17 by the GDR Government and the Berlin Senate. In return for the East German issuance of holiday passes, the Erhard Government declared that "in 1964 the DM-West currency area will compensate the DM-East currency area for up to 582,000 tons of fuel at DM 129/ton, a total of DM 75,000,000."[92] Some improvement was also discernible in 1964, as the two governments reached agreement on the repairing and maintenance of the Hirschberg autobahn bridges in August, with the participation of the Trade Trustee, and the opening of a new railroad crossing point at Hof. The GDR was made responsible for the actual construction of the bridge, while the Federal Republic contributed a lump-sum of 5.5 million VE. A September 9 Protocol between the Federal Railway and the East German Ministry of Traffic Service provided for the alternate use of East and West German trains for the shipment of freight to and from the FRG, specified the crossing points to be utilized for this purpose, and initiated prior inner-German agreement on the amount of freight to be transported during each rail schedule. The above agreement was reached one day after a statement by the GDR Council of Ministers that permitted East German pensioners to make annual visits to the Federal Republic of up to four weeks.[93]

These agreements culminated in the September 24 "Permit Agreement" once more concluded by the GDR and the Berlin Senate, but which in addition to allowing Christmas and New Years' visitation of relatives also secured West Berliners' travel to East Berlin for two weeks during Easter and Pentecost. Chancellor Erhard, of course, approved the agreement but accompanied this approval with an emphatic statement on the illegitimacy of the GDR and the assertion that "the importance of the regulation lies in the human area."[94] Both the SED decision to permit pensioners' travel to West Germany and the "Wall Pass" agreement were preceded by the September 2 West German announcement of First Secretary Khrushchev's willingness to visit Bonn. The November 25 East German introduction of a compulsory minimum currency exchange for Western travellers into the GDR, six weeks after Khrushchev's ouster, stood in sharp contrast to these earlier travel-expansion intiatives. In unilaterally imposing these payments, the

Ulbricht regime inaugurated a series of inner-German travel hindrances in keeping with East Berlin's heightened efforts towards a change in the status of Berlin and West German recognition of GDR sovereignty within its borders. Two important exceptions to this tendency were the continuation of the "Wall Pass" understanding for the Christmas and New Year holidays in 1965-66 and for Easter and Pentecost in 1965 and 1966.[95] Again, however, it was the Senate of West Berlin and not the Erhard Government which played the leading role in these negotiations.

These successes preceded a series of setbacks for the West German Government concomitant with a developing East German program to secure international recognition. The resulting breakdown in inner-German transportation was first reflected in SED termination of the mutual List of Fares for Inter-zonal Railway Traffic on June 30, 1965. This action, ostensibly implemented by the Ulbricht leadership to obtain the recognition of international transportation law for inner-German traffic and receive full membership in international transport organizations, placed new impediments in the way of freight transportation. (It will be recalled that June was also the period of East German interruption of transportation routes to West Berlin and extreme verbal objections to the Federal presence there). In 1966 toll fees retroactive to 1961 were demanded by the SED authorities from the Federal Railway, a condition that was only to be set aside after long negotiations and compensation in September 1969.[96] Perhaps the most serious inner-German confrontation of 1968, a year replete with tensions in the face of the Prague Spring, resulted from the East German imposition of traffic and visa requirements in June. In addition to the visa requirements, which necessitated a more time-consuming process of acquisition for West German citizens, authorities added an "equalization tax" to the already enacted road toll and certain groups were denied entry onto East German territory altogether.[97]

Even the bestowal of some important trade concessions on the GDR in December of 1968, treated earlier, and several other conciliatory West German gestures did not relieve East German pressure on inner-German travel; new fees were introduced on January 1, 1969 for items brought across the GDR border in tourist traffic. SED opposition to the holding of the FRG Presidential election in West Berlin not only took the form of a ban on the travel of the electors, the General Assembly (Bundesversammlung), to West Berlin but reportedly also led to Ulbricht's offer of a further "Wall Pass" agreement if the election were transferred to another city.[98] The failure of the East German-West Berlin negotiations toward this end were followed by the holding of the election on March 5, a "partial blockade" by East German soldiers, and roadblocks obstructing the land routes to West Germany but allowing the Assembly to arrive in Berlin by airplane.[99] Although the Soviet Government had protested the Presidential election along with the GDR leadership, its lack of desire for an East-West confontation in Berlin in 1969, particularly after the Soviet-Chinese border clashes in early March,[100] ensured that the most severe travel restrictions were limited in time. Indeed, in the midst of growing possibilities for FRG-Soviet force renunciation talks, the East German Government agreed on September 10 to begin talks with the Federal Republic on transportation questions, which commenced on September 16.

MAIL AND TELECOMMUNICATIONS

The postal and telecommunications authorities of the four occupation powers were transformed into the German Federal Postal Service and the German Postal Service after the proclamation of the Federal Republic and the German Democratic Republic in 1949. What was in the first postwar years a relatively intensive period of consultation between postal authorities in the western and eastern zones, from the high authorities down to district directors, gave way to increasingly infrequent meetings once the political division of the two Germanys became apparent in the 1950's. One of the earliest and most conspicuous instances of the disruption took place in May of 1952, when the East German Government accompanied its lock-out measures along the "line of demarcation" with disconnection of the approximately 4,000 telephone lines connecting the eastern and western sectors of Berlin. Postal deliveries, on the other hand, continued in a relatively smooth fashion until 1954, although the transportation of mail was limited to letters, postcards, printed matter, braille mailings, and parcels. The August 5 "Ordinance on the Mailing of Gifts and Parcels along the Postal Routes to West Germany, West Berlin, and Foreign Countries" symbolized a much tougher SED policy on mailings into the GDR. As a result of the strict enforcement of this regulation, mail sent to the GDR was increasingly confiscated or returned to the sender.[101]

Telephone service between the Federal Republic and East Germany was during this period subject to special limitations, not least of which was the paucity of connecting lines between the two parts of Germany. It was not unusual for callers to experience a waiting period of four to fifteen hours for connection to be made or for calls to be refused altogether. East

German authorities were compelled to introduce time limitations on each call due to the considerable number of prospective callers. Inner-German telegraph and teleprint transmissions were similarly subject to a shortage of lines and the fact that, particularly on days of heavy usage, delays arose from the necessity of directing West German or West Berlin transmissions to the GDR or East Berlin through the main telegraph office in East Berlin, where they were re-telegraphed.[102]

In 1966 the SED regime also began to make a number of financial claims on the West German Government for postal services rendered earlier. Towards the end of 1966, East Berlin demanded several hundred million DM from the Federal Government and approximately 100 million DM from the Berlin Senate, essentially for East German package deliveries, West German use of a long-distance cable to West Berlin, and interest payments; these payments were to cover services calculated from the year 1949. Not surprisingly, the East German fees were reputedly determined according to "international" costs.[103] The response of the Federal Minister for Mail and Telecommunications was to refuse payment on the basis of international principles, but to agree to compensation from 1967 onward. These suggestions were not heeded by the Ulbricht Government, which on February 9, 1968 demanded 630 million DM in postal fees and on May 23 raised the total for West German payments from 1948 to 1967 to over 1 billion DM. Bonn, in fact, did remit 16.9 million in postal fees to the GDR Postal Authority in East Berlin on October 28, 1968 as a settlement for the year 1967 and paid 5.1 million DM in February 1969 for the first half of 1968. It was not until September of 1969, however, that SED assent to negotiations between East and West German postal authorities was secured, and the final resolution of this dispute awaited postal agreements in 1970 and 1971.[104]

SPORTS

East-West German athletic events were quite numerous prior to 1961 but suffered considerable stagnation from 1961 to 1965. This is not to imply, of course, that athletic contacts in the early years remained insulated from the political purposes of each government; reports surfaced in the spring of 1952, for example, that West Berlin athletes desiring to compete in East German sporting events would be required to utter declarations condemning the newly-drafted "general war treaty" and "the Reuter-Adenauer splitter regime."[105] Yet the East German "German Sports Committee" (DSA) agreed later in the year not to

subject West Berlin athletes to "special regulations,"
a reversal of its earlier operative premise of a "three
states theory,"[106] and All-German teams participated in
both the 1956 and 1960 Olympic Games. (This last
arrangement was a precondition for the GDR's continued
provisional membership in the International Olympic
Committee). A December 12, 1952 agreement between the
DSA and the German Federation of Sports (DSB), its West
German counterpart, laid the foundation for later
sporting activities: it prohibited "the misuse of the
Olympic ideal and of sports" for political purposes as
well as established Berlin's participation in athletic
events.[107] Moreover, inner-German events from 1957 to
1961 attained a numerical level not even remotely
approached in any year through 1969. In the area of
the Federal Republic alone, 1,530 such events were held
in 1957, decreasing to 738 in 1961, while from the year
1966 to 1969 the maximum number of events held in both
the FRG and GDR for one year amounted to only 88.[108]

In retrospect, it is to be observed that these
athletic contacts never recovered from the blows
inflicted in 1960 and 1961. The East German "two
states policy," it will be recalled, culminated in the
creation of a coat-of-arms and state flag in 1959, the
former of which was to be carried by East German
athletes alongside the insignia of their club.
Although impasses resulted after the West German
refusal to allow such representations in events on the
soil of the Federal Republic, it was the building of
the Berlin Wall that triggered the interruption of All-
German sporting events. A joint communique of the DSB
and the National Olympic Committee (NOK) of the FRG
announced the suspension of these contacts on the
grounds that since "only those persons obedient to the
system have the possibility of athletic meetings with
the Federal Republic,"[109] it was the SED that prevented
an authentic All-German exchange. Statements
attributed to Adenauer and von Brentano, however,
clearly expressed a West German desire to terminate the
sporting events prior to August 1961,[110] and Willi
Daume, President of the DSB, had engaged in a critical
exchange of letters with his East German counterpart,
Manfred Ewald, over the attempts to use sports for
political propaganda.[111] For the next four years, joint
East-West German athletic participation was limited to
the inclusion of German teams in the 1964 Olympics, albeit with the same national symbols, and the "illegal
sports activities" which were technically prohibited by
the August 1961 DSB and NOK decision but which did not
prevent some few inner-German events in the GDR.

As a result of an October 11, 1965 IOC decision in
Madrid, however, the DSB was at the end of the month
able to announce the resumption "of sporting events
with the organizations of the (East German) Federation

of German Gymnastics and Sports." The DSB specifically
cited the IOC ruling, which established a separate East
German Olympic team for the 1968 Olympics but also
included West Berlin athletes on West German teams, as
sufficient reason to restore "the movement of human
beings in divided Germany" on the athletic level.[112]
Although the Federal Government pledged to remove all
obstacles to the promotion of inner-German sports and
West German athletes began to participate in
international events where GDR symbols were used, the
contacts could hardly be termed extensive in comparison
to the 1950's. The East German DTSB, despite the
Madrid declaration, persisted in refusing to include
the Berlin Sports Federation along with the member
organizations of the DSB in prospective athletic
agreements. This position precluded the realization of
more ambitious DSB plans. The West German Government,
for its part, adopted the policy of tolerating the use
of GDR symbols in international sporting events but not
in inner-German events, a course of action that
appeared unavoidable once the IOC in 1968 sanctioned
the displaying of a separate East German flag, hymn,
and emblem at the 1972 Olympics.[113]

LEGAL ASSISTANCE

The Federal Republic, unlike the GDR, established
practices for responding to requests for legal
assistance from governmental bodies in the other part
of Germany early in its history. This foundation was
provided by way of a May 2, 1953 "Law on Inner-German
Legal and Official Assistance in Criminal Cases."
Legal and administrative assistance would be extended
to East German authorities if: 1) the proposed action
did not conflict with Federal laws; 2) no doubt existed
that the assistance was compatible with "constitutional
state principles"; and 3) "no considerable
disadvantages accrued" to the person affected by the
assistance that were "incompatible with constitutional
state principles."[114] A further condition for legal
assistance prevented the return of a legal offender to
the GDR who had committed a capital offense unless it
could be proven that there would be no death penalty
imposed. Generally, any contemplated legal assistance
also had to be approved by the local West German
Prosecutor General.
East German policy regarding legal and official
assistance exhibited a reliance on the assumption of
the Federal Republic as a foreign state after 1955. It
was therefore predictable that, after 1965 in
particular, the SED leadership treated requests for
assistance from West German courts according to the
criteria applied in inter-state relations. As a result

of a 1965 judicial decree by the Minister of Jusice, such requests were to be submitted to the Ministry and would be refused if they injured "the sovereign rights or the security of the GDR" or ran counter to the "bases of the legal order of the GDR."[115] A second decree in 1969 also required West German and West Berlin courts seeking assistance from East German courts and notaries to direct requests through the Ministry; additional legal requests from the FRG had to be first placed with the Federal Ministry of Justice or the Land justice ministries.[116] The consequence of directing legal requests of West German courts to courts in East Germany was thus the failure of any GDR judicial disposition.

SPECIAL ARRANGEMENTS FOR THE RELEASE OF EAST GERMAN PRISONERS

Any discussion of this area of East-West German activity is necessarily problematical, primarily because the sensitivity of such exchanges has dictated an unusually high degree of governmental silence. Thus there are no "official" statistics on the number of East Germans released into the Federal Republic since 1963, the first year for which the arrangements reportedly assumed significant proportions, nor for the sums of money and merchandise extended to East Berlin by the Federal Government. (The fact that espionage agents have often been a part of these transactions supplies an additional impetus for secrecy).[117] A book by Michel Meyer, Des hommes contre des marks, represents the most extensive treatment of the "human trade" (Menschenhandel) based on the author's personal contacts with the East Berlin and West Berlin lawyers directly negotiating these agreements, Wolfgang Vogel and Juergen Stange. Meyer asserts that the number of East German prisoners released from 1963 to 1969 was in the range of 5,500 to 6,000, with the average price for prisoners "purchased" in 1964-1965 equalling almost 50,000 DM per person.[118] Rainer Barzel, on the other hand, gives no more precise information on these activities than that 100,000 DM was delivered to the GDR after the release of "some" prisoners during his tenure as Inner-German Minister in 1963.[119] In addition to Vogel and Stange, who have not held formal governmental positions, the Evangelical Church of Germany has performed a key role in the transmission of goods into the GDR in fulfillment of the terms of the special arrangements.[120] The West Berlin Tagesspiegel reported that deliveries of these items began in 1963 and consisted of "goods which the GDR could otherwise not obtain in inter-zonal trade, such as gold bars or quicksilver."[121] Moreover, Meyer has provided some details on products that the West German Government was permitted to substitute for cash payments to East Berlin during Mende's term as Inner-German Minister, consisting primarily of machine tools, chemical products, and food commodities.[122]

---

[1]Bundesministerium fuer innerdeutsche Beziehungen, Zehn Jahre Deutschlandpolitik (February 1980), p. 205-211.

[2]Amos J. Peaslee, ed., Consitutions of Nations, 4 vols., 4th ed.(The Hague: Martinus Nijhoff, 1968): 3:361.

[3]Ibid.

[4]". . . Vielmehr ist aus dem Vorspruch fuer alle politischen Staatsorgane der Bundesrepublik Deutschland die Rechtspflicht abzuleiten, die Einheit Deutschlands mit allen Kraeften anzustreben, ihre Massnahmen auf dieses Ziel auszurichten und die Tauglichkeit fuer dieses Ziel jeweils als einen Masstab ihrer politischen Handlungen gelten zu lassen . . . Nach der negativen Seite bedeutet das Wiedervereinigungsgebot, dass die staatlichen Organe alle Massnahmen zu unterlassen haben,die die Wiedervereinigung rechtlich hindern order faktisch unmoeglich machen. Das fuehrt aber zu der Folgerung, dass die Massnahmen . . . verfassungerichtlich auch darauf geprueft werden koennen, ob sie mit dem Wiedervereinigungsgebot vereinbar sind." KPD-Prozess Dokumentarwerk zu dem Verfahren ueber den Antrag der Bundesregierung auf Feststellung der Verfassungswidrigkeit der Kommunistischen Partei Deutschlands vor dem Ersten Senat des Bundesverfassungsgerichts, 1956, Band 2, p. 605ff, quoted in : Achim von Winterfeld, "Potsdamer Abkommen, Grundgesetz und Wiedervereinigung Deutschlands," Europa Archiv 11 (5 October 1956): 9211-9212.

[5]"Interview des Leiters der Politischen Abteilung des Auswaertigen Amtes," in: Auswaertiges Amt, Die Auswaertige Politik der Bundesrepublik Deutschland (Koeln: Verlag Wissenschaft und Politik, 1972), p. 315.

[6]Report on the Tripartite Conference of Berlin (Potsdam Conference) Official Gazette of the Control Council for Germany (1946), Suppl. No. 1, pp. 13ff., in: Jens A. Brueckner and Guenther Doeker.ed., The Federal Republic of Germany and the German Democratic Republic in International Relations, 3 vols. (Dobbs Ferry, N.Y.: Oceana Publications, 1979), I:47.

[7]Peaslee, 391. <u>Constitutions</u> <u>of</u> <u>Nations</u>, III: 363, 391.

[8]Ingo von Muench, <u>Dokumente</u> <u>des</u> <u>geteilten</u> <u>Deutschland</u> (Stuttgart: Alfred Kroener Verlag, 1968), p. 99.

[9]Peaslee, III: 382, 392, 394-395.

[10]

"Ich stelle folgendes fest. In der Sowjetzone gibt es keinen freien Willen der deutschen Bevoelkerung. Das, was dort jetzt geschieht, wird nicht von der Bevoelkerung getragen und damit legitimiert.
Die Bundesrepublik stuetzt sich dagegen auf die Anerkennung durch den freibekundeten Willen von rund 23 Millionen stimmberechtiger Deutschen. Die Bundesrepublik Deutschland ist somit bis zur Erreichung der deutscher Einheit insgesamt die alleinige legitimierte staatliche Organisation des deutschen Volkes... Die Bundesrepublik fuehlt sich auch ver-antwortlich fuer das Schicksal der 18 Millionen Deutschen, die in der leben... Die Bundesrepublik Deutschland ist allein befugt fuer das deutsche Volk zu sprechen.
Sie erkennt Erklaerungen der Sowjetzone nicht als verbindlich fuer das deutsche Volk an.
Das gilt insbesondere auch fuer die Erklaerungen, die in der Sowjetzone ueber die Oder-Neisse Linie abgegeben worden sind." "Erklaerung der Bundesregierung vor dem Bundestag zur Bildung der Deutschen Demokratischen Republik und zur Lage Berlins vom 21 Oktober 1949," in: Muench, <u>Dokumente</u>, p. 204.

[11]"Statement by the United States' Secretary of State, Dean Acheson, on the Illegality of the East German Government," in Beate Ruhm von Oppen, <u>Documents</u> <u>on</u> <u>Germany</u> <u>under</u> <u>Occupation</u> (London: Oxford University Press, 1955), pp. 424, 517-518.

[12]"Statement by the Soviet Government on the Relations between the Soviet Union and the German Democratic Republic, Berlin, March 26, 1954," in: Brueckner and Doeker, eds., <u>The</u> <u>Federal</u> <u>Republic</u> <u>of</u> <u>Germany</u>, I:160.

[13]"Erklaerung der Bundesregierung und Entschliessung des Deutschen Bundestages ueber die Nichtanerkennung der 'Souveraenitaet' der Sowjetzon-enregierung, 7 April 1954, in: Auswaertiges Amt, <u>Die</u> <u>Auswaertige</u> <u>Politik</u> <u>der</u> <u>Bundesrepublik</u> <u>Deutschland</u>, pp. 253-254.

[14]"Declaration by the Allied High Commission Denying the Sovereignty of the 'East German Regime,'" in U.S. Congress, Senate, Documents on Germany, 1944-1970, 92nd Congress, 1st sess., 1971, p. 243.

[15]Theodor Maunz, Deutsches Staatsrecht (Muenchen: Beck, 1955): 15-16.

[16]"Bericht ueber die aussenpolitische Lage vom Bundesminister des Auswaertigen, Dr. Heinrich von Brentano, vor dem deutschen Bundestag am 28 Juli 1956," in: DAA, Die Auswaertige Politik, p. 322.

[17]Bundesverfassungsgericht. "Urteil vom 13 Juni 1952," Sammlung der Entscheidungen des Bundesverfassungsgerichts 1 (1952): 341.

[18]Bundesverfassungsgericht, "Urteil vom 19.12.1953," Juristenzeitung 9 (5 February 1954): 80.

[19]"Das Deutsche Reich, welches nach dem Zusammenbruch nicht zu existieren aufgehoert hatte, bestand auch nach 1945 weiter. Wenn auch die durch das Grundgesetz geschaffene Organisation vorlaeufig auf einen Teil des Reichsgebiets beschraenkt ist, so ist doch die Bundesrepublik Deutschland identisch mit dem Deutschen Reich," quoted in BFIB, Dokumente zur Deutschlandpolitik 6 (1975): 267-268.

[20]Peaslee, Constitutions of Nations, 3: 334.

[21]Peaslee, Constitutions of Nations, 3: 334, 351, 352; Muench, Dokumente, p. 309.

[22]Ministerium fuer Auswaertige Angelegenheitn der Deutschen Demokratischen Republik, Dokumenten aus den Jahren 1945-1949 (Berlin: Staatsverlag der Deutschen Demokratischen Republik, 1968), p. 789. This "imperative," however, did not become a binding legal obligation on GDR state organs as was the case in West Germany.

[23]"Urteil des Obersten Gerichts vom 31 Oktober 1951," Neue Justiz 6 (May 1952): 223.

[24]OLG Schwerin, "Urteil vom 18 Juni 1951," Neue Justiz 5 (October 1951): 469.

[25]"Urteil vom 31 Oktober 1951": 223.

[26]See, for example, Sozialistische Einheitspartei Deutschlands, Beschluesse und Dokumente des III Parteitages der SED (Berlin: Dietz Verlag, 1950), pp. 5-32; SED, Beschluss des V. Parteitages der SED

(Berlin: Dietz Verlag, 1958), pp. 7-9; Walter Ulbricht, Die gegenwaertige Lage und der neuen Aufgaben der Sozialistischen Einheitspartei Deutschlands (Berlin: Dietz Verlag, 1952).

[27]Ulbricht, Die gegenwaertige Lage, p. 152.

[28]Herbert Kroeger, "Adenauer's 'Identitaetstheorie' und die voelkerrechtliche Stellung der DDR," in BFGF, Dokumente zur Deutschlandpolitik 3 (1967): 693-703.

[29]Johannes Dieckmann, In Deutschlands Entscheidungsvoller Zeit: Reden und Aufsaetze (Berlin: Kongress Verlag, 1958), pp. 110, 112; Walter Ulbricht, Die Entwicklung des deutschen volksdemokratischen Staates, 1945- (Berlin: Dietz Verlag, 1958), pp. 350-352; Wilhelm Pieck, Reden und Aufsaetze, 4 vols. (Berlin: Dietz Verlag, 1954), III: 621; Nationale Front des Demokratischen Deutschland, Programmatische Dokumente der Nationalen Front des demokratischen Deutschland, (Berlin: Dietz Verlag, 1967), p. 160.

[30]"Aus der Erklarerung des Ersten Stellvertretenden Ministerpraesidenten Ulbricht," in BFGF, Dokumente zur Deutschlandpolitik 1 (1963): 417.

[31]"Aus der Erklaerung der Regierung der DDR," in BFGF, Dokumente zur Deutschlandpolitik 2 (1963): 683.

[32]"Wortlaut der neuen Verfassung der DDR," Deutschland Archiv 1 (February 1968): 166.

[33]Quoted in Bundesministerium fuer innerdeutsche Beziehungen, Dokumente zur Deutschlandpolitik 12 (1981): 417.

[34]Neues Deutschland, 5 March 1964. The above scholar was Research Director of the German Academy of Sciences in East Berlin.

[35]"Erklaerung des Bundeskanzlers Dr. Konrad Adenauer, 16 Oktober 1951," in: Auswaertiges Amt, Die auswaertige Politik der Bundesrepublik Deutschland, p. 185.

[36]"Draft Election Law of the East German Volkskammer, January 9, 1952" in U.S. Senate Committee on Foreign Relations, Documents on Germany, 1944-1961, 87th Congress, 1st sess., pp. 102-113.

[37]Oppen, Documents on Germany, p. 499.

[38]Ibid., p. 500.

[39]Ibid., p. 545.

[40]Ulbricht, Die gegenwaertige Lage, pp. 46-49.

[41]Muench, Dokumente, pp. 230, 400.

[42]"Statement by the Soviet Government on the Relations between the Soviet Union and the German Democratic Republic," in: Oppen, Documents on Germany, p. 597.

[43]"Vorschlaege des ZK der SED zur Wiedervereinigung Deutschlands," in: Ibid., 74-75.

[44]"Ich muss unzweideutig feststellen, dass die Bundesregierung auch kuenftig die Aufnahme diplomatischer Beziehungen mit der DDR durch dritte Staaten, mit denen sie offizielle Beziehungen unterhaelt, als einen unfreundlichen Akt ansehen wuerde." BFGF, Dokumente zur Deutschlandpolitik 1 (1961): 20-22, 338-340.

[45]Ibid., p.388.

[46]"Aus der Erklaerungen des Ersten Stellvertretenden Ministerpraesidenten Ulbricht." Ibid., 417. "Die Deutsche Demokratische Republik besitzt als einziger deutscher Staat die volle Souveraenitaet"; Noble Frankland, ed., Documents on International Affairs, 1955 (London: Oxford University Press, 1958), pp. 200-202; 203; 201; 203.

[47]Siegler, ed., Dokumente zur Deutschlandfrage 3 (April 1966): 221.

[48]It is not impossible to see the effects of the Schirdewan group, in particular, on East German policy in 1956; these could be discerned, for example, in the May 29 Volkskammer "8 Point Program for Inner-German Detente" and a June 28 decision by the Council of Ministers to reduce the size of the Volksarmee from 120,000 to 90,000 men. "Beschluss des Ministerrates der 'DDR,'" in: BFGF, Dokumente zur Deutschlandpolitik 2 (1963): 496; "Entschliessung der Volkskammer der DDR," in: ibid., 409.

[49]"Gesetz ueber die Vervollkommnung und Vereinfachung der Arbeit des Staatsapparates in der Deutschen Demokratischen Republik vom 11 Februar 1958," in Muench, Dokumente, pp. 332-355.

[50]See Neues Deutschland, 30 December 1956; "Erklaerung der Regierung der 'DDR,'" in: BFGF, Dokumente zur Deutschlandpolitik 3 (1967): 1299-1304;

"Note der Regierung der 'DDR' an der Regierung der Bundesrepublik Deutschland, in: <u>Dokumente</u> <u>zur</u> <u>Deutschlandpolitik</u> 4 (1969): 1548-1549.

[51]BFIB, <u>Dokumente</u> <u>zur</u> <u>Deutschlandpolitik</u> 1 (1971): 184-191.

[52]The subsequent breaking off of relations was by no means complete, however. The West German decision to punish Belgrade, which had dispatched an envoy to East Berlin, did not prevent the Tito Government from maintaining general consulates in Hamburg and Munich thereafter. See <u>Der</u> <u>Spiegel</u>, 17 March 1965, pp. 29-33.

[53]<u>Frankfurter</u> <u>Allgemeine</u> <u>Zeitung</u>, 14 November 1958. <u>Parlamentarisch-Politischer</u> <u>Pressedienst</u>, 23 November 1960, quoted in Dean, <u>West</u> <u>German</u> <u>Trade</u> with <u>the</u> <u>East</u>, p. 61.

[54]Intergovernmental Conference on the Common Market and Euratom, <u>Treaty</u> <u>Establishing</u> <u>the</u> <u>European</u> <u>Economic</u> <u>Community</u> <u>and</u> <u>Connected</u> <u>Documents</u> (date not given), p. 243.

[55]Several authors have noted that the acts of demarcation by the SED and Soviet leaderships did not put an end to Adenauer's efforts toward progress on the German question. Klaus Gotto, "Adenauer's Deutschland- und Ostpolitik: 1954-1963," in Rudolf Morsey and Konrad Repgen, ed., <u>Untersuchungen</u> <u>und</u> <u>Dokumente</u> <u>zur</u> <u>Ostpolitik</u> <u>und</u> <u>Biographie</u> (Mainz: Matthias-Grunewald Verlag, 1974), pp. 67-78; Griffith, <u>The</u> <u>Ostpolitik</u> <u>of</u> <u>the</u> <u>Federal</u> <u>Republic</u>, pp. 94-95.

[56]"Erklaerung der Regierung der Bundesrepublik Deutschland zur Lage im Nahen Osten," in: BFIB, <u>Dokumente</u> <u>zur</u> <u>Deutschlandpolitik</u> 11 (1978): 263-264...."durch jeweils dem Einzelfall angemessene Massnahmen beantwortet werden."

[57]"Interview mit dem Minister fuer Gesamtdeutsche Fragen, Dr. Erich Mende," <u>Der</u> <u>Spiegel</u>, 18 April 1966, pp. 26-27.

[58]"Reden Ulbrichts und Chruschtschows anlaesslich des VI. Parteitags der SED," in: Siegler, ed., <u>Dokumente</u> <u>zur</u> <u>Deutschlandfrage</u> 3 (April 1966): 221.

[59]That the elected coalition would persist in upholding these positions could be observed in such measures as the Bundestag's May 1967 passage of a law concerning the fixing of value-added tax (Mehrwertsteuer). In determining the law's application, the pertinent section read: "The area of

the German Reich in the borders of December 31, 1937 is the home country in the sense of this law." "Unter Inland im Sinne dieses Gesetzes ist das Gebiet des deutschen Reiches in den Grenzen vom 31. Dezember 1937.... zu verstehen." Sammelblatt 18 (9 June 1967): 849.

[60]"Erklaerung des Staatssekretaers fuer westdeutsche Fragen der Deutschen Demokratischen Republik," Staatsverlag der DDR, Dokumente zur Aussenpolitik 15: 252-259; New York Times, 15 January 1967.

[61]New York Times, 4 February 1967; Dokumente zur Aussenpolitik der DDR 15 (1967): 56-87.

[62]Sueddeutsche Zeitung, 3 February 1967.

[63]"DDR Staatsrat Erklaerung," in: BFGF, Texte 2 (1968): 246-247.

[64]Bundesanzeiger 1 (11 October 1949): 1.

[65]Bundesanzeiger 1 (11 October 1949): 1.

[66]Bundesanzeiger 2 (6 May 1950): 2-7; Holbik and Myers, Postwar Trade, pp. 58-59.

[67]Holbik and Myers, Postwar Trade, p. 62.

[68]Sieben, ed., Interzonenhandel, pp. 89-95.

[69]Lambrecht, "Die Entwicklung des Interzonenhandels," p. 33.

[70]BFIB, Zehn Jahre Deutschlandpolitik, p. 29. East German deliveries benefitted from their special, inner-German duty-free status, a principle endorsed in the Rome Treaty. Thus East Berlin willingly accepted this designation despite its inconsistency with the "two states" doctrine. Sieben, ed., Interzonenhandel, pp. 98-99; Bundesanzeiger 10 (25 November 1958): 1.

[71]"Mitteilung der Regierung der Bundesrepublik Deutschland," in: ibid., p. 525. The East German attempt to force separate negotiations could be detected in the distinctions made between West Berlin and the Federal Republic by the Departmental Director of the GDR Ministry for Foreign and Inner-German Trade. Ibid., pp. 460-462, 683; "Aus den Erklaerungen des Staatssekretaers von Eckardt," in: Dokumente zur Deutschlandpolitik 6 (1975): 31, 330-331.

[72]Sueddeutsche Zeitung, 14/15 August 1961.

[73]Frankfurter Allgemeine Zeitung, 24 May 1962; Die Welt, 5 January 1963; "Reden Ulbricht und Chruschtschows," Siegler, ed., Dokumente zur Deutschlandfrage 3 (1966): 221.

[74]"Erklaerung des Stellvertretenden Finanzministers Kaminsky vor der Volkskammer der DDR," in: Dokumente zur Deutschlandpolitik 10 (1980): 1135.

[75]The total volume of goods and services reached a level of 2.3 billion VE, exceeding the previous peak of 2.03 billion in 1960. BFIB, Zehn Jahre Deutschlandpolitik, p. 29.

[76]Times (London), 1 October 1964.

[77]From 1964 to 1966, for example, British and Italian exports to the GDR roughly doubled in value and French exports increased by a factor of three-and-one-half. United Nations, UN Yearbook of International Trade Statistics (New York: United Nations, 1967), p. 287.

[78]Frankfurter Allgemeine Zeitung, 30 March 1966.

[79]This course of action was favored in particular by Mende, who remarked that the political responsibility for the "structurally modified" Trade Trustee should lie with the Inner-German Ministry or the Chancellor. See "Pressekonferenz des Bundesministers Mende," in: Dokumente zur Deutschlandpolitik 10 (1980): 887-888.

[80]BFIB, Zehn Jahre Deutschlandpolitik, p. 29.

[81]Frankfurter Allgemeine Zeitung, 22 August 1967; Berliner Morgenpost, 17 August 1967; Frankfurter Allgemeine Zeitung, 2 September 1967; Die Welt, 28 October 1967; Inner-German trade declined from approximately 3 billion VE in 1966 to 2.75 million in 1967 and 2.9 million in 1968. BFIB, Zehn Jahre Deutschlandpolitik, p. 29.

[82]"Zusatzvereinbarungen fuer Interzonenhandel bis 1975," Siegler, ed., Dokumente zur Deutschlandfrage 5 (1970): 375-376.

[83]BFIB, Zehn Jahre Deutschlandpolitik, p. 28.

[84]"Vermerk ueber die Besprechung betr. Interzonen-Omnibusverkehr zwischen dem Vereinigten Wirtschaftsgebiet und der sowjetischen Besatzungszone am 4.10.1949 in Helmstedt," Offenbach/M., 5 October 1949.

[85]Muench, Dokumente, p. 400. A Volkskammer decision of that year also prohibited West Berliners' travel into the GDR without East German identity papers. New York Times, 2 June 1952.

[86]"Vertrag zwischen der Deutschen Reichsbahn und dem Deutschen Reisebuero GmbH, Berlin, Verwaltungssitz Frankfurt (Main)," Berlin, 8 July 1954, pp. 40-44.

[87]BFIB, Zehn Jahre Deutschlandpolitik, p. 38.

[88]Lawrence L. Whetten, Germany East and West: Conflicts, Collaboration and Confrontation (New York: New York University Press, 1980), p. 170.

[89]Dokumente zur Deutschlandpolitik 5 (1973): 191-192.

[90]Dokumente zur Deutschlandpolitik, 6 (1975): 742.

[91]Zehn Jahre Deutschlandpolitik, p. 42.

[92]Frankfurter Rundschau, 23 January 1964. The Inter-zonal Trade Trustee, significantly, did not take part in these negotiations.

[93]Dokumente zur Deutschlandpolitik 10 (1980): 856, 963-966.

[94]"Erklaerung der Regierung der Bundesrepublik Deutschland," in: ibid., p. 986.

[95]Dokumente zur Deutschlandpolitik 11 (1978): 953-955; Zehn Jahre Deutschlandpolitik, p. 43.

[96]"Verhandlungen ueber Verkehrsfragen zwischen der Bundesrepublik Deutschland und der DDR," in: Siegler, ed., Dokumente zur Deutschlandfrage 5 (1970): 691-692.

[97]Zehn Jahre Deutschlandpolitik, p. 38; Sueddeutsche Zeitung, 12-13 June 1968.

[98]Der Spiegel 23 (3 March 1969), p. 27.

[99]Berliner Morgenpost, 4-6 March 1969.

[100]See Eberhard Schulz, "Die sowjetische Deutschlandpolitik," in: Dietrich Geyer, ed., Osteuropa Handbuch: Sowjetunion, Teil: Aussenpolitik II, 3 vols. (Koeln: Bohlau Verlag, 1976): 280.

[101]Zehn Jahre Deutschlandpolitik. p. 33.

[102]Ibid., p. 34.

[103]Ibid.

[104]"Zeittafel vom 1. bis zum 15. Februar 1968, 15. bis zum 31. Mai 1968," Europa Archiv 23: Z44, Z122; Frankfurter Allgemeine Zeitung, 29 October 1968; Dokumente zur Deutschlandfrage 5 (1970): 423.

[105]Karl Ihmels, Sport und Spaltung in der Politik der SED (Koeln: Verlag Wissenschaft und Politik, 1965), p. 84.

[106]Frankfurter Allgemeine Zeitung, 6 February 1963. According to this theory, the FRG, GDR, and West Berlin were to be regarded as separate political entities.

[107]Frankfurter Allgemeine Zeitung, 6 February 1963. Thus West Berlin, a founding DSB member, participated on the West German side.

[108]The above figures, however, relate only to those events registered with the DSB for those years and financially supported by it. DSB, "Gesamtdeutscher Sportverkehr von 1966 bis 31.12.1969," Informationsblatt, Frankfurt/Main, 5.1.70, quoted in Wilfried Lemke, Sport und Politik (Ahrensburg bei Hamburg: Verlag Ingrid Czwalina, 1971), p. 37, and Karlheinz Gieseler und Ferdinand Mans, Sport als Mittel der Politik (Mainz: Institut fuer staatsbuergerliche Bildung in Rheinland-Pfalz, 1966), p. 69.

[109]BFIB, Dokumente zur Deutschlandpolitik 7 (1973): 59.

[110]Lemke, Sport und Politik, p. 16.

[111]BFIB, Dokumente zur Deutschlandpolitik 6 (1976): 744, 1364.

[112]Sueddeutsche Zeitung, 2 November 1965.

[113]Siegler, ed., Dokumente zur Deutschlandfrage 5 (1970): 328; Frankfurter Allgemeine Zeitung, 23 July 1969.

[114]"Gesetz ueber die innerdeutsche Rechts- und Amtshilfe in Strafsachen," Bundesgesetzblatt, Teil I (7 May 1953), pp. 161-164.

[115]BFIB, Zehn Jahre Deutschlandpolitik, p. 51.

[116]Ibid.

[117]One notable instance of this "mixed" exchange

was the 1981 return of the "Chancellor spy" Guenter Guillaume. See _Suedeutsche Zeitung_, 28 September 1981.

[118]_Des hommes contre des marks_ (Donoel: Stock, 1976), p. 225.

[119]Rainer Barzel, _Es ist noch nicht zu spaet_ (Muenchen: Droemer Knaur, 1976), p. 39.

[120]_New York Times_, 6 October 1975; _Die Welt_, 2 October 1975.

[121]_Der Tagesspiegel_, 22 June 1976, quoted in Jacobsen, et. al., _Drei Jahrzehnte Aussenpolitik der DDR_, p. 426.

[122]Meyer, _Des hommes_, p. 138.

2
The Formulation
of the Basic Treaty,
October 1969–June 1973

The West German policy of non-recognition of the GDR underwent slight modification in the 1960's but was not altered substantially until the formation of the Social Democratic-Free Democratic government coalition late in 1969. The latter's acknowledgment of East Germany as a state and subject of international law was already foreshadowed in speeches by Chancellor Brandt upon his accession to office, but both the materialization of the Basic Treaty negotiations and the agreement's content could not have been predicted in advance. Both were contingent upon the approval of the four former occupation powers in Germany, the receptivity of the SED leadership to Brandt's proposals and thus Moscow's willingness to exert itself vis-a-vis East Berlin in support of its own interests, and the emergence of sufficient support for the new government's policy in the West German population and political parties.

THE BRANDT INITIATIVES

On October 28, 1969, Brandt unveiled his government's modified program towards inner-German cooperation in a broad statement of policy. Of central importance to the Chancellor was the necessity to "prevent any further alienation of the two parts of the German nation, that is, arrive at a regular modus vivendi, and from there proceed to cooperation (Miteinander)."[1] This recognition entailed the active extension of new overtures to the East German Government:

The Federal Government will continue the policy
initiated in December 1966 and again offers the
Council of Ministers of the GDR negotiations at
Government level without discrimination on either
side, which should lead to contractually-agreed
cooperation.[2]

Nevertheless, the above was not intended to
constitute an unqualified recognition of East German
state sovereignty:

International recognition of the GDR by the Federal
Republic is out of the question. Even if there
exist two states in Germany, they are not foreign
countries to each other; their relations with each
other can only be of a special nature.[3]

Brandt also asserted the Federal Republic's
"readiness for binding agreements on the reciprocal
renunciation of the use or threat of force" with the
GDR, and care was taken to reemphasize the Federal
support for a Four Power Berlin accord and the
viability of West Berlin.[4]
As if to make visible the new government's
departure from earlier versions of Deutschlandpolitik,
the Chancellor also announced that the Ministry for
All-German Questions was to be re-named "the Ministry
for Inner-German Relations."[5] With regard to the object
of an East-West German "modus vivendi," Inner-German
Minister Egon Franke identified the following goals:

to contribute to the easing of daily life for the
people in both parts of Germany as well as to
measures towards strengthened economic, transportation, and political cooperation, and, to
obtain contractual agreements concerning framework
arrangements for scientific, technical, and
cultural exchange.[6]

It is instuctive to pay careful attention to the
former Chancellor's October 1969 declaration to
ascertain the degree to which it represented a
departure from or continuation of the legal and
doctrinal principles adhered to by earlier West German
governments. As was discussed earlier, the operative
premise of the Grand Coalition's Deutschlandpolitik was
that the alleviation of living conditions for East
Germans should assume a high priority for Bonn and
could be partially fulfilled through the offering of
positive incentives to East Berlin, such as trade
credits and the possibility of negotiations at the
governmental level. Recognition of the GDR, however,
was enacted only in the sense of Kiesinger's
acknowledgment of the Ulbricht Government as the

effective East German leadership in the Chancellor's letter exchange with Willi Stoph, given the conflicting policy views within the Grand Coalition. In addition, if one is to compare Kiesinger's December 1966 government declaration with Brandt's policy statement, it is immediately observable that the latter, unlike the former, does not contain the word "reunification" in the section on inner-German relations.[7] For Brandt it was less important to promote the notion of a still-existing state unity, an aim that can be detected in the All-German provisions of the Basic Law as well as in decisions of the Federal Constitutional Court, than it was to emphasize the unity of the German nation and its right to self-determination. In line with this preference and the concept of "two states in one German nation," the reunification imperative was not construed by Brandt as requiring that Bonn foreswear mutual inter-state representation with the GDR, although an international recognition was specifically excluded.

Brandt's declaration, like Kiesinger's, affirmed that "the questions that have arisen for the German people out of the Second World War" could only be definitively solved in a European peace settlement.[8] It was nevertheless made clear that Kiesinger's admonition against a "retreat" from "our legal standpoint"[9] was modified by Brandt in favor of cooperation between the two German states within the German "house." Whereas the former asserted that the Federal Government is the only German government that is "freely, lawfully, and democratically elected and which is therefore entitled to speak for the entire German people,"[10] this statement of All-German legitimacy was absent in the latter's 1969 declaration. Brandt's statement of support for the German right to self-determination,[11] of course, clearly implied that the new government would continue to pursue this in its policies even while advancing a "special" inter-state relationship with the GDR. While Kiesinger's above statement tacitly expressed FRG maintenance of the state identity of the former German state, an interpretation supported by the April 1954 Bundestag resolution and the Constitutional Court, Brandt attributed the "special nature" of the two states' relations to a common "language," "history," and "responsibility to ensure peace among us and in Europe."[12]

Walter Ulbricht's response to this modified West German policy on December 17 brought into sharp focus the incompatibility of positions held by the two leaderships. The First Secretary's letter to FRG President Gustav Heinemann contained a draft treaty for equal inner-German relations which provided for mutual international recognition, recognition of the existing European state borders (including the East-West German border and the Oder-Neisse Line), the exchange of ambassadors and embassies by the two governments, and recognition of West Berlin as "an independent political entity."[13] Without specifically commenting on any of these East German maximal goals, Brandt suggested to Willi Stoph on January 22 that the two German states begin negotiations on force renunciation statements and, ultimately, on regulating practical questions. A further Stoph-Brandt letter exchange created the prospect of meetings between the two, the first of which took place in the East German city of Erfurt on March 19.

The Erfurt meeting as well as the later Brandt-Stoph meeting in Kassel, West Germany, did not produce evidence of a thaw in the relationship. The Chairman of the Council of Ministers in both cases repeated SED demands regarding "the full sovereignty" of both German states, recognition of European frontiers by the FRG, mutual international recognition, and West German abandonment of the right of sole representation of Germans.[14] In spite of this insistence, the meetings were of considerable importance within the context of the history of inner-German relations and the negotiation of the Basic Treaty articles. The actual face-to-face encounters of the two leaders amounted to an unequivocal West German confirmation of the GDR as an equal negotiating partner, which Brandt had laid a foundation for in his October 28 speech. In addition, the Chancellor made more specific the policy content of the modified inner-German program in his morning statement during the Kassel meeting. Brandt advocated "a treaty which regularizes the relations between the two states in Germany, reinforces the links between the population and the two States, and helps to remove existing handicaps."[15] After repeating his October assertions concerning FRG-GDR equality in negotiations, the renunciation of force, and two states in one German nation, the Chancellor declared the need for the two states to respect one another's "independence and autonomy" and not "act on behalf of, or represent, the other." Brandt thus showed a willingness to concede to the GDR leadership its separate authority in East German foreign and domestic policy at the same time that he continued to emphasize the unity of the nation and preferred an exchange of "plenipotentiaries of ministerial rank" instead of ambassadors.[16] Brandt's acknowledgment of the GDR's "autonomy" as well as his expressed desire to include both states in international organizations thus meant that the Federal Government might no longer obstruct GDR efforts to acquire the outward prerogatives of statehood so long as the "special nature" of East-West German relations could be reflected in mutual inner-German representation. What is more, five of the Chancellor's "Twenty Points" of Kassel aimed at the improvement of cooperation in practical areas, such as family reunification, travel, postal service, and the regulation of border-related problems.

THE MOSCOW NEGOTIATIONS AND THE REMOVAL OF INNER-GERMAN OBSTACLES

Stoph's rather strident tone as well as the intensity of East German demands at the two meetings amounted to proof of the improbability that the SED leadership would eventually respond positively to Brandt's proposals without Soviet urging. For this reason, the Soviet-West German negotiations of 1970 had considerable bearing on inner-German progress. In order to understand the formulation of the Basic Treaty, one must first assess what can be considered its prototype, the August 1970 Moscow Treaty, as well as the Bahr Paper, a far-ranging document of intent concerning FRG relations with the Warsaw Pact states. It should be noted first of all that the Moscow Treaty is the first agreement ever signed by a West German government which refers to the German Democratic Republic as a state. The signatories to the treaty

regard today and shall in the future regard the frontiers of all States in Europe as inviolable such as they are on the date of signature of the present Treaty, including... the frontier between the Federal Republic of Germany and the German Democratic Republic.[17]

In so doing, however, the Brandt-Scheel Government avoided the obligation to recognize the GDR as a foreign state and thus prevented the realization of one of East Berlin's main aims. Furthermore, the "Letter on German Unity" recorded the West German position that the treaty did not conflict with the political objective of the Federal Republic to work for a state of peace in Europe in which the German nation will recover its unity in free self-determination.[18] This letter, submitted to Soviet Foreign Minister Andrei Gromyko by West German Chancellor's Office State Secretary Egon Bahr, was not included in the Moscow Treaty text. The Bahr Paper, on the other hand, simply represented a draft treaty under consideration by the two which was leaked to the West German press in June 1970. The paper is useful, however, for ascertaining some FRG inner-German purposes and anticipating some of the Basic Treaty's provisions.

First of all, the document's assent to respecting the frontiers of all states in Europe, including the East-West German border, was incorporated into the Moscow Treaty, as has been indicated. Second, the

Federal Republic expressed its " readiness to conclude an agreement" with the GDR "that shall have the same binding force, usual between States, as other agreements the Federal Republic of Germany and the German Democratic Republic conclude with third countries."[19] The use of the phrase "the same binding force" would have upgraded the status of such an agreement over earlier East-West German undertakings that implied a more unique relationship. Third, both the Soviet Union and the Federal Republic announced their preparedness "to take steps... to support the accession of the FRG and GDR to the United Nations," and the paper declared that "neither of the two (German) states can represent the other abroad or act on its behalf."[20] These two statements of intention left no room for even a formal continuation of the Hallstein Doctrine, which had been practically eliminated under the Grand Coalition. Each of these inner-German provisions was to have its counterpart in the Basic Treaty negotiations affirming the West German Government's respect for East German autonomy in internal and external affairs, although allowance is also made in the treaty for the West German position regarding the unity of the nation.

While the Bahr Paper represented a basis for agreement on general principles between the Soviet and West German Governments, this did not automatically guarantee East Berlin's acceptance. Indeed, for the SED leadership West German acknowledgment of the GDR in the Moscow Treaty was overshadowed by the Kremlin's failure to insist on international recognition of the GDR as it had done in previous years.[21] Inner-German cooperation was complicated not only by East Berlin's visible resistance to what it perceived as a neglect of its true interests, demonstrated, for example, in traffic slowdowns along the Berlin access routes in late 1970, but also by the prospect of a Berlin settlement. This latter consideration assumed importance first of all in the announcement of East-West German talks on October 29 by the GDR Council of Ministers. The materialization of these conversations meant that the Ulbricht leadership was compelled to withdraw its precondition of legal recognition of the GDR prior to negotiations which the First Secretary had required for a "regular coexistence." Yet even though the Quadripartite talks on Berlin had been in progress since March 1970, it was soon reported that the SED leadership aimed at making Berlin access a subject of inner-German negotiation.[22]

Since the West German Government maintained its position that the Berlin question was a matter for resolution by the Four Powers, an impasse developed in the negotiations that lasted until the conclusion of the Quadripartite Agreement in September 1971. In the

interim period, East German authorities had continued
to interfere sporadically with the FRG-West Berlin
traffic, but after the removal of Walter Ulbricht from
the position of First Secretary at a May 3 Central
Committee meeting, it was clear that the East German
strategy regarding relations with the Federal Republic
would be subject to some change. Ulbricht, unlike some
of his SED colleagues,[23] had shown few deviations from
his virulent criticisms of the FRG. It is true, of
course, that his successor as First Secretary, Erich
Honecker, continued to seek legal recognition of East
Germany by West German governments and implement a
policy of "Abgrenzung." Yet after Ulbricht's
"retirement" the Soviet Government proceeded to assume
responsibility for Western transportation access to
West Berlin and underwrite follow-up negotiations
between East and West German representatives towards
implementation of the Four Power accord.[24]

Another outgrowth of the Quadripartite Agreement
was thus implicit Western acknowledgment of the GDR as
a state, subject to Four Power legal rights and
responsibilities. The "German Democratic Republic" is
consistently referred to throughout the agreement in
juxtaposition with the Federal Republic and Four
Powers. This verbal upgrading of the GDR is not
entirely surprising in view of an already concluded
East-West German postal agreement of April 1970 which
did not contain such earlier face-saving designations
as "currency areas" but referred to "the Federal
Republic of Germany" and "the German Democratic
Republic."[25] Inner-German negotiations in
implementation of the Quadripartite Agreement's
sections on the transportation of civilian persons and
goods between the FRG and West Berlin, however, were
specifically based on mandates bestowed by the Four
Powers.

It was not until after the signing of the
Quadripartite Agreement that inner-German negotiations
began to yield significant results. Four Power
agreement in September 1971 was followed not only by
the December 1971 FRG-GDR and Berlin Senate-GDR
implementations of the Quadripartite Agreement but also
by several other agreements. Among these were the
September 1971 postal and radio transmission
agreements,[26] an April 26, 1972 understanding relating
to the settlement of damages from motor vehicle
accidents,[27] and a May 26, 1972 traffic treaty.[28] This
last document was particularly noteworthy in that,
unlike earlier East-West German agreements, the "two
states" in the preamble agreed "to develop normal, good
neighborly relations to each other as are customary
between states independent of one another."[29] The two
parties also expressed their intention to regulate
questions regarding border-crossing travel and

commercial traffic "in and through their sovereign
territories."[30] Through its approval of the treaty in
Bundestag voting on September 22, even the CDU/CSU
opposition concurred in the designation of inner-German
relations as "inter-state" (zwischenstaatlich), yet the
language of the agreement was carefully phrased so as
to avoid a characterization of those relations as
"international" (voelkerrechtlich).

FOUR POWER INTERESTS AND THE MODIFIED EAST GERMAN
POSITION

Before proceeding to the Basic Treaty negotiating
process, it is first necessary to identify some of the
external limitations imposed on the policies of the two
governments as well as explain the East German
negotiating position after the fall of Ulbricht. The
Federal Republic's Deutschlandpolitik had, of course,
been established in Brandt's early government
declaration and was made somewhat more explicit in the
Erfurt and Kassel meetings. The notions of the
"special relations" of two states in one German nation,
West German exercise of the German right to self-
determination, an exchange of representation that would
not constitute international recognition, and the
creation of an acceptable level of practical
cooperation between the two states in areas of
interests were recognizable components of that policy.
These first two points as well as the fourth were
confirmed by the West German cabinet on August 8 as
being non-negotiable elements in the prospective
treaty.[31] In return, Bonn conceded to the SED regime in
principle the respecting of both states' independence
and autonomy, their equality of status, and
renunciation of international representation of the
partner state as well as the use of force against it.
Aside from Bonn's purely inner-German priorities,
external concerns also dictated to a great degree the
West German negotiating position. East Berlin clearly
would have to accept a formula acknowledging Four Power
rights and responsibilities in any German agreement, as
Brandt repeatedly stressed. This requirement was not
only a consequence of the wartime allies' desire to
maintain their legal authority in Germany and Berlin
but also lent credence to the Chancellor's thesis of
"special relations" by calling to mind the provisional
nature of the division of Germany. For this reason, it
was also necessary that any inner-German treaty not
encroach on issues that could only be settled in a
peace treaty between the Four Powers and Germany, such
as the final establishment of German borders. Finally,
the legal status of Berlin could not be regulated by
East and West German representatives.[32]

While the above-stated goals of the Federal
Republic received their clear expression in public
statements, it was by no means obvious what form such
objectives might assume in a bilateral FRG-GDR
agreement. Undoubtedly their formulation had by the
time of the Basic Treaty negotiations been influenced
by the fact of official East-West German meetings and
negotiations and, especially, by the phraseology of the
Traffic Treaty. In an important sense, then, a "floor"
of recognition had been established prior to the June
1972 negotiations from which, SED spokesmen asserted,
relations would be "normalized."[33] Yet the minimum
demands of the Honecker leadership at the onset of
negotiations were not at all as unambiguous as had
appeared those fixed by Walter Ulbricht in the December
1969 draft treaty. The First Secretary's April 18,
1972 Sofia speech, which was frequently referred to by
GDR spokesmen as the basis for the subsequent inner-
German negotiations, called for "the creation of normal
relations" and the concluding of "international
agreements" between the Federal Republic and the GDR.[34]
The address did not contain references to the
establishment of diplomatic relations or an exchange of
embassies, as had the 1969 draft treaty, and the demand
for international recognition (voelkerrrechtliche
Anerkennung) disappeared from East German announcements
from the time of the speech through the Basic Treaty
negotiations. Furthermore, Honecker, in referring to
the Brandt Government, declared that

> peace and security can only be guaranteed when one
> proceeds from the assumption of the reality and
> non-infringement of the existing frontiers in
> Europe and of non-interference in the affairs of
> other sovereign states.[35]

The above statement failed to mention either the
inner-German border or the GDR specifically.
It can thus be seen that the SED had verbally
retreated from Ulbricht's maximum demands for full
recognition in its public statements. Nevertheless,
since the Traffic Treaty was later described as "a step
on the way towards the normalization of relations"[36]
between East and West Germany, it appeared certain that
the status definition of the two states contained
therein would not be considered sufficient in later
agreements. In calling for the creation of "normal
relations... which correspond to generally valid
international principles" on June 6, the First
Secretary's phraseology was not incompatible with
Brandt's Kassel remarks suggesting that the two "adjust
their relations on the basis of human rights, equality
of status... as universal rules of international
law."[37] Yet these East German statements did not answer

the question of what precise form the representation
would take, although Kohl's reference to FRG-GDR
"sovereign equality" implied that recognition on an
international basis would have to be reciprocated by
the Federal Republic.[38]

On other matters, East Berlin emphatically denied
that FRG-GDR relations could have a "special" or
"inner-German" character, and asserted that "the people
of the German Democratic Republic realizes its self-
determination through the socialist revolution."[39] The
SED, corresponding to the notion of the "nation"
developed in the 1960's that was described earlier,
plainly intended to resist West German attempts to
include explicit terms proclaiming the unity or even
the existence of the German nation. Furthermore,
significant upgrading of West German recognition of the
GDR clearly implied both Bonn's acceptance of the two
states' United Nations membership and non-recognition
of the GDR. Other claims advanced by Stoph at these
last two talks, including the payment of debts by the
Federal Government to the GDR, renunciation of the
acquisition of or disposal over nuclear weapons, and
the removal of "discriminatory laws" in West German
legislation were not specifically repeated by the SED
leadership in public immediately prior to the
negotiations. (This is not, of course, to imply that
they were to be excluded from inner-German bargaining).
In the same way that Stoph had declared "the creation
of equal relations between the GDR and the FRG on the
basis of international law (Voelkerrecht)" to be "the
main question" at Erfurt, statements by Kohl continued
to emphasize the "creation of normal relations" or, of
"normal international relations" as the "main goal" of
the inner-German negotiations.[40]

The East German Government also perceived an
interest in preventing in an East-West German agreement
a direct reference to Four Power rights and
responsibilities in Germany as a whole; this priority
assumed significance in that it would weaken Bonn's
claim of "special" inner-German relations as well as
support the legal concept of a sovereign East German
state. The fact that the Soviet Union had not been
wholly consistent in its espousal of this authority in
"all of Germany" probably strengthened East Berlin in
its belief that confirmation of it could be avoided in
the upcoming negotiations.[41]

THE NEGOTIATION PROCESS AND RATIFICATION

The East-West German negotiations towards a
framework treaty, which formally extended from June 15
to November 8, 1972, were thus heavily influenced by
East-West issues and interests, West German domestic

politics, and the East German drive to secure
international recognition. At the beginning, however,
both Egon Bahr and Michael Kohl restored the language
of the Traffic Treaty in their joint June 15 statement,
defining FRG-GDR relations as "normal and good
neighbourly relations customary between states
independent of one another."[42] This basis for verbal
agreement was obviously intended as a starting point
for discussion, rather than a statement of the ultimate
framework of relations. Kohl continued to adhere to
Honecker's ambiguous Sofia formula of "normal
relations" simultaneous with "international agreements"
in public statements, although on August 31 the State
Secretary was quoted as stressing that the exchange of
ambassadors was "a precondition for normal relations,"
and, in mid-September, that "international relations
should be created" between the FRG and the GDR.[43]

This renewed East German effort to portray the two
German states as foreign lands to one another proceeded
in part from concurrent international recognition of
the GDR, this time by non-Communist states. The East
German Foreign Ministry was able to announce the
establishment of diplomatic relations with Finland and
India on September 6 and October 7. The SED leadership
also attempted to secure East German membership in the
United Nations without first finalizing an inner-German
agreement and thus sought to cut the linkage required
by the Brandt-Scheel Government. Yet the larger policy
priorities of East-West security as well as West German
diplomatic activity soon began to interfere with East
German attempts to circumvent the Basic Treaty
negotiations. The visit of U.S. Special Adviser for
National Security Affairs Henry Kissinger to Moscow
from September 10-14 resulted in Soviet-American
agreement to begin preliminary discussions for both the
Conference for Security and Cooperation in Europe, a
long-time goal of Soviet policy, and the Mutual and
Balanced Force Reduction talks. Since the first CSCE
discussions were to be held on November 22, the Kremlin
clearly perceived an interest in removing any East-West
German obstacles still existing by this date. It
followed that this Soviet compulsion could only set
limits to a GDR demand for full recognition by Bonn,
which Kohl had enunciated without qualification on
September 13, although it is also true that the
impending FRG election on November 19 increased the
West German stake in concluding the negotiations
rapidly as well.

West German policy thus had to contend with
external initiatives by East Berlin towards U.N.
membership in addition to reconciling often
incompatible positions in the inner-German talks. On
this first account, American insistence to Moscow that
an East German membership would be vetoed without GDR

recognition of Four Power rights and responsibilities
in Germany[44] made ineffective much of the SED's
diplomatic activities in third states. Bonn also
strengthened its position vis-a-vis the East German
Government through Egon Bahr's October 8-10 visit to
Moscow, an event which occurred only seven days after
the State Secretary reported difficulties with his East
German counterpart over "central questions."[45] Bahr
indicated publicly that his discussions there would
treat the issues of Four Power authority in Germany and
the U.N. membership of East and West Germany.
Furthermore, the Federal Republic's diplomatic
recognition of the People's Republic of China on
October 11 made it unlikely that the latter would veto
a U.N. admission of the FRG and GDR that confirmed the
Four Powers' German authority.

In the face of these external developments, East
Berlin was compelled to recognize that its ability to
force West German international recognition of the GDR
had diminished, but it had also left room for a face-
saving retreat through its inconsistent and vague
assertion of this aim. Hence, Albert Norden simply
referred to international recognition of East Germany
as "a cardinal problem of detente on our continent,"
while Willi Stoph on October 6 expressed the fallback
position by declaring that there existed FRG-GDR
"international agreements already concluded, in
particular the Traffic Treaty."[46] SED Central Committee
Secretary Werner Lamberz emphasized on October 12 that
while the Bahr-Kohl negotiations concerned "normal
international relations," the East-West German treaty
"must take account of the realities of international
law."[47] Consequently, the Traffic Treaty was hailed in
the East German press as an "international
agreement."[48] By October 27 Bahr made explicit what had
already been suspected: GDR negotiators no longer
raised the demand for an international recognition
"because the GDR leadership knows very well that they
cannot attain this goal as long as there are Four Power
rights for all of Germany."[49] Michael Kohl, following
suit, employed the language of the Traffic Treaty to
describe East-West German relations on October 31.

Both the Soviet Union and the three Western powers
affirmed their interest in preserving their rights and
responsibilities in Germany with the agreement to Four
Power discussions beginning October 23 on entry of the
two German states into the United Nations. An impasse
developed, however, in both the Four Power and inner-
German talks. The Soviet Ambassador objected to the
inclusion of a reference to Four Power rights and
responsibilities "in all of Germany," as this might
imply support for the principle of German
reunification. East-West German difficulties, on the
other hand, were reported by Bahr on November 2

regarding "the text of the treaty, including the preamble, all the way down to the inclusion of West Berlin."[50] Although this inclusion was resisted by East Berlin, meetings between the four ambassadors and Bahr were followed by a November 5 announcement that differences over the disputed points had been cleared up. A further Bahr-Kohl meeting was necessitated on November 6, however, and the joint statement on Four Power responsibilities only appeared alongside the published Basic Treaty provisions after the initialing of the treaty in Bonn on November 8. It was signed by the two chief negotiators on December 21.

The numerical strengthening of the SPD-FDP coalition's Bundestag majority after the November 19 election preceded a series of sharp criticisms of the treaty by the opposition CDU/CSU. This behavior is to be contrasted with CDU leader Rainer Barzel's pre-election suggestions to the Federal Government that the treaty be excluded from the campaign discussion in favor of the themes of inflation and radicalism.[51] Although the opposition's objections were too numerous to be treated in great detail here, three specific criticisms assumed unusual prominence: the negotiations were said to have been conducted "too early, too quickly, and too noisily," the absence of the terms "Germany" or "the German nation" in the treaty's text was held to have excluded acknowledgment of German national unity, and the inclusion of West Berlin in future agreements was judged as insufficiently safeguarded.[52] More fundamentally, however, CDU/CSU spokesmen such as Barzel expressed the apprehension that the Government's commitment to "change through rapprochement" might backfire in a "change in the Federal Republic"; the practical and humanitarian sections of the treaty were thus attacked as contributing to possible East German ideological infiltration and even to the growth of "socio-political neutralism" in the FRG.[53]

Notwithstanding an almost total CDU/CSU opposition to the treaty, a 268-217 ratification by the Bundestag was forthcoming on May 11, 1973. Yet the persistent opposition of the Bavarian Land Government resulted in attempts to invalidate or delay the treaty's entry into effect, first in the Bundestag's Conference Committee and then in the Bundesrat. The Bavarian Government was then twice repulsed by the Senate of the Federal Constitutional Court in its strategy to postpone the counter-signing, preparation, and announcement of the treaty's consenting law and exchange of notes with the GDR leadership.[54] Thereafter, a May 28 parallel application petitioning the Court for a legal ruling on the constitutional validity of the treaty culminated in the landmark July 31 decision that declared it compatible with the Basic Law, the so-called "Karlsruhe

Decision." In the meantime, both the Bundestag and East German Volkskammer passed consenting laws to the treaty on June 6 and 13, allowing it to enter into force on June 21.

AN INTERPRETATION OF THE INNER-GERMAN TREATY PROVISIONS

In interpreting the results of the June 15-November 8 East-West German negotiations, it is useful to compare the relevant sections of the Basic Treaty with the December 1969 Ulbricht draft treaty, the Traffic Treaty, and available information containing FRG or GDR negotiating positions as well as the stated positions of the heads of government. The Moscow Treaty, while not an inner-German agreement, is in many respects a forerunner of the Basic Treaty in its sections relating to the respecting of existing European frontiers and the renunciation of force; this in itself allows one to draw distinctions between the formulation of such provisions by two states with full diplomatic relations, the Soviet Union and the Federal Republic, and two whose relations are subject to legal and political contention, East and West Germany. The following pages will thus explain how the already elaborated East and West German doctrinal and political positions were preserved in the treaty as well as focus on the envisioned cooperation in practical and humanitarian areas.

The preamble of the Basic Treaty, unlike the 1969 Ulbricht draft, makes no particular reference to the legal status of East and West Germany beyond characterizing them as "the two German states," nor does it specify the nature of their relations. Also instructive in this respect is the Moscow Treaty's preamble, which describes the cooperation between the two signatories "on the basis of the purposes and principles of the Charter of the United Nations" with regard to "the ardent desire of nations (Voelker) and the general interests of international peace."[55] The omission of any reference to "Voelker" in the Basic Treaty reflects the extent to which the West German Government was at pains to avoid the impression that an East German "Volk" had become a legal reality. Acts in support of the goal of reunification would otherwise become meaningless and leave Bonn open to charges of interference in the affairs of a sovereign state. In this sense, the reunification imperative was to be preserved, although in the crucial following section of the preamble both East and West German views regarding the nation are implicitly allowed for:

Proceeding from the historical facts and without prejudice to the different views of the Federal

Republic of Germany and the German Democratic
Republic on fundamental questions, including the
national question,[56]

Such a formulation in and of itself continued to
permit Bonn to pursue the right of the German people to
self-determination just as it allowed East Berlin to
promote the idea of a separate nation defined according
to socialist criteria. At the same time, both
negotiating parties failed to attain their preferred,
and opposite, objectives: the West German delegation
did not succeed in including the phrase "the German
nation" and the East German attempt to preclude the
acknowledgment of the nation as an inner-German concern
was frustrated. Only in the "Letter on German Unity,"
presented to Michael Kohl on December 21, was the
Federal Republic's policy relating to national unity
recorded.

Altogether, the Brandt-Scheel Government limited
the registering of a significant demarcation between
the FRG and the GDR in the preamble beyond what had
already been acknowledged in the Traffic Treaty,
namely, that of two states "independent of one
another." This conclusion is supported in particular
by an examination of the preambles of the 1969 draft
treaty and the East German proposal published in the
periodical Quick in October 1972. The former declared
the FRG and GDR to be "equal, sovereign states" with
"relations of equal rights" and counted among its
signatories the foreign ministers of both states. The
latter included references to "peaceful coexistence"
and "the different social orders" of East and West
Germany; relations were to be "formed," not "developed"
as in the Basic Treaty, on the basis of equal rights.[57]
One finds in the Basic Treaty preamble, on the other
hand, an emphasis on the state character of the FRG and
GDR, reflected, for example, in the term "High
Contracting Parties," the respecting of the
inviolability of frontiers and the "territorial
integrity and sovereignty of all States in Europe," and
the imperative that the two states refrain from the use
of force.[58] Such passages are normally applicable to
the affairs of sovereign states, but no conclusions
relating to mutual relations and recognition are drawn
from them in the preamble, and "the national question"
was formally left open.

Article 1 states that the FRG and the GDR "shall
develop normal, good-neighbourly relations with each
other on the basis of equal rights."[59] It should be
pointed out that the language "normal, good-neighbourly
relations" was identical with that chosen by Honecker
in his Sofia address and subsequently included in East
German announcements, yet the First Secretary also
added that "agreements under international law" would

be concluded by the two states as an important qualification. The development of relations "on the basis of equal rights," however, does not address this issue of recognition or dealings between the Federal Republic and the German Democratic Republic; the article's wording is thus far less strong than Ulbricht's treaty declaration of "normal, equal relations." This last phrase lacks the precise legal definition which would be clear, for example, in the phrase "normal, diplomatic relations." To give another example, the Warsaw Treaty's third article declared that the Federal Republic and the People's Republic of Poland "shall take further steps towards full normalization and a comprehensive development of their mutual relations,"[60] an unmistakable expression of the goal of diplomatic recognition.

The second article of the treaty establishes that the FRG and GDR

> will be guided by the aims and principles laid down in the United Nations Charter, especially those of the sovereign equality of all States, respect for their independence, autonomy and territorial integrity, the right of self-determination, the protection of human rights, and non-discrimination.[61]

The above declaration of intent is in keeping with the prior characterization of the FRG and the GDR as states and closely resembles the second articles of the Moscow and Warsaw Treaties, with one exception. In the latter, the aims and principles of the Charter are to be specifically applicable in the signatories' "mutual relations."[62] Therefore, although Article 2 of the Basic Treaty emphasizes that East and West Germany are to undertake the responsibilities of states, there is no direct acknowledgment by either that the two states are "sovereign equals." To this extent, the article avoids a recognition of an irrevocable legal splitting of "Germany," since "the sovereign equality of states" is not presented as a joint precept in inner-German relations. Additionally, the Quick draft's reference to "non-interference in internal and external affairs" in its second article was not included in the Basic Treaty. Nevertheless, it corresponded to East German interests to record the above principles relating to the sovereign prerogatives of states in that, together with Articles 3, 4, and 6, a cumulative expression of state sovereignty can be interpreted.

Articles 3, 4, and 6 might be most appropriately defined as the "state autonomy" provisions in that they offer the most explicit formulations of East and West German status, representation in third states, and domestic jurisdiction. The two German states agreed in

Article 3 to "reaffirm the inviolability now and in the future of the frontier existing between them and undertake fully to respect each other's territorial integrity."[63] The foundation for this inclusion was laid in Article 3 of the Moscow Treaty which also affirms the inviolability of the inner-German frontier. With respect to representation in third states, Article 4 obligates the East and West German leaderships "to proceed on the assumption that neither of the two States can represent the other in the international sphere or act on its behalf."[64] Article 6 is the most unambiguous expression of the domestic authority of the two German states. In it, the signatories

> proceed on the principle that the sovereign jurisdiction of each of the two states is confined to its own territory. They respect each other's independence and autonomy in their internal and external affairs.[65]

Although Article 3 proclaims the territorial integrity of the two states and the inviolability of their common frontier, it is possible to defend the West German position that a final establishment of German frontiers was avoided. This position rests largely on two considerations: the choice of words selected in the article and the existence of Article 9. The inner-German frontier was declared to be "inviolable," as opposed to "unalterable" and, as such, does not necessarily preclude a final settlement achieved peaceably. The Ulbricht draft treaty had employed the word "non-infringement" (Untastbarkeit) of frontiers, a much stronger designation. West German policy, as was explained in the earlier chapter, consistently assumed the validity of the Potsdam provisions and the October 1954 treaty with the Western Powers regarding the final determination of borders at a peace conference. The territorial integrity of the FRG and the GDR was "respected," rather than "recognized" as in the Ulbricht draft, and the East German Government was unable to include the Quick draft's provision that the two states "have no territorial claims whatsoever against each other and will not assert such claims in the future."[66] Such a declaration was included in the 1970 Warsaw Treaty. More importantly, Article 9 of the Basic Treaty states that the treaty "shall not affect the bilateral and multilateral international treaties and agreements already concluded by them or relating to them."[67] Thus the respecting of territorial integrity already provided for is, it can be argued, subject to the limitations imposed by the treaty provisions of Potsdam and the 1954 treaty, which not only defer the ultimate resolution of the frontier question but declare Four

Power rights and responsibilities in "Germany as a whole."[68] An exchange of letters between the two chief negotiators on the day of the treaty's signing referred directly to Article 9 in confirming that "the rights and responsibilities of the Four Powers and the corresponding, related Quadripartite agreements, decisions and practices cannot be affected by this Treaty."[69]

In identifying the preservation of the East German position, on the other hand, the final sentence of Article 3 did not differ from Article 1, paragraph 2 of the Warsaw Treaty, a treaty in which the Federal Republic and Poland agreed to fully normalize their relations eventually. Inclusion of the phrase "territorial integrity," a term used in reference to the relations between foreign states, in itself distinguishes between the FRG and the GDR and could be cited to reinforce SED objection to the depiction of East-West German relations as "special."

Article 4 explicitly establishes that neither of the two German states can represent the other internationally or "act on its behalf." Through this article, the Brandt Government thus recognized that on the soil of the area of the former German Reich, a second subject of international law has come into being for which West German governments cannot speak.[70] The point was given unambiguous emphasis through an exchange of letters on November 8 in which Bahr and Kohl declared that each government "initiates the necessary steps in conformity with domestic legislation to acquire membership of the United Nations Organization."[71] It is important to realize, however, that this article concerns non-representation of another state internationally and does not specifically proscribe West German actions in support of the right of self-determination, particularly in view of the preamble's requirement that the treaty be agreed on "without prejudice to the different views" of the FRG and the GDR "on fundamental questions, including the national question." One implication of Article 4 is that, as Georg Ress asserts, "the Federal Republic, if understood to be identical with the German Reich, may claim all rights of the Reich which do not comprise acting for the other state, the GDR."[72] Acts on behalf of the German nation, then, would presumably be permissible so long as this threshold is not crossed. Ress, however, proceeds to state that Article 4 invalidates the former West German legal position to the extent that the latter claimed "that the Federal Republic alone is authorized to act effectively as the German Reich" as defined by the 1937 frontiers.[73]

If, as the author emphasized, the "identity theory" became legally untenable as a result of Article 4 after the Hallstein Doctrine had been practically abandoned under the Grand Coalition, this recognition still fails to answer the question of when West German acts on behalf of the German nation constitute action in the name of the GDR. Article 4 did provide sufficient clarity towards including both states in the United Nations, however, and it should be pointed out that Article 6's reference to the two states' "independence and autonomy in their internal and external affairs" reinforces the notion of separate international representation.

Articles 3 and 4 anticipate Article 6, which contains the most specific reference to the nature and extent of the mutual sovereignty recognized by each German leadership. In stating that "the sovereign jurisdiction of each of the two states is confined to its own territory" and that "independence and autonomy" internally and externally is respected, it is difficult to see how the treaty avoided the sharpest of demarcations according to state criteria. The authority of the East German leadership within the territory of the GDR receives unqualified confirmation here. One possible interpretation of this passage, for example, might support the contention that past activities of the West German Government which by extension applied FRG legislation to East Germany, such as the 1967 value-added tax law, could no longer be continued. Thus the Federal Government would possess no lawmaking authority within the territory of the GDR.

In spite of the passage's relatively unequivocal language, the West German position of "special relations" is still not wholly negated as long as the "offsetting" character of Article 9 is recognized. In considering the question of whether the FRG and the GDR were portrayed as foreign states, it should also be noted that the word "international" is not employed in this article as well as the earlier articles relating to state autonomy. As was apparent elsewhere in the treaty, the Brandt-Scheel Government was prepared to concede passages that accented the inter-state quality of East-West German relations in return for keeping the national question open. The presence of Article 9 once again can be cited as setting limits to Article 6 through the treaty-sanctioned invocation of Four Power authority.

Through the mutual representation agreed to in Article 8, the Federal Republic was, at best, able to put into effect its claim that inner-German relations were of a special nature or, at worst, defer the practical question of representation. It was agreed that the two states "shall exchange Permanent Missions. They shall be established at the respective Government's seat."[74] Formulation of this last sentence avoided the Ulbricht draft's usage of "the capital cities Bonn and Berlin" in favor of the more nondescriptive term. This article also stipulated that "practical questions relating to the establishment of the Missions shall be dealt with separately."[75]

The agreement to exchange Permanent Missions instead of embassies represented the major argument against defining inner-German relations as "international" as a result of the Basic Treaty. Thus the Chancellor's Erfurt suggestion that "permanent representatives" be exchanged was literally given expression in the treaty. That such an arrangement resulted from the Basic Treaty negotiations is, in retrospect, not incomprehensible given the somewhat more flexible SED policy after Ulbricht's removal, the rather vague and inconsistent manner in which East German leaders publicly called for international recognition by Bonn through October 1972, and the interest of the Kremlin as well as Brandt and Bahr in concluding the inner-German negotiations rapidly.[76] It was through Bonn's acknowledgment of East German territorial integrity and sovereign jurisdiction but accreditation to the SED regime of representation less than that normally accorded to sovereign states that the doctrine of "special relations" can be maintained in which there is no suggestion of separate East and West German nations. However, inasmuch as the practical questions were to be "dealt with separately," it was not to be excluded that the Permanent Missions would perform many of the same functions as embassies, as Kohl suggested in a May 1974 interview.[77]

It would be no exaggeration to state that the practical cooperation between the Federal Republic and the German Democratic Republic envisioned in Article 7 was the most important aim of SPD-FDP German policy. In return for its inclusion, Bonn, as was indicated, agreed to the "state autonomy" provisions subject to their unusual wording and the restrictions that may be applied to them as a result of Article 9. In Article 7, both states

> declare their readiness to regulate practical and humanitarian questions in the process of the normalization of their relations. They shall conclude agreements with a view to developing and promoting on the basis of the present Treaty and for their mutual benefit cooperation in the fields of economics, science and technology, transport, judicial relations, posts and telecommunications, health, culture, sport, environmental protection, and in other fields. The details have been agreed in the Supplementary Protocol.[78]

The above formula elaborated intended areas of cooperation far beyond any specified in the Ulbricht draft treaty, which had simply declared that "relations in other areas will be separately regulated by treaty."[79] In addition, it represented an improvement, from the West German viewpoint, over the Quick draft's condition that this cooperation develop "according to the rules of international law (entsprechend den Normen des Voelkerrechts).[80] In another respect, this last draft also concurred in the broad range of activities contained in Article 7. The Supplementary Protocol to the article outlines in some detail specific objectives of the two governments in the practical areas, the greater part of which concerns family reunification and facilitation of inner-German travel and the exchange of goods. The majority of statements listed in Part II of the Protocol simply registers the East and West German intention to conclude agreements or enter into negotiations in the indicated practical areas, with two noticeable exceptions. The first consists of the pronouncement that inner-German trade "shall be developed on the basis of the existing agreements."[81] In proceeding from this understanding, East Berlin gave implicit assent to the West German standard of "special relations," since Bonn could thereby continue to regard the trade as "internal German trade" under the EEC provisions as well as deal with the GDR through the Inter-zonal Trade Trusteeship. The second exception was the agreement "to conclude an agreement on posts and telecommunications on the basis of the Constitution of the Universal Postal Union and the International Telecommunication Convention."[82] Regulation of the area of posts and telecommunications would therefore conform to international, as opposed to inner-German, rules and principles. It was also agreed that "owing to the different legal positions," questions of property and assets "could not be regulated by the Treaty."[83]

An exchange of letters between Bahr and Kohl on the day of the treaty's signing confirmed that after its entering into effect, "steps to regulate matters in the following fields" would be taken: family reunification, border crosssing travel and visitor traffic, and the non-commercial goods traffic.[84] The provisions of the first allowed the re-uniting of married couples, parents who must be cared for by their children, and, in special cases, the granting of permission for marriage. Visitor traffic and border crossings were given the most detailed regulation through an expansion of travel grants to GDR citizens in "cases of family urgency," West German use of the East German Travel Office, visits to the GDR of up to thirty days per year by West German inhabitants living in the proximity of five designated border districts, and new allowances for some items accompanying travellers' to East Germany and for postal packages. To be sure, the prospective future travel was largely for West Germans: new permission for East Germans to travel to the Federal Republic was extended only for cases of family urgency, specifically silver and golden wedding anniversaries, and half-sisters were for the first time included among those eligible for such travel.[85]

Finally, with the issuance of the FRG-GDR "Oral Agreement on Political Consultation," both governments agreed

> to consult each other in the process of the normalization of relations between the Federal Republic of Germany and the German Democratic Republic on questions of mutual interest, in particular on those important for the safeguarding of peace in Europe.[86]

Although the above declaration was not included in the treaty in connection with any specific article, it can be viewed in the context of Article 1's reference to "good-neighbourly relations" and the intended "contribution to security and cooperation in Europe" of Article 5. Through this measure, it became possible to theoretically continue the inner-German dialogue in another formal channel. Such a provision could also not have been unwelcome to Soviet leaders in view of their advocacy of the upcoming Conference on Security and Cooperation in Europe.

One other area of practical cooperation, that of "working possibilities for journalists" of each state, was to be regulated by assurances given in another Bahr-Kohl letter exchange. Each government affirmed that the present correspondents from either state "will be entitled to the same treatment as correspondents from other states," rather than providing for reciprocal treatment. Further principles established the journalists' freedom of movement within the country as well as unhindered departures, the accessibility of the media and official information to newspersons, and permission for journalists to carry the equipment and documents necessary for their work. Yet allowance for such activity was also circumscribed by the requirement that journalists "be accredited or established in accordance with the applicable modalities" of each state and "observe regulations and ordinances issued in the interests of security, crime prevention, protection of public health and of the rights and liberties of others."[87]

For a number of reasons, it cannot be stated with certainty which German government succeeded in attaining its near or ultimate objectives in greater measure in the Basic Treaty. In "proceeding from the historical facts and without prejudice to the different views" of the two states, the negotiators ensured that rarely was there unambiguous phraseology which could

not be offset or qualified by statements elsewhere in
the treaty. This is especially true of the "state
autonomy" provisions, Articles 3, 4, and 6, which
provide for a specific FRG and GDR state independence
and autonomy vis-a-vis one another, but which can be
held to be subject to Article 9, which in a later
protocol directly affirmed Four Power rights and
responsibilities that legally restrict some East and
West German prerogatives. In addition, a final
judgment on East or West German success in the treaty
work must await future developments in inner-German
relations. For Brandt and his main negotiator Bahr, the
instrumental value of the treaty toward practical and
humanitarian cooperation was all-important.

It would be accurate to say that neither side
realized its inner-German goals in the form that these
had been stated publicly. The SED leadership could not
(and did not) claim that full diplomatic relations were
created betwen the two German states as a result of the
Basic Treaty, since embassies were not exchanged. On
the other hand, the Federal Government's requirement
that the "unity of the nation" be upheld in an
agreement was only implicitly satisfied, as the
preamble simply indicated the existence of a "national
question" and the "Letter on German Unity" took the
form of a unilateral declaration. East Berlin never
succeeded in obtaining a direct reference to the GDR as
a "sovereign state" but an interpretation of "special
relations" is supported mainly by making inferences
from the treaty's passages, particularly the preamble
and Article 9.

The treaty thus created a framework for possible
future inner-German cooperation and consultation but
did not clarify a number of status and doctrinal
questions that had existed prior to the Brandt-Scheel
diplomacy. The agreement to disagree on the "national
question" guaranteed that Bonn would continue to
advance All-German unity while possible, while East
Berlin would not cease to claim a separate nationhood.
In approaching the question of whether or not East and
West Germany had established "relations under
international law," on the other hand, little more
clarity has been forthcoming because of the highly
political usage of the word "voelkerrechtlich." As was
observed earlier, First Secretary Honecker
intentionally did not specify what was meant by
"agreements under international law"; scholarly
pronouncements, on the other hand, differ widely in
their answers to this question. Richard Loewenthal,
for example, has written that the May 1972 Traffic
Treaty was "the first autonomous international treaty
between the two German states."[88] Yet the FRG and GDR
had not yet agreed to establish or define their
relations through the exchange of Permanent Missions,

let alone embassies. The legal analyst Helmut Rumpf sees "a recognition of the GDR as a state within the meaning of international law" primarily as a result of Article 1's description of East-West German relations and the cumulative effect of Articles 3, 4, and 6.[89] Georg Ress, as was observed, presents the view that the "special" nature of relations contained in the Basic Treaty cannot be rejected because of Article 9's provision for the "incomplete" separation of Germany, an inclusion limiting the effect of the "state autonomy" articles. As for the assessment of the two chief negotiators on the day of the treaty's signing, Bahr declared that the document "takes into account the international situation in the center of Europe in which there are two states that call themselves German."[90] Kohl, on the other hand, stressed that the treaty created "a general basis according to internatioinal law for normal good-neighbourly relations" between the two states and mutually recognized in "unlimited fashion" the sovereignty and independence" of the two.[91] Bearing these last two statements in mind, it can be inferred that inner-German relations were not explicitly declared to be "international" in the treaty but could later be modified in this direction through the practical status accorded to the Permanent Missions.

Probably the most obvious lacunae arising from the "agreement to disagree" was the lack of a citizenship regulation. In producing this outcome, both German leaderships thus avoided giving a sharper definition of their relations and also ensured that the citizenship issue would remain as a point of contention in the future.

Despite the flexible formulations of the Basic Treaty and the offsetting character of a number of its articles, one practical consequence of the understanding should not be overlooked. Although the GDR was never specifically described as a sovereign state, the SED leadership did receive West German confirmation of its sovereign jurisdiction and autonomy that was hitherto only obtained through unilateral or Warsaw Pact declarations as well as diplomatic recognition by, for the most part, Communist countries. While the Brandt/Scheel Government's modification of the reunification imperative to some extent removed the communication barrier separating the two German governments since 1949, whether or not the "recognition" of East Germany contained in the Basic Treaty can coexist with the long-term goal of reunification depends to a great degree on the agreement's implementation. Of particular importance is the West German Government's practical observance of SED "sovereign jurisdiction" and "autonomy in internal affairs"; a literal interpretation of Article 6 by Bonn would require that it refrain from criticizing objectionable internal measures by the East German leadership, such as the suppression of political dissent or shootings of fleeing Germans along the border. At the least, this would seriously impair West German attempts to promote the unity of the nation.

OTHER INNER-GERMAN AGREEMENTS

Several additional understandings were concluded by the two German governments in this period outside the framework of the Four Power and Basic Treaty negotiations. Two postal agreements of April 1970 and September 1971 fulfilled an essential purpose of each negotiating party. For the East German Government, a basis was achieved for resolving the question of payment claimed by the GDR for postal services provided in border-crossing mail. It will be recalled that in the late 1960's, East German demands for payment of such fees by the Federal Republic steadily escalated alongside SED opposition to Bonn's modified Hallstein Doctrine. By 1970, East Berlin required separate payments for postal services extended before 1966, from 1966 to 1969, and in 1970. The first postal accord in 1970 established the figure of approximately 22 million DM as a charge for the 1967-1969 period, while the lump-sum of 30 million DM was to be paid by the FRG for the year 1970 and each succeeding year through 1973. In the September 1971 agreement, a further payment of 250 million DM was fixed for the period up to and through 1966, and the earlier established payment of 30 million DM per year was also extended through 1976.[92]

West German interests, on the other hand, found expression to a greater degree in measures undertaken "toward the improvement of transactions in mutual border-crossing posts and telecommunications." The September 1971 agreement proved its value in this area, especially in the upgrading of East-West German telephone and telegraph connections. The SED leadership committed itself to the installation of thirty new telephone lines with a "half-automatic method of operation" by the end of 1971 and sixteen further lines by March 31, 1972. Telephone service between the two German states was to be fully automated by January 1972 with the setting in place of forty-five additional wires as well as twelve lines for telex transmissions and the erection of new telecommunication installations by the East German Government.[93] Finally, a protocol registered the commitment of GDR authorities to shorten the delivery time for letters, parcels, and packages. On the same day of its signing, a related agreement opened the possibility of exchanges of radio and television programs between East and West Germany

"as well as between Eurovision and Intervision," the
European broadcasting networks; the exact broadcast
parameters were to be later agreed upon by the two
sides.[94]
    In terms of practical and symbolic effect,
however, the May 1972 Traffic Treaty must be considered
the most important inner-German undertaking in this
period other than the Basic Treaty. This document not
only contained the first joint acknowledgment by the
two German states that they were "independent of one
another" but confirmed the GDR's pledge to "allow
repeated annual visits to the German Democratic
Republic by relatives and acquaintances from the
Federal Republic."[95] The precise fulfillment of this
commitment, of course, was detailed in the Basic Treaty
supplementary pronouncements on family reunification
and travel, in addition to similar promises regarding
permission for packages brought into the GDR and East
German travel to the Federal Republic. A letter by
Kohl on the day of the Traffic Treaty's signing also
foresaw increased allowance for the use of personal
motor vehicles by West Germans while in East Germany.
    The Traffic Treaty, a comprehensive document
containing thirty-three articles and a protocol,
consists of general regulations for reciprocal
treatment in inner-German travel as well as specific
provisions relating to rail and motor traffic and river
and sea navigation. The treaty at the outset
establishes that the two states are not bound to pursue
practices in these areas on the basis of reciprocity.
Each government agreed to permit the use of railway by
its neighbor for certain purposes; including West
German transportation of potash through the GDR. The
two sides also clarified procedures for the submission
of documents in inner-German river navigation, the
docking of ships from one state in the ports of another
during emergencies, and "the use of sea ports and other
establishments of sea transportation for the
transporting and sale of goods."[96] East and West German
negotiators also agreed to regulate the exchange of
travellers, luggage, and freight according to two
international agreements which, as was observed
earlier, had been one of the chief goals of the SED
leadership since 1966.[97]
    Three additional agreements relating to
transportation were concluded between the FRG and GDR
in this period. The first, signed on September 25,
1972, reaffirmed the applicability of international
practices for the inner-German commercial and motor
vehicle traffic.[98] The second and third agreements
concerned the settlement of damages resulting from
motor vehicle accidents and the financing of services
provided in the assistance of victims of such
accidents. An April 26, 1972 accord between the West

German Ministry of Justice and the East German Ministry of Finance committed the authorized insurance institution in each state to assess the damage inflicted on "a person with domicile, residence or usual abode in the area of business" of the institution by motor vehicles registered in the neighboring German state.'' The agreement also provided that the appropriate institution would oversee the payment of damages to the injured party as well as the extension of medical and road assistance to inhabitants of the other German state involved in accidents.

Finally, a May 10, 1973 agreement between the West German Association of Liability, Accident, and Motor Vehicle Insurance and the State Insurance of the GDR formulated standards for compensation as well as legal and technical assistance in the case of traffic accidents. This understanding, like the above agreement, avoided usage of the word "citizens" and committed both governments to mutual consultations and final payment of accident-related fees at the end of the year.[100]

---

[1]Willy Brandt, "German Foreign Policy," Survival 11 (December 1969): 370.

[2]Ibid.

[3]Ibid.

[4]Ibid.

[5]Bundesrepublik Deutschland, Presse- und Informationsamt der Bundesregierung, Bundeskanzler Brandt: Reden und Interviews (Melsungen: A. Bernecker, 1971), p. 15.

[6]"zur Erleichterung des taeglichen Lebens fuer die Menschen in den beiden Teilen Deutschlands beizutragen sowie ueber Massnahmen zur verstaerkten wirtschaftlichen und verkehrspolitischen Zusammenarbeit und ueber Rahmenvereinbarungen fuer den wissenschaftlichen, technischen, und kuturellen Austausch vertragliche Vereinbarungen zu erreichen." "Bundesminister Franke: Rede vor dem Deutschen Bundestag," in: Texte 4: 59-60.

[7]Brandt, "German Foreign Policy,": 370; Texte 1: 25.

[8]Brandt, "German Foreign Policy,": 370.

[9]Texte 1: 25.

82

[10]Ibid.: 24.

[11]"However, no one can dissuade us from our conviction that the Germans have a right to self-determination just as has any other nation." "German Foreign Policy": 370.

[12]Ibid.

[13]BFIB, Zehn Jahre Deutschlandpolitik, p. 120.

[14]Press and Information Office of the Federal Republic of Germany, Erfurt, March 19, 1970: A Documentation (1971), pp. 32-33, and Kassel, May 21, 1970: A Documentation (Opladen: Dr. Middelhauve GmbH, 1971), pp. 32-34.

[15]FRG Press and Information Office, Kassel, p. 13.

[16]Ibid., pp. 13-15.

[17]"Treaty between the Federal Republic of Germany and the Union of Soviet Socialist Republics," in: Karl E. Birnbaum, East and West Germany: A Modus Vivendi (Westmead, Farnborough, Hants, England: D.C. Heath Ltd., 1973), p. 110.

[18]Ibid., p. 111.

[19]Ibid., p. 115.

[20]Ibid.

[21]For this reason, the GDR Council of Ministers' commentary on the Moscow Treaty underlined much more the value of the treaty in "opening the possibility of the consolidation of European security" than it elaborated on the status-enhancing effect of FRG acknowledgment of East German statehood and territorial inviolability. Dokumente zur Aussenpolitik der Deutschen Demokratischen Republik 13 (1972): 674-677.

[22]"Ansprache des Vorsitzenden des Staatsrates der Deutschen Demokratischen Republik, Walter Ulbricht, am 9 Januar 1970 in Berlin," in: Dokumente zur Aussenpolitik der DDR 18 (1972): 577. Der Spiegel 24 (23 November 1970): 118. Moscow needed to offer concessions in the Berlin negotiations, thus reaffirming its often ambiguous responsibility for transit access, in order to secure West German approval of the Moscow Treaty.

[23]Stoph on February 4, 1971 proclaimed the GDR's readiness "under corresponding provisions" to conclude

agreements providing for, among other things, the maintenance of "economic, technical-scientific, and cultural links" between West Berlin and the Federal Republic. "Zeittafel vom 1. bis zum 15. Februar 1971," *Europa Archiv* 26 (1971): 245.

[24]"Quadripartite Agreement (on Berlin)," in: Birnbaum, *East and West Germany*, pp. 125-129.

[25]BFIB, *Zehn Jahre Deutschlandpolitik*, p. 135.

[26]Ibid., pp. 163-165.

[27]Ibid., pp. 181-182.

[28]Ibid., pp. 183-188.

[29]"in dem Bestreben, einen Beitrag zur Entspannung in Europa zu leisten und normale gutnachbarliche Beziehungen beider Staaten zueinander zu entwickeln, wie sie zwischen voneinander unabhaengigen Staaten ueblich sind." Ibid., p. 183.

[30]Ibid.

[31]*Sueddeutsche Zeitung*, 9 August 1972.

[32]Ibid., pp. 98, 100.

[33]See, for example, the October 16, 1972 speech by Foreign Minister Otto Winzer before the Volkskammer, *Dokumente zur Aussenpolitik der DDR* 20 (1975): 870.

[34]*Dokumente zur Aussenpolitik der DDR* 20 (1975): 197-200.

[35]Ibid.

[36]See the April 25 Honecker interview in *Neues Deutschland* and the declaration by Kohl after the conclusion of the Traffic Treaty negotiations. Ibid., pp. 837, 842.

[37]"Interview des Ersten Sekretaers des Zentralkomitees der SED, Erich Honecker, fuer die Nachrichtenagentur der DDR, ADN, vom 6 Juni 1972," Ibid., p. 991. Press and Information Office of the Government of the FRG, *Kassel*, p. 13.

[38]*Dokumente zur Aussenpolitik der DDR* 20: 866.

[39]Ibid., pp. 866-867; "Interview des Ersten Sekretaers des Zentralkomitees der SED, Erich Honecker, vom 6 Juni 1972," ibid., pp. 989-990.

84

⁴⁰Dokumente zur Aussenpolitik der DDR 20:   866,
868; Erfurt, p. 30.

⁴¹The Kremlin in the past had seen the need to
reconcile the competing interests of maintaining its
Four Power authority in all of Germany and seeking
sovereign recognition for the GDR. Hacker, Der
Rechtsstatus Deutschlands aus der Sicht der DDR, p.
419.

⁴²Neues Deutschland, 16 June 1972.

⁴³"Interview   des   Staatssekretaers   beim
Ministerrrat der Deutschen Demokratischen Republik zum
Stand der Verhandlungen zwischen der DDR und BRD, vom
13 September 1972," Dokumente zur Aussenpolitik der DDR
20 (1975): 869; Neues Deutschland, 1 September 1972.

⁴⁴Sueddeutsche Zeitung, 9 October 1972.

⁴⁵Frankfurter Allgemeine Zeitung, 3 October 1972.

⁴⁶Neues Deutschland, 3, 7 October 1985.

⁴⁷Ibid., 13 October 1972.

⁴⁸"Rede   des   Ministers   fuer   Auswaertige
Angelegenheiten der DDR, Otto Winzer, auf der 6. Tagung
der Volkskammer am 16 Oktober 1972," Dokumente zur
Aussenpolitik der DDR 20 (1975): 871.

⁴⁹Sueddeutsche Zeitung, 27 October 1972. The SED
had also moved to meet Bonn's concerns through the
Council of State's grant of an amnesty to thousands of
political prisoners on October 6. Neues Deutschland, 7
October 1972.

⁵⁰Sueddeutsche Zeitung, 3 November 1972.

⁵¹Die Zeit, 17 November 1972.

⁵²Bundesrepublik Deutschland, Deutscher Bundestag,
Verhandlungen des Deutschen Bundestages 81: 551; 82:
1443, 1638.

⁵³Verhandlungen 81: 136; "Ministerpraesident Dr.
Filbinger: Rede vor dem Bundesrat," in: Texte 12: 121.

⁵⁴Karlheinz   Niclauss,   Kontroverse
Deutschlandpolitik (Frankfurt: Alfred Metzner Verlag,
1977), pp. 101-102.

⁵⁵Press and Information Office of the Government
of the Federal Republic of Germany, The Bulletin 20,

no. 38 (14 November 1972), p. 294.

⁵⁶Birnbaum, East and West Germany, p. 109, and BFIB, Zehn Jahre Deutschlandpolitik, p. 156.

⁵⁷"Entwurf Vertrag ueber die Grundlagen der Beziehungen zwischen der Deutschen Demokratischen Republik und der Bundesrepublik Deutschland," in Quick, 25 October 1972, pp. 12-13; Zehn Jahre Deutschlandpolitik, p. 120.

⁵⁸The Bulletin, pp. 293-294.

⁵⁹Ibid., p. 294.

⁶⁰Birnbaum, East and West Germany, p. 118.

⁶¹The Bulletin, p. 294.

⁶²Birnbaum, East and West Germany, pp. 109, 117.

⁶³The Bulletin, p. 294.

⁶⁴Ibid.

⁶⁵Ibid. The treaty's Supplementary Protocol authorizes the formation of an East-West German commission to supervise the marking of the inner-German frontier and to "contribute to regulating other problems connected with the course of the frontier." Ibid., p. 295; Zehn Jahre Deutschlandpolitik, p. 211.

⁶⁶Ibid., p. 120; "Entwurf Vertrag," Quick, p. 12.

⁶⁷The Bulletin, pp. 294-295.

⁶⁸Brueckner and Doeker, The Federal Republic of Germany and the German Democratic Republic, I: 41, 47, 111, 113.

⁶⁹The Bulletin, p. 297.

⁷⁰With regard to German citizenship, however, provision was made only for separate declarations by each side. The West German Government declared that citizenship questions are not regulated by the treaty while the East German position proceeded "from the assumption that the treaty will facilitate a regulation of citizenship questions." Zehn Jahre Deutschlandpolitik, p. 207.

⁷¹The Bulletin, pp. 296-297.

⁷²"Die Bundesrepublik, als identisch mit dem

Deutschen Reich gedeutet, darf alle Rechte des Reiches in Anspruch nehmen, die nicht ein Handeln fuer den anderen Staat, die DDR, einschliessen." Ress, Die Rechtslage Deutschlands nach dem Grundlagenvertrag vom 21 Dezember 1972 (Berlin-Heidelberg-New York: Springer Verlag, 1978), p. 306.

[73]Ibid., p. 303.

[74]The Bulletin, p.294.

[75]The Bulletin, p. 294.

[76]This sense of urgency was reportedly not shared by the Social Democrats' coalition partners, who feared that undue haste in the treaty formulation could impair the quality of the agreement as well as the prospects for its success in the Bundestag. Der Spiegel (9 October 1972): 22.

[77]Deutschland Archiv 7, (June 1974): 650.

[78]The Bulletin, p. 294.

[79]Zehn Jahre Deutschlandpolitik, p. 120.

[80]"Entwurf Vertrag," Quick, p. 13.

[81]The Bulletin, p. 295.

[82]This intention was also conveyed in an exchange of letters between the two chief negotiators on the day of the initialing of the treaty. Ibid.

[83]Ibid.

[84]The Bulletin, pp. 297-298. East Berlin's "first installment" on the family reunification cooperation was reported on November 13 with the re-uniting of 308 East German children and their parents in West Berlin; Bonn committed itself to paying approximately $10 million in "guardship" money for 1,000 East German children with fathers in the Federal Republic. New York Times, 5, 13 November 1972.

[85]Fifty-four GDR crossing points were also listed in this protocol, and a Bahr-Kohl letter exchange obligated each party to open four further crossing points with the treaty's entry into effect. Ibid., pp. 208-210.

[86]The Bulletin, p. 296.

[87]Ibid., pp. 299-300.

[88]"den ersten selbststaendigen, voelkerrechtlichen Vertrag zwischen den beiden deutschen Staaten." Richard Loewenthal, _Vom kalten Krieg zur Ostpolitik_ (Stuttgart: Seewald Verlag, 1974), p. 87.

[89]Helmut Rumpf, _Land ohne Souveraenitaet_, (Karlsruhe: Verlag C.F. Muller, 1973), p. 189.

[90]"Er traegt der voelkerrechtlichen Situation in der Mitte Europas Rechnung, in der es zwei Staaten gibt, die sich deutsch nennen." Erklaerung der Verhandlungsfuehrer bei Unterzeichnung des Grundvertrages," _Zehn Jahre Deutschlandpolitik_, p. 212.

[91]"Die DDR und BRD erkennen mit diesem Vertrag gegenseitig uneingeschraenkt die Souveraenitaet und Unabhaengigkeit der Vertragspartner," Ibid.

[92]_Zehn Jahre Deutschlandpolitik_, pp. 135, 164.

[93]Ibid., p. 164.

[94]Ibid., p. 165.

[95]Ibid., p. 188.

[96]Ibid., pp. 184-186.

[97]Ibid.

[98]"Uebereinkommen zwischen der Deutschen Bundesbahn, vertreten durch die Hauptverwaltung, und dem Ministerium fuer Verkehrswesen der Deutschen Demokratischen Republik ueber den Eisenbahngrenzverkehr," ibid., pp. 192-198.

[99]Ibid., p. 181.

[100]Ibid., pp. 220-221.

3
Implementing the Basic Treaty

There are a number of ways in which the Federal
Republic of Germany and the German Democratic Republic
have implemented the inner-German provisions of the
Basic Treaty. The most obvious have been the bilateral
agreements reached in the practical and humanitarian
areas of Article 7. Also to be included as
implementation, however, are some unilateral actions of
FRG and GDR governments and judicial organs. The
treaty, as was explained in the previous chapter,
failed to resolve a number of questions of vital
interest and thus ensured that each government would
adhere to its former state conceptions, albeit often
with new innovations. General statements of government
policy offer a third index of implementation, in
particular since they frequently disclose what status
each has accorded the Basic Treaty, what emphasis has
been placed on specific articles, and how the treaty as
a whole has been interpreted. The first section of
this chapter will attempt to answer the question of the
treaty's overall status, inasmuch as it is the prism
through which inner-German practices pass in subsequent
pages.

Before undertaking the discussion of
implementation, it is first necessary to transform the
general language of the treaty articles into concrete
areas of government activity. Implementation with
regard to the preamble and "the national question"
relates to the two governments' policies on German
self-determination and the legal relationship of the
two states. The question of citizenship will also be
included in this discussion since this issue, although
not regulated by the Basic Treaty, has a direct bearing
on the national question. Article 1's provision for
"normal, good-neighborly relations" serves simply as a
general statement of intent and thus does not relate to

the treaty's implementation.

Article 4 is concerned with East and West German policies regarding the membership of both states in international organizations as well as the representation of Germans in third states. Application of Articles 2 and 6, on the other hand, raises the issues of sovereign jurisdiction and internal autonomy. Here what is essential are the questions of the applicability of West German laws to the GDR, Bonn's approach to the escapes of East Germans from the GDR, and each leadership's interpretation of the principle of "sovereign jurisdiction" broadly speaking. The discussion of Article 7 will identify inner-German agreements reached in the practical and humanitarian areas and assess the degree of progress attained. Finally, the treatment of Article 8 will extend to the accreditation and functions of the Permanent Missions, while the discussion of the Oral Agreement on Political Consultation will examine the frequency and scope of FRG and GDR consultations by the heads of state and ministers.

THE BASIC TREATY AS A POINT OF ORIGIN IN INNER-GERMAN RELATIONS

In practice, the Basic Treaty has frequently receded into the background as an inner-German reference point even when disputed questions are almost entirely of a bilateral nature. This statement holds true for both leaderships and requires some explanation. First, both governments have drawn attention to the treaty's validity within the larger framework of West German-Warsaw Pact states treaties concluded in the 1970's, although the SED leadership has stressed much more that the agreement "represents an important constituent part of the entire treaty work of the socialist states with the FRG."[1] This East German emphasis serves the purpose of drawing attention to the GDR's ideological and political bonds with the Warsaw Pact nations as well as tacitly equating the sovereign state relations adopted between those states and West Germany with inner-German relations. Federal Minister Franke, on the other hand, has described "contractually-agreed cooperation with the states of the Warsaw Pact, including the GDR," as a "policy of relaxation" which "does not impair the rights and responsibilities of our partners in the (1954) Germany Treaty."[2] Both Bonn and East Berlin have thereby of necessity acknowledged the influence of non-German states in German affairs and emphasized the treaty's existence within a broader political framework. Such an acknowledgment has the effect of precluding a literal interpretation of the Basic Treaty's "state autonomy" or national sections.

Second, the SPD-FDP coalition's determination "to proceed from postwar realities," notably East Germany's importance in Soviet political and security calculations, has further mitigated against a consistent West German interpretation or application of the treaty's articles. West German governments under Brandt and Schmidt repeatedly drew attention to the difficulty of negotiating with East Berlin and the limits which existed with respect to inducing changes in GDR internal practices.[3] Implicit in this recognition was the further proposition that verbal criticism of the GDR leadership for treaty violations might only produce a hardening of its attitude towards Bonn and thus prevent any further practical cooperation. Thus Bonn did not cite the violation of Article 2, which in addition to other precepts provided for FRG and GDR observance of human rights, during periods of restrictive SED measures against political dissent and Western journalists in East Germany. In the face of a January 1977 interdiction by GDR policemen of East German inhabitants seeking to enter the FRG Permanent Mission, for example, the Federal Government invoked only the more general Article 1.

Finally, the Basic Treaty is by no means all-inclusive with respect to the range of inner-German issues that fall within its area of applicability. It regulates neither the questions of West German-West Berlin travel and political ties, absolutely vital objects of West German policy, nor German citizenship, although the East German Government has declared the validity of Article 4 in support of its own citizenship policy. Even if one examines the two most dramatic setbacks in areas specifically covered by the Basic Treaty in this period, the doubling of the GDR minimum currency requirements for Western travel to East Germany in November 1973 and October 1980, the treaty itself is not at issue. In the first instance, Egon Bahr stated only that the increase was not compatible with "the spirit of the agreements" already reached[4] without referring to the Basic Treaty. In the second, Foreign Minister Hans-Dietrich Genscher described the East German action as a violation in the context of "the CSCE (Conference on Security and Cooperation in Europe)."[5] This method of response also proved to be the case in most other disputes that produced an official West German protest of some East German act. On the occasions of the eviction of two West German journalists from the GDR in 1975 and 1976, the Schmidt Government's formal objection to their expulsion was based on a specific reference to the Final Act of the Helsinki Agreement and "the agreements between both states." In addition, the activities of the "Chancellor spy," Guillaume, as well as the 1976-1977 restrictions

on East German authors and those seeking to enter the
Permanent Mission were described by Helmut Schmidt as
"encumbrances" to the inner-German relationship but not
as violations of the Basic Treaty.

It is also instructive to observe that in the
presence of marked East-West political tension in the
spring of 1980, the period in which the NATO allies
considered economic and political sanctions against the
Soviet Union, Bonn placed emphasis on the international
salience of inner-German cooperation. The May 1980
FRG-GDR traffic treaty was interpreted by at that time
State Secretary Hans-Juergen Wischnewski as evidence
that the two German states were "conscious of their
special responsibility for the preservation of peace in
Europe and...the policy of detente."[6] Wischnewski thus
valued the agreement less as a fulfillment of the Basic
Treaty than of the Federal Republic's international
obligations. One can detect in such practices Bonn's
desire to "multilateralize" diplomacy in line with its
recognition of continued Four Power rights and
responsibilities in Germany that preclude solely
bilateral inner-German relations, its traditional
desire to avoid isolation within the West on major
foreign policy issues, and the necessarily pan-European
scope of the Ostpolitik as a long-term strategy for
overcoming the German division. Also to be perceived
in the FRG's reliance on the Final Act is West German
championing of an international document whose
expressed provision for expanded human contacts could
prove more effective than the Basic Treaty in promoting
the GDR's liberalization. The latter document, after
all, openly declares East German sovereign jurisdiction
as an inner-German premise.

When the Brandt and Schmidt Governments did cite
specific applications of the treaty, these took the
form, not surprisingly, of testimonials to the
enhancement of inner-German contacts after 1972.
Minister Franke enumerated four separate achievements
in this area during his "Five Years of the Basic
Treaty" address of December 20, 1977: the exchange of
the Permanent Missions, the commencement of border-
district travel, family reunification, and West German
press reporting from the GDR.[7] Franke praised "the
continued and permanent exchange between the Germans in
East and West" while conceding that the Federal
Government's successes "measured according to the ideal
of freedom of movement are insufficient."[8]

The Federal Government has thus made little use of
the treaty's "bilateral" articles, especially Articles
2,4, and 6, and has for the most part invoked Article
1, as in the case of the 1980 currency exchange
increase. Conversely, East Berlin has utilized
Articles 2, 4, and 6 in alleging West German
interference in its external affairs and has cited

Article 7 in warning against a possible modification of West German trade policy. Both leaderships have acclaimed Article 5 as a constructive tool for the preservation of peace, given its provision for East-West German consultation on European security matters.

The Federal Government's rather sparing use of the treaty offers one indication of the conscious shift of SPD-FDP governments away from a strict reliance on legal formulas, in contrast to frequent practices of the 1950's and 1960's. A related feature of this revision was, of course, an avoidance of earlier terminology that proved especially offensive to the East German regime; with the onset of Brandt's inner-German policy, phrases such as "Pankow"[9] or "the so-called GDR" disappeared from the public utterances of chancellors and ministers. This general practice was departed from only slightly by Chancellor Schmidt's occasional remarks regarding the "zonal frontier area" (Zonenrandgebiet) and GDR shooting installations along the frontier.[10] In this connection, it is interesting to note that in a February 1977 interview with the West German publication _Stern_, Schmidt did not take exception to his interviewer's reference to East Germany as "a sovereign state,"[11] although the Chancellor himself avoided such phraseology publicly.

THE NATIONAL QUESTION

As was indicated in the previous chapter, the Deutschlandpolitik of the Brandt-Scheel coalition embraced attempts to enhance the unity of the nation through increased physical contacts between Germans on both sides of the inner-German frontier. Concomitant with this revised policy was a de-emphasis on the exclusive claims of the FRG as the only legitimate German government and on past assertions that a German state unity continued to exist in a strict legal sense. Bonn's re-definition of the nation compelled East Berlin to refine somewhat its earlier conception of the socialist nation. However, since the Basic Treaty's preamble allowed both governments to continue to profess separate national doctrines and the perceived interests of the two leaderships demanded this, it is not surprising that East and West German versions of national unity continued to show little resemblance.

The FRG position on reunification and the self-determination of Germans found its expression in the earlier "Letter on German Unity," where it was declared that the Federal Republic would strive for German unity "in free self-determination." Yet the most comprehensive West German statement on the legal relationship of the two German states appeared only with the July 1973 "Karlsruhe Decision" of the Federal

Constitutional Court. The Court, in declaring the compatibility of the Basic Treaty with the Basic Law, was at pains to harmonize the Federal Government's goal of German self-determination with the treaty's designation of the GDR as an autonomous state and subject of international law. These competing purposes produced a legal ruling that was not always free of ambiguity. Once more a West German judicial organ declared that the GDR was not considered to be a foreign country and that the Federal Republic was "identical with the state German Reich." An important proviso was added to this last formulation, however, since the FRG "in relation to its spatial expanse is, to be sure, partially identical, thus to that extent the identity lays no claim to exclusivity."[12]

The Court thus laid down an interpretation of the two states' status that presupposed a German "roof," the nation, under which both states could administer their affairs autonomously. It proclaimed the GDR "a state within the meaning of international law and as such a subject of international law." Yet inhabitants of East Germany continued to be considered German citizens "within the meaning of the Basic Law." This association was limited only insofar as practical judicial jurisdiction was concerned, since it was required that a German be "in the protective area of the state order of the Federal Republic"[13] in order for him to pursue his rights before a West German court. The Court thereby denied the existence of a separate East German citizenship and asserted that the two German states were to be understood as "parts of a still-existing, even if indisposed (because not reorganized), All-German state with a uniform Staatsvolk."[14] How this understanding of an All-German state was to co-exist with the prior reference to the GDR as "a state within the meaning of international law" was not immediately clear. The reference to the inner-German frontier also raised a legal question: the Court explained that the Basic Treaty's depiction of the frontier as a "state frontier" was subject to the qualification that the two states' existence on the basis of the still-existing state "Germany as a whole" altered the intrinsic status of the frontier. It was held to be "similar to those (frontiers) that run between the Laender of the Federal Republic of Germany."[15] Such an understanding of the frontier could only be harmonized with sections of the Basic Treaty with great difficulty, such as the force-renunciation clause of Article 3. It was testimony to the ambiguous nature of the Court's ruling that the GDR could be considered a state but that the inner-German frontier should be described as akin to a Land boundary.

In other respects, the decision reaffirmed the West German Government's authorization to act in support of the German nation's interests and its obligation to refrain from acts that might hinder reunification. The "Karlsruhe Decision" can thus be viewed as a judicial adjunct to the Brandt Government's German policy in that it strove to emphasize the "special" nature of inner-German relations while denying to the Federal Republic an All-German jurisdictional authority. Even though the two states had by 1973 signed a treaty which set limits to the Federal Republic's sovereign jurisdiction, the Court ruled against the Bavarian Land Government's claim that the SPD-FDP government had violated the Basic Law through its "recognition" of the GDR. Rather than committing the latter violation, the Court maintained, the Federal Government had only chosen "not to politically make use of this legal title or consider it suitable as a political instrument at the moment or in the foreseeable future."[16]

An examination of West German political, as opposed to legal, precepts regarding the unity of the nation provides evidence of Bonn's reordering of priorities after the formation of the SPD-FDP coalition in 1969. In Brandt's first government declaration after the concluding of the Basic Treaty, the Chancellor emphasized that

the preservation of the peace ranks higher than the question of the nation... Only the long and arduous way from coexistence- to cooperation by the two states offers the nation its chance.[17]

Even more noteworthy than this rhetorical shift in accent from the phraseology of earlier West German governments, who avoided such a clear statement of choice, was Bonn's post-1972 observance of the "Day of German Unity." Throughout the 1950's and 1960's, the June 1953 uprising of workers in the GDR had been commemorated in official ceremonies, including an annual address by the Federal Chancellor. The "Day of Unity" was intended as a symbol of the Federal Republic's will to sustain its commitment to Germans in the GDR, but its observance was no longer automatic with the coalescence of an SPD-FDP Bundestag majority in 1969. On June 12, 1974, the Federal Government announced that it would not observe the twenty-first anniversary of the event; Chancellor Schmidt expressed his preference for a parliamentary session in place of the usual commemoration. The necessity to compromise with the opposition CDU/CSU in the Bundestag eventually produced an alternative outcome, as both the commemoration and the parliamentary session were cancelled.[18]

The governing coalition's disinclination to observe the "Day of Unity" paralleled its proven

willingness to trade off All-German claims in return
for the possibility of practical cooperation. In a
June 17, 1973 declaration, Willy Brandt referred to the
1953 upheaval in the following way:

> We should recognize this day in its importance,
> transcending party boundaries and other competing
> conceptions, and remember the victims that it
> claimed. However, it should not be degraded for
> the purpose of almost unrelated, to a certain
> degree antiquarian hours of ceremony.[19]

Brandt then repeated a familiar tenet of SPD-FDP
Ostpolitik: "This (the division of Germany) may be
bitter but according to my conviction it is our primary
German interest to give highest priority to the
maintenance of peace."[20] The Chancellor thus admonished
against any use of the "Day" that ignored either
international realities or the lessons of German
history.

Although the Basic Treaty does not directly
regulate the matter of German citizenship, some
explanation of the problem is demanded because of its
relation to the national question and the importance of
citizenship as a state prerogative. Here one finds an
exception to, in particular, Brandt's predisposition to
de-emphasize past West German legal positions. The
Federal Government in the 1970's was no less energetic
than earlier governments in striving to protect the
integrity of one German citizenship and was supported
in this attempt by the "Karlsruhe Decision." The
Federal Constitutional Court ruled that a bifurcation
of jurisdictional authority in the two German states
had not led to the creation of separate citizenships.
In line with this continued validity of Articles 1, 16,
and 116 of the Basic Law, Bonn continued to issue
special entry slips to East Germans travelling to the
FRG rather than stamping GDR passports.[21] Analogous to
this activity was the continued West German extension
of legal and consular assistance to East German
residents in third states as well as Foreign Minister
Genscher's active opposition to the concluding of an
Austrian-East German consular treaty that recognized an
East German citizenship in January 1975.

If the "Karlsruhe Decision" is to be regarded as
the single most important official enunciation of the
Federal Republic's position on the two German states'
legal relations and national ties, one must then
consider the September 1974 GDR constitution for the
corresponding East German doctrinal conception. It is
notable that this amended document contained the first
modifications of the 1968 constitution, thus following
the conclusion of the Basic Treaty and the inauguration
of some closer inner-German contacts. Unlike the

earlier constitution, this later version omitted any reference to the German nation, declaring instead in Article 1 that the GDR "is a socialist state of workers and farmers." The pertinent passage in the 1968 constitution declared East Germany to be "a socialist state of the German nation."[22] Every other All-German reference contained in this earlier constitution was deleted.

The SED leadership also moved to strike passages proclaiming the goal of German unity from "friendship treaties" concluded with other members of the Warsaw Pact. Upon examining the previously mentioned 1967 treaties agreed to between the GDR, on one hand, and Poland, Czechoslovakia, and Bulgaria, on the other, one finds a passage aiming at "the peaceful settlement of the German question" and "the creation of a unified, peace-loving, and democratic German state."[23] This provision was removed from similar treaties signed between these parties in 1977 and no equivalent sections were inserted. In addition, while the 1964 Soviet-East German Friendship Treaty declared the GDR to be "the first workers' and farmers' state in the history of Germany" and registered the aim "to promote the unity of Germany,"[24] the October 1975 "Treaty of Friendship, Assistance and Cooperation" referred to East Germany as "a sovereign, independent socialist state"[25] and contained no All-German phraseology.

Other official East German measures in 1976 and 1977 must necessarily be seen as extensions of East Berlin's demarcation policy in the aftermath of the Basic Treaty and the Helsinki Final Act-inaugurated contacts with the Federal Republic. The SED's May 1976 Party Program omitted the traditional references to the aim of German reunification and national ties with West Germans. A similar motivation could be discerned in a July 1976 East German travel requirement that West German visitors to East Germany in the future describe their citizenship as "FRG" instead of "German" in filling out travel applications. In January of 1977, the same month in which the SED leadership began to remove the physical vestiges of a Four Power status for East Berlin, GDR inhabitants were granted entry into the FRG Permanent Mission in East Berlin only after they had first acquired permits from the East German Foreign Ministry.[26]

The GDR leadership's characteristic tendency to de-limit the two German states above all on an ideological basis remained unchanged, and the notion of a still open "German question" was persistently dismissed by SED Central Committee members. Politburo member Hermann Axen supported this outlook in an article printed in Pravda on March 6, 1973:

"The so-called German question has been

definitively solved in agreement with the
principles of international law. All that was to
be regulated was unambiguously and precisely
regulated through many international treaties,
including the Basic Treaty. As a consequence no
German question exists at all anymore, rather,
there are two sovereign, socially-opposite German
states, independent of one another and with two
nations as was confirmed by the Eighth Party
Congress of the SED.[27]

Yet the SED leadership did perceive the need to
provide some more precise explanation of the East-West
German relationship beyond ideological oppositions. In
December 1974, General Secretary Honecker declared:

We have already advanced a historical epoch in
comparison to the Federal Republic of Germany. To
express it concisely, we represent, in contrast to
the Federal Republic of Germany, the socialist
Germany... This difference is the decisive one.
Our socialist state is called the German Democratic
Republic because its citizens are according to
nationality Germans in the overwhelming majority...
The answer to questions of this type resounds
clearly and without any ambiguities: citizenship--
GDR, nationality-- German. Thus is the state of
affairs.[28]

This speech contrasts somewhat with the earlier remarks
made by Axen in that it was recognized that the denial
of affinities between the two parts of Germany could
not be carried to the most absurd lengths. The
official terminology of the East German leadership, for
example, continued to speak of the GDR railroad service
as the "Reichsbahn," or Imperial Railway.
Nevertheless, although the General Secretary referred
to the Rome Treaty's inner-German trade provision as
"one of the few particularities which continue to exist
in the (inner-German) relations" in November 1972,[29]
East Berlin persisted in its denunciation of the West
German promotion of "special" relations.[30] Albert
Norden took note of "so-called special relations
towards the anti-socialist subversion of the GDR and as
a battle-cry against the true unity of the people in
socialism."[31] Axen advanced the explanation that inner-
German relations "are not determined by any sort of
'common character' but rather by insurmountable
oppositions, by the irreconcilable opposition between
socialism and capitalism."[32] This extended lecture on
the historical conflict between capitalism and
socialism, which allegedly received its stamp after the
1848 upheavals in the German states, was testimony to
the SED leadership's concern over the possible

viability of Brandt's "unity of the nation" thesis in the presence of increasing, if gradual, West German visits to the GDR. East German internal measures in the two years after the signing of the Basic Treaty were thus characterized by a heightened campaign of ideological education. One of the first manifestations of this policy decision could be found in SED Politburo member Kurt Hager's December 1972 "Report on Ideology and Culture" which openly lauded the development of "the free, broadly educated and highly qualified socialist personality" and "the imprinting of a spiritual life that does justice to the requirements of the developed socialist society."[33] Regarding the ideological consequences for inner-German relations, Axen was more succinct:

> The Leninist principles of peaceful coexistence are more and more being implemented as the general rules of relations between the socialist states, among them the GDR, on one hand, and the capitalist states on the other... However, by law peaceful coexistence includes the further-executed Abgrenzung between the socialist GDR and the capitalist FRG.[34]

The East German pursuance of a separate citizenship has accompanied SED exhortations for ideological and physical Abgrenzung. This can be observed most directly in East Berlin's requirement that West German travellers to the GDR display their passports upon entry as well as in the passage of the October 16, 1972 law withdrawing East German citizenship from those who have escaped to the West. Also representative of this desired effect in SED policy was the August 16, 1973 commentary on the "Karlsruhe Decision" in <u>Neues Deutschland</u>,[35] which quoted the autonomy provision of Article 6 in rejecting the notion of one German citizenship.

The traditional postwar irreconcilability of East and West German positions on the citizenship question was not removed in the aftermath of the Basic Treaty, as the preceding pages testify. Nevertheless, it would be incorrect to assume that this issue has been a major factor in sharpening the points of conflict between Bonn and East Berlin on a day-to-day basis. While it is true that Honecker verbally linked improvements in inner-German travel to the Federal Government's recognition of a GDR citizenhip in February of 1977,[36] SED demands in this area have not recurred with the persistent regularity of earlier statements by Ulbricht. Indeed, during the stiffening of East German public policy toward Bonn in October 1980, the General Secretary called specifically for the "respecting" rather than recognition of the separate citizenship, implying that some mutually acceptable arrangement might be attainable.[37] It is only in the area of legal assistance that the citizenship dispute has emerged as an obstruction to practical inner-German cooperation, in spite of the fact that formal policies were not altered in this period.

THE FRG AND GDR IN INTERNATIONAL ORGANIZATIONS AND REPRESENTATION OF GERMANS

Both German states became members of the United Nations Organization on September 18, 1973. Despite unequivocal acceptance of the GDR as a full and equal member by the majority of the world's states, the West German Government continued to publicly proceed from the understanding that "the simultaneous membership of both states in Germany in the U.N.... does not prejudice the special situation in Germany."[38] The only international organizations in which this recognition of unique German conditions was given practical acknowledgment, however, continued to be the General Agreement on Tariffs and Trade and the European Economic Community in the sense that FRG-GDR trade was declared to be "internal German trade."[39]

There is no evidence that Bonn at any time attempted to obstruct East German efforts to gain membership in an international organization after the Basic Treaty's entry into effect. Such preventive measures would clearly have jeopardized the prospects for a new inner-German relationship and violated Article 4 of the treaty. By the end of 1973 alone, both German states had secured membership in such organizations as the U.N. Conference on Trade and Development, the International Telecommunications Union, the World Health Organization, the Universal Postal Union, and the International Atomic Energy Agency. Meetings between the East and West German foreign ministers at the United Nations, although infrequent,[40] confirmed the Federal Government's acceptance of the principle of non-representation of the East German state internationally.

Although it has not been a regular practice of the two German governments to attach inner-German problems to the agendas of international organizations, there did arise several occasions when the Schmidt Government brought practices of the East German leadership to the attention of a broader public. In a September 28, 1976 address to the U.N. General Assembly, Foreign Minister Genscher took note of fresh incidents along the FRG-GDR frontier: "The Federal Government does not resign itself to the reality of a frontier on the other side of which shots were recently fired."[41] This indirect reference to, among other events, the August 1976 shooting of an Italian truck driver by GDR border guards substituted for calls by the West German opposition that Bonn file a protest with the U.N. Human Rights Commission. Such a response was rejected by Chancellor Schmidt on the grounds that the GDR was a party to neither the U.N. Human Rights Convention's "state grievance" article, which allows such a grievance to be lodged against a state by another signatory, nor its Facultative Protocol, which authorizes the Commission to consider the charges against a state.[42]

Other contentious policies pursued by the GDR leadership became the subject of discussion at the two follow-up conferences to the 1975 Helsinki Conference. The Federal Republic's spokesman, Per Fischer, declared that the January 1978 closing of the Spiegel office and the denial of entry to East Berlin for several CDU politicians "could not advance the realization of the Helsinki Final Act"[43] at Belgrade in early 1978. During the later conference in Madrid, the West German delegation took up the problems posed by the October 1980 compulsory currency exchange increase for Western travellers into the GDR as well as incidents along the inner-German frontier. The East German delegation reportedly levelled the charge of the deprivation of economic and ethnic rights in Western countries but directed many of these specifically at the FRG.[44]

In approaching the question of the representation of Germans internationally, it is once more essential to point out that the Basic Law's imperative for German self-determination has coexisted with the Federal Republic's renunciation of acting on behalf of or speaking for the GDR only with difficulty. As was observed in the previous chapter, acts "on behalf of the German nation" are not easily distinguishable from acts "on behalf of the GDR." In agreement with respective national policies, Bonn in this period continued to issue West German papers to East German travellers to the Federal Republic that desired them, an object of East Berlin's repeated criticism. A similarly divergent application of Article 4 was evident in the West German extension of consular and legal assistance to East Germans in third states and Honecker's insistence that this practice be discontinued.

The Federal Government also outwardly strove to gain third states' validation of its All-German consular authority. After the conclusion of a British-East German consular treaty in May 1976, the British ambassador to the FRG provided Genscher with a letter stating that the agreement did not "affect the authority of West German consular officials to assist all Germans, based on the July 30, 1956 British-West

German consular treaty, in accordance with Article 116
of the Basic Law."[45] In addition, Bonn at one point
severely tested the Basic Treaty's provision for East
and West German "autonomy in external affairs" in an
action opposed by Vienna as well as East Berlin.
Genscher publicly contested the January 1975 Austrian-
East German consular treaty due to its recognition of a
GDR citizenship, although West German efforts to have
this section deleted met with no success. The East
German Government, on the other hand, interpreted the
Federal Government's intervention as a violation of
Articles 2, 4, and 6.[46]

SOVEREIGN JURISDICTION

Article 6 confined the jurisdiction of each German
state to the area within its post-1945 frontiers, a
principle reinforced by the guarantee of "independence,
autonomy and territorial integrity" contained in
Article 2. One of the main points of controversy
between the two governments at the 1970 Kassel meeting
stemmed from the East German desire that
"discriminatory legislation" be removed from West
German lawbooks; much of this entailed statutes that by
extension applied FRG legal provisions to the GDR. The
value-added tax law passed in 1967, it will be
recalled, was declared valid for the German Reich as
defined by its 1937 frontiers even though the Federal
Government took no practical steps to implement it as
such. Rather, what was at issue was the symbolic
recognition of a still-existing, even if latent, German
state unity.
Given the Brandt-Scheel preference for relegating
many of these legal formulations of unity to the
background after 1969, it was not unexpected that such
West German legislation would undergo alteration in the
course of the search for "Miteinander" with the GDR.
The change of priority could be detected in the passage
of legislation in the Bundestag, in which a majority of
deputies were members of the governing SPD-FDP
coalition. The July 14, 1971 reading of a wine law
declared its "area of validity" to be "the home country
within the meaning of this law."[47] Foreign lands were
understood to be "the areas which belong neither to the
area of validity of the law nor to the currency areas
of the mark of the German Democratic Republic."[48]
Although the Basic Treaty was not concluded until a
year-and-a-half later, the passage of this law plainly
suggested a limited interpretation of FRG jurisdiction
that was not acknowledged in earlier laws.
The emergence of the Basic Treaty as a "fait
accompli" further reinforced the tendency to dispense
with formalistic inclusions of the GDR in West German

legislation. With the conclusion of deliberations by the Bundestag Conference Committee, a new version of the former sales-tax law was passed on November 8, 1979. This compromise succeeded in taking into account the opposition CDU/CSU's objections that the governing coalition had categorized the GDR as "foreign land" (Ausland) for the purpose of the law. The "area of validity" of the law was explicitly equated with "the area of collection" of the tax except for "customs-exempt areas," a reference to West Berlin; as in the earlier wine law, "foreign territory" corresponded to areas outside the area of collection and those not situated in the GDR or East Berlin.[49]

SPD Bundestag Deputy Heinz Westphal, in defending the Conference Committee's decision, justified this reading with the explanation that the earlier version was incompatible with Article 6 of the Basic Treaty and that the principle of pacta sunt servanda represented a West German obligation.[50] Thus the Federal Republic's pursuit of "special relations" with the GDR translated into a designation of East Germany as neither "Inland" nor "Ausland" in legislative practice.

The same application of an intermediate status to the GDR was enacted in the judicial sphere. As was explained earlier, the "Karlsruhe Decision" confined FRG lawmaking jurisdiction to the actual area of the Federal Republic while denying the validity of an East German citizenship. A later ruling by a Federal Court of Justice on November 26, 1980 established that East Germany could not be considered "Inland" in the realm of criminal law but that West German criminal law protects East Germans who have been the victims of acts that are punishable under this law.[51] Thus an East German escapee who spied on a fellow escapee for the GDR Ministry of State Security was condemned to imprisonment by the Court, even though the offense had been committed in East Germany.[52]

A related facet of the question of "sovereign jurisdiction" concerns West German disposition of East Germans who have fled the German Democratic Republic and arrived in the Federal Republic. All such attempts are regarded by East German authorities as illegal[53] whether or not the escapee has committed a violent act, as is sometimes the case, that would be punishable in a West German court. Therefore West German approaches to the problem must necessarily conceive of it as a legal as well as political matter the resolution of which would vary in each case. One can also find instances of East German shootings of Western inhabitants along the border. All-important for the purpose of examining Article 6's implementation are the judicial decisions of West German courts in addition to practices of the executive branch relating to these incidents.

Both German governments have adhered to a policy

of lodging formal protests with the other during instances of perceived border violations. This type of rejoinder was most in evidence in the summer of 1976; the Federal Goverment cited GDR border guards' shooting of an Italian truck driver near the frontier and East German apprehension of three West German tourists as "encumbering" the inner-German relationship.[54] During the same interval, the GDR Permanent Mission charged that three members of the Federal Border Guard had committed a trespass violation on East German territory, which the East German leadership construed as a violation of Article 6.[55] (Such disputes were followed in 1978 with steps by the Frontier Commission toward a more precise marking of the frontier).

On the other hand, it has been the West German judiciciary that has decided the fate of East German escapees who appeared to have left the GDR under more questionable circumstances. This occurred, for example, in the much-publicized case of Werner Weinhold, who in December 1975 shot two East German border guards in escaping to the FRG. After initially being acquitted of manslaughter by the Essen Land Court in December 1976, Weinhold was later sentenced to five years in prison by a Hagen Land Court in December 1978, a decision that was subsequently upheld by a Federal Court of Justice. An extradition of Weinhold to the GDR by West German authorities, however, did not come into consideration. Such a course of action was rejected both because of the absence of an inner-German extradition treaty, in line with Bonn's promotion of German unity, and because GDR authorities had made known their intention to impose the death penalty in this case.[56]

In connection with other East German escapes, the FRG judiciary has in principle upheld the legality of "escape contracts" agreed to between fleeing Germans and West Germans assisting them for a fee. This principle was established in a decision by a Federal Constitutional Court of Justice on September 29, 1977. The legal ruling to some degree ran counter to the principle of East German sovereign jurisdiction, since it legitimated an activity legally proscribed by East Berlin. Yet the West German executive has been careful not to support unauthorized activities by Germans on the FRG-Berlin access routes. While Erich Honecker publicly rebuked the Brandt Government for its "officially tolerated and even promoted misuse" of these transit routes,[57] such utterances as Minister Franke's December 1978 warning against such commercial undertakings[58] are indicative of the degree of restraint advocated by the Federal Government in areas outside West German jurisdiction.

Broadly speaking, SPD-FDP governments have not called into question the East German authority to regulate affairs inside the GDR. This guideline has not only been observed in FRG legislation, noted earlier, but corresponded more generally with Bonn's preference for renouncing the direct undermining of the SED leadership. As Chancellor Schmidt stated in a 1977 interview, "detente policy is only possible when both partners are stable."[59] This premise found reinforcement in other statements, as in the Chancellor's reaction to the question of the authorship of an alleged "opposition manifesto" of middle- and higher-level SED functionaries in January 1978:

> We have clearly explained that, regardless of whom you think sent (the manifesto), the Federal Government has nothing to do with it. Only the political reaction of the SED and GDR leadership is of importance to me.[60]

General Secretary Honecker has also frequently stressed the necessity that both states adhere to the principle of respect for one another's sovereign jurisdiction as it was inscribed in Article 6 of the Basic Treaty. After making a specific reference to the article, Honecker, in a July 1978 interview, expressed the view that "it would be entirely unreal if one (state) tried to force the other against its will on this or that question."[61] In practice, as will be discussed more fully in a later chapter, this doctrinal observance of Article 6 has not prevented the surfacing of East German charges of West German interference in GDR internal affairs. In view of East Berlin's only grudging acceptance of inner-German contacts and its potential vulnerability vis-a-vis the more populous and economically more powerful FRG, it was predictable that the SED leadership would define "sovereign jurisdiction" in a much broader sense. Although the Basic Treaty does not contain the term "non-interference" (Nicht-Einmischung), the Helsinki Final Act upholds the principle of non-intervention[62] and East Berlin has invoked this form of state behavior as a professed norm in its dealings with the Federal Republic.[63]

The East German Government has in fact recorded the position that there has been West German interference, although not always <u>government</u> interference, in GDR internal affairs. Such charges originated in events relating to West German journalistic activity in East Germany, incidents along the inner-German frontier,[64] FRG promulgation of the doctrine of "special relations,"[65] and the West Berlin Government's protest against East German increases in the minimum currency requirement.[66] Respecting East German sovereign jurisdiction from Bonn's vantage point, on the other hand, has not been interpreted as

dictating that the Federal Government refrain from such
activities as the maintenance of a border "listening
post" to monitor attempted escapes from East Germany, a
source of repeated protests by East Berlin.[67] Neither
government, it should be remembered, has effected any
noticeable decrease in espionage activities directed at
the other and thereby interpreted Article 6 as
restricting such behavior.

TRADE

It bears restating that inner-German trade gave
rise to asymmetrical interests in East and West German
policy calculations for at least two reasons. The
first is that in terms of its relative commercial
importance, it impacted more heavily on the GDR economy
than that of the Federal Republic, averaging about 9.3%
of total East German external trade in the 1960's.[68]
For the FRG the corresponding percentage was less than
2%.[69] The second divergence in the respective trade
outlooks could be seen in Bonn's subordination of trade
to its political purposes, immediately observable in
the onerous system of licensing and goods quotas
imposed by the Federal Government. The maintenance of
this practice guarded against both the unauthorized
transfer of sophisticated technology to the Warsaw Pact
states and preserved for the FRG the option of altering
by gradations the level of trade with the GDR if
political developments justified such a course. The
SED leadership's participation in the trade, on the
other hand, had been predominantly economic in
motivation in the pre-1969 period. Both asymmetries
persisted to a great degree from 1973 through 1980,
except that with the West German Government's expansion
of the "swing" credit to 850 million DM-West in 1974
and the participation of a number of West German
businesses in inner-German trade, the economic
incentives for these firms to continue to do so also
strongly affected the government's appraisal of the
trade's value. This consideration increased in
importance in the presence of slower growth rates and
higher unemployment in the Federal Republic in the mid-
and late 1970's.
The Basic Treaty's foundation for the transaction
of inner-German trade "on the basis of the existing
agreements" allowed the West German Government to
continue to pursue and implement its policy standard of
"special" German relations. This was accomplished in a
number of ways. Bonn continued to utilize the Inter-
zonal Trade Trusteeship in its trade negotiations with
East Berlin. Internationally, both the EEC and the
General Agreement on Tariffs and Trade formally
regarded the trade as "internal German trade,"[70]

although the EEC Council of Ministers decided to deal with the GDR as a third state in prospective Community trade treaties with the members of COMECON.[71] While this October 1974 decision provided for the continuation of duty-free inner-German trade,[72] it was nevertheless testimony to the Federal Government's increasing difficulty in promoting an All-German appearance in the face of growing international recognition of the GDR.

Inner-German trade can genuinely be characterized as "special," however, because of the West German grant of a long-term, 7-year credit, the unique taxing policy employed by the Federal Government, and the preponderance of administrative controls over these exchanges which have exceeded even those in place for FRG-East European trade.[73] The December 1974 trade-stimulating package fixed the interest-free "swing" credit at a level of 850 million DM through 1981. The agreement required that the two sides negotiate over the further shaping of the trade for the years subsequent to 1981 and that East German deliveries of mineral oil products provided for in the Berlin Agreement be fixed at 140 million DM.[74] Regarding the taxation policy for West German "purchases" of East German goods, trade economist Horst Lambrecht has drawn attention to the unusual FRG practice of subjecting these products to neither the sales-tax levied for foreign goods nor that which is applicable for domestic sales.[75] Rather, the West German importer of such East German deliveries receives a discount in his payment of the value-added tax.[76] Here there is considerable incentive for mutual transactions, since the latter receives what is in effect a pre-tax discount. The tax is calculated according to, in most cases, only 89% of the value of an industrial product and 97.5% of that of an agricultural product.[77]

There are thus no import levies on GDR agricultural deliveries to the Federal Republic. The cumulative effect of Bonn's tax concessions is to encourage somewhat the sale of certain East German goods that are generally treated restrictively in third countries: GDR textile and clothing deliveries, for example, amounted to 13% of total East German deliveries in 1980.[78] West German deliveries are also favored by special provisions, as a May 1973 sales-tax law applied only a 3-6% range to industrial deliveries and declared agricultural deliveries tax-free.[79]

The expansion of credit to the GDR unfolded against the familiar backdrop of a meticulous West German regulation of inner-German trade. The SPD-FDP coalition no less than its predecessors maintained numerous preconditions for East-West German exchanges, including lists of specific goods permitted in the trade, quotas on particular items, separate clearing accounts, a price-monitoring system, the fixing of precise values to each good, and an elaborate procedure of application and licensing for intended commerce.[80] One can detect in such practices a West German interest in keeping trade flows roughly balanced, preventing the unauthorized extension of credit to the GDR, and prohibiting unfavorable and excessive East German trade practices, notably dumping. In addition to the political and security rationale, one can surmise that West German decisionmakers perceived an interest in preventing a too-rapid expansion of inner-German trade for budgetary reasons. Bonn had earlier established a relationship between the amount of East German deliveries and the level of the "swing" credit until the December 1974 agreement fixed the latter at 850 million DM. A decisive rise in the volume of inner-German trade might well have prompted SED insistence that the "swing" be raised correspondingly. Heightened opposition to such an increase by the FRG Bundesbank, which has already registered its objection to the 850 million DM figure as too excessive,[81] would have been a predictable outcome.

Political and budgetary motivations have thus come into play in this area. As could be observed already in the policies of the Erhard Government, however, SPD-FDP governments clearly refrained from using putative trade leverage for momentary reprisals against the SED leadership in this period. Although press reports surfaced in 1974 that the Federal Government contemplated reducing the GDR's trade benefits in retaliation for the November 1973 currency increases for Western travellers,[82] the year ended with Bonn's guarantee of the 7-year "swing" credit to East Berlin. This step was taken even though the higher currency payment had been only partially reduced. Nor did the Schmidt Government yield to the opposition CDU/CSU's calls for a stiffer trade policy towards the GDR in 1976. It did nevertheless register its position that further extension of the "swing" represented a part "of a total connection...in West German Deutschland- and Ostpolitik"[83] after a second currency exchange doubling in 1980.

Bonn's reluctance to avail itself of a trade "lever" for maximum political effect discloses one additional goal of West German policy compared with those of East Berlin. Alongside the Federal Government's traditional interest in maintaining a tangible link with and offering economic support for the East German population, the purely economic importance of the approximately 6,000 West German firms concluding 50,000 separate agreements with East German state trading companies yearly[84] must also be weighed in the balance. Here the "swing" has been the key element in perpetuating West German deliveries to East

Germany manufactured in considerable part by middle-sized companies. Given the reality of periodic downturns in the West German economy during worldwide recessions as well as the Federal Republic's extensive reliance on its export industries,[85] it cannot be said that Bonn's interest in trade with the GDR is wholly attributable to its continued promotion of German unity.

Yet the differences in the goals sought by each government in this activity have persisted. Numerous statements by General Secretary Honecker have not only prized trade cooperation with the FRG[86] but, as on the occasion of the 1977 Leipzig Fair, also recorded his position that the trade should develop independent of the political relationship.[87] (This denial of linkage is, of course, also reminiscent of Ulbricht's earlier insistence that the Inter-zonal Trade Trusteeship only treat trade matters). However, Honecker's positive attitude towards the mutual participation in this area should not obscure the reality that East Berlin has had to exercise no less caution than before in calibrating its degree of involvement in inner-German trade. The SED's perceived necessity to reduce the possibility of political pressure from Bonn and to preempt a flood of FRG deliveries that could encourage popular comparisons of the two German economies cannot be lightly dismissed. Moreover, goods exchanges with Western countries in general may interfere with the mid- and long-term allocation requirements in the centrally-planned East German economy.[88]

Nevertheless, the incentives for East-West German trade from the GDR leadership's perspective have remained powerful, particularly the acquisition of Western technology, basic materials, and production goods. Equally important is the fact that East Berlin can find a ready market in the FRG for many products that would otherwise encounter difficulty in gaining trade outlets, a result made possible by virtue of the special West German tax provisions for the trade. Other advantages enjoyed by East Germany in inner-German trade compared with exchanges with other Western states derive from the FRG's sheer geographical proximity. Transportation cost-intensive products, such as construction materials, fuel, and agricultural goods, are naturally more competitive in West Germany and West Berlin. The GDR also enjoys lower costs in the Federal Republic for advertising, distribution, marketing, and customer assistance.[89]

One can use several standards of comparison in assessing the development of inner-German trade-- its volume in relation to earlier levels, its importance as a percentage of both states' total external trade, and the size of annual trade deficits and debt sustained. A realistic appraisal of these transactions would also

contrast their growth with that of FRG trade with the
other members of COMECON, since the West German program
of "change through rapprochement" aimed at wider links
with all European Communist states'[0] and such a
comparison can make more visible the unique quality of
inner-German trade. The following paragraphs will
pursue these categories.

Trade between the two German states expanded
continuously in the 1970's, especially for East German
products. From 1969 through 1980, the value of East
German deliveries into the Federal Republic increased
by approximately 354% while the corresponding
percentage for West German deliveries to the GDR was
approximately 283%.[1] These results compare with
increases of only 56% for the former and 105% for the
latter in the 1960's.[2] In the eight years after the
signing of the Basic Treaty alone, GDR deliveries
expanded by over 240% and those from the FRG by almost
100%.[3] If one calculates inner-German trade totals
with an eye to real rates of increase, however, a
considerably different picture emerges. Adjusting the
above figures to reflect the annual price rises in West
German exports and imports, with 1962 as the first year
for which such figures are available, trade actually
expanded more rapidly in the earlier decade. From 1962
through 1969 GDR deliveries to the Federal Republic
rose in real terms by 7.9%, while West German
deliveries increased by 23%.[4] These proportions are to
be weighed against real increases in the 1969-1980
period of only 4.1% for both states' deliveries; from
1973 to 1980 the percentages were 3.2% for East German
deliveries and 4.4% for those from the Federal
Republic.[5]

It can therefore be seen that the setting of a
progressively higher "swing" ceiling each year through
1974 by the Federal Government did contribute to annual
increases in the inner-German trade volume but proved
incapable of keeping pace with the higher inflation
rates of the 1970's. In 1980, for example, the trade
total rose by the largest absolute amount ever and the
GDR balanced its trade, yet West German deliveries grew
in real terms by only 2.4%, with those from East
Germany only about 1.5 % higher.[6]

In addition, East-West German trade has declined
sowewhat as a percentage of the GDR's total external
trade. (In the case of West German trade, it will be
recalled, its actual share was never large). In 1970
this amounted to 10.2% then declined to 9.2% in 1973
and only 8.5% in 1977.[7] This last year also showed an
expansion of East German trade with the non-Soviet
members of COMECON from 28.2 to 32.5% of total GDR
foreign trade.[8] The experience of the 1960's
nevertheless indicates that the amount of inner-German
trade may fluctuate downward somewhat but not below the

minimum threshold of 8%, given the substantial payoffs from the trade for both sides.''

With regard to East German debt to the Federal Republic, data is relatively scarce as a result of Bonn's refusal to make accessible complete information on each aspect of the economic relationship with the GDR.[100] Available statistics nevertheless provide a number of indications that East Germany's credit position was not an unfavorable one in the 1973-1980 period. Of chief importance here is the fact that the GDR leadership narrowed and finally eliminated its annual trade deficits with the FRG by 1980; as Lambrecht has observed, it is not a trading partner's "absolute credit or debit position that is decisive but the relation of deliveries and counter-deliveries or the relation of the cumulative trade balance to annual deliveries."[101] When considered according to these criteria, the overall East German credit position improved perceptibly between 1970 and 1976. In the latter year, the total GDR cumulative debt was covered by approximately two-thirds of East German deliveries. By the year 1980, when East German debt to the Federal Republic rose to 3.9 billion DM,[102] the GDR leadership could still cover this amount with 69% of its deliveries to West Germany.[103]

With the exception of the Soviet Union, a country approximately sixteen times as populous as East Germany,[104] there is no European Communist state which maintains a trade volume with West Germany as high as that of the GDR. This can be said with confidence despite the fluctuating and often uncertain values of most East European currencies. Polish-West German trade in the entire period under consideration here did not once attain even the minimum level of inner-German trade that existed in 1973.[105] The Federal Republic's goods trade with the Soviet Union tripled in the 1973-1980 period at the same time that inner-German trade barely doubled, but, computed on a per capita basis, the former only amounted to about 9.3% of the latter by 1979. West German trade with Hungary and Czechoslovakia, the two next most important COMECON trading partners of the FRG, also lagged well behind the East-West German goods trade although the CSSR more than doubled its West German trade between 1973 and 1980. Seen from an alternative perspective, the GDR's goods trade with the Federal Republic amounted to 10.4 billion DM in 1980 compared with an East German trade with all other OECD countries of only 8.7 billion DM.[106]

In examining the composition of inner-German trade in this period, it is at first observable that the GDR continued to import roughly the same proportion of goods within the major trading categories. Basic materials and production goods as well as investment

goods comprised about three-quarters of all West German
deliveries throughout.[107] East Berlin chose to purchase
less iron and steel but proportionately increased its
total of West German chemical and engineering products,
in particular. Interestingly, West German deliveries
of consumer goods declined as a percentage of total
deliveries.[108] Despite press reports of "intershop
socialism," SED policymakers seem to have opted for a
controlled opening of the East German market, with 1973
and 1974 as the peak years for the importing of these
consumer products.[109]

By contrast, East German deliveries to the Federal
Republic underwent three long-term shifts in terms of
the mix of goods. First, basic materials and
production goods rose from 37% of GDR deliveries in
1973 to 52.8% in 1980, with mineral-oil products
expanding by over 250%.[110] Second, the percentage of
GDR agricultural deliveries to the Federal Republic
dropped by over 50% in this period.[111] East German
agriculture was thus outpaced by the overall expansion
of inner-German trade. Third, East German engineering
products, while increasingly exported to other OECD
countries,[112] steadily decreased in importance in the
inner-German trade.[113] Of course, this result was not
simply a function of these items' competitiveness in
West Germany but was conditioned by the COMECON
requirement that the bulk of GDR investment goods be
exported to the other socialist members.[114] With
respect to the FRG-GDR services balance, East Germany
has sustained annual deficits consistently, but this
sector remains fairly small in terms of the total trade
(7% in 1980).[115]

TRAFFIC AND TRANSPORTATION

The Basic Treaty sections for the facilitation of
inner-German travel and improvements in the non-
commercial goods traffic formally took effect June 21,
1973 after the ratification of the treaty by both
states earlier. A series of executive decisions
announced by the GDR Interior Ministry on June 14
entered into force the same day; these provided for the
commencement of inner-German border-district travel as
well as the cross-border mail flow, the carrying of
gifts across the border, and simplification of the
approval policy for the cross-border relocation of
inherited and household goods. On July 5 the border-
district traffic was opened for those residing in the
East and West German districts enumerated in the Basic
Treaty and four new crossings were made accessible to
ease this travel.[116]

After several months, however, growing tensions
between the two governments, reflected in SED

objections to several cases of misuse of the transit
routes between the FRG and West Berlin,[117] were
destined to have their impact on East-West German
travel. The first major setback thus took the form of
East Berlin's November 5, 1973 doubling of the
compulsory currency exchange requirement for West
Germans and West Berliners travelling into the GDR and
East Berlin.[118] This measure resulted in a downturn in
West German visits to East Germany and East Berlin,[119]
thus producing a deterrent effect similar to the
physical obstruction of inner-German routes by the
People's Police in years past.

It was not until November 5, 1974, exactly one
year after the raising of the requirememt, that the GDR
Finance Ministry reduced the increase by approximately
two-thirds. Foreign Minister Genscher described this
response as unsatisfactory, yet the measure's entry
into force on November 15 preceded agreement between
Bonn and East Berlin on a fairly wide range of
activities the next month, including the new "swing"
regulation.[120] The West German Government had in the
meantime attempted to gain a payment exemption for West
German travellers who were pensioners or under the age
of 16, a concession which was forthcoming in a December
10 announcement of the GDR Finance Ministry.[121] This
action did not materialize, however, before Neues
Deutschland claimed that the agreed adjustment
represented a "pre-concession" by the Federal
Government in return for the exemption.[122] This
interpretation of events was emphatically denied by
West German spokesman Armin Gruenewald, who claimed the
East German Government had agreed to the exemption at
the end of November, days before the initialing of the
"swing" regulation.[123] Since the SED regime had not
completely restored the "status quo ante" in terms of
travellers' payments, Bonn was compelled to prevent an
attenuation of its own psychological linkage of trade
and travel lest "reverse linkage" be applied by East
Berlin.

Up to this point in time, West German use of
private motor vehicles in the GDR was largely
restricted to those with special needs, such as
handicapped citizens or those with children under the
age of three. Simultaneous with conclusion of the
"swing" agreement on December 20, 1974, GDR authorities
permitted the use of the automobile for travel into
East Germany on a broader basis.[124] However, it was not
until the Federal Government's September 11, 1976
announcement of a more flexible inner-German travel
understanding that all prohibitions on the use of motor
vehicles in border-district traffic were abolished. As
a result of the 1974 agreement, the GDR leadership did
permit West German travel into the entire area of East
Germany. Prior to this understanding, inner-German

travel on a regular basis had been limited to several
East German districts close to the frontier. These
travel-facilitation measures were connected to one
other issue: the taking up of negotiations on rail and
motor traffic. The East German insistence that joint
projects in this area bring "no additional economic
burdens" to the GDR implied a predominantly West German
economic contribution in the transportation
agreements.[125]

Thus it can be seen that East Berlin's opening of
the GDR to new travel contacts emerged gradually
between 1972 and 1976, suffered some setbacks, and
unfolded in the presence of financing concessions by
the Federal Republic. The SED leadership's delay in
removing all motor vehicle restrictions for border-
district traffic placed particularly severe limitations
on this activity inasmuch as, in most cases,
automobiles offered the sole possibility for
undertaking such daily visits. The September 1976
withdrawal of this prohibition was accompanied by
several other travel-promoting practices, including a
shortening of the waiting period for East German
commuter trains and for acceptance of West German
travel applications, new facilitation of the procedure
for carrying inherited and household goods across the
border, and the announcement of FRG-GDR negotiations in
the non-commercial payments area.[126]

It soon became apparent, however, that an ensuing
"freeze" in the two German states' relations would
limit further activity on the traffic and travel
question. The next two years saw the intervention of a
number of developments which subjected inner-German
relations to renewed strains: reports of mass
applications for emigration by GDR inhabitants, the
January 1977 incident involving the FRG Permanent Mission, and increasing invocation of the Helsinki Final
Act by dissenting East Germans.[127] In this time there
were no inner-German travel agreements except for a
December 1977 exchange of letters on construction of a
section of the Helmstedt-Marienborn autobahn.
Beginning in mid-December 1976 it was reported that
East Germans who had emigrated from the GDR to the
Federal Republic in accordance with GDR statutes were
denied permission to re-enter East Germany. Later East
German statements described the action as completely
within East Berlin's right.[128] This policy clearly ran
counter to the December 20, 1971 traffic agreement
between the GDR and West Berlin and coincided in time
with a stepped-up SED campaign against East German
dissidents as well as the expulsion of West German
television correspondent Lothar Loewe. Not unrelated
to these de-limiting actions were concurrent steps by
GDR authorities to abolish the military control points
between East Berlin and adjacent parts of East Germany

on January 1, 1977, thus attempting to invalidate a Four Power status for the city.

Throughout 1977 and much of 1978, such East German internal practices continued to complicate inner-German relations. In late 1978 it nevertheless became possible for both governments to sign a transportation agreement which chiefly provided for completion of the Berlin-Hamburg autobahn. Two new border-crossing points were also opened to traffic at Zarrentin and Stolpe-Dorf, and the two sides committed themselves to the resumption of negotiations toward travel alleviations in 1980. The Federal Government stated that it "foresees a payment contribution of up to 500 million DM for still to be agreed-upon construction measures and services for the period after 1981."[129]

It is significant that further transportation agreements were not precluded in 1979, another year in which East-West German relations were subject to repeated stress. The SED leadership's post-Helsinki sensitivities to the East German population's new contacts with Western visitors were reflected not only in the passing of a much stiffer criminal law regulation in July, but also in two July 20 regulations on the transmission of written materials into and from the GDR. These last two measures forbade the introduction into or transporting from East Germany of "publications, manuscripts, and other materials that are designed to damage the interests of the German Democratic Republic" and were applied specifically to travellers and those transporting goods during changes of residences.[130] Nevertheless FRG Permanent Mission Director Gaus and a representative of the GDR Finance Ministry, Hans Nimmrich, signed an October 31 agreement initiating the Federal Government's lump-sum payment for West German motorists' use of East German streets. The document established a price of 50 million DM per year from 1980 through 1989 to be deposited in a West German bank account in the name of the East German Foreign Trade Ministry.[131] This payment was thus substitited for earlier on-the-spot payments by West German motorists and truck drivers. Five West German border districts with 1.2 million inhabitants were in addition now eligible for border-district travel for the first time.

For the remaining fourteen months, however, progress in transportation was confined to further regulation of the Berlin traffic, in particular the April 1980 traffic agreement.[132] One of the major turning points in inner-German transportation, the second raising of the minimum currency requirement for visitors to East Berlin and the GDR, was announced in an October 9, 1980 regulation of the East German Finance Ministry. The compulsory amount was doubled for visitors to the GDR and almost quadrupled for visitors to East Berlin; the East German leadership, in line with steps taken from 1977 to 1979, no longer calculated the payments for the GDR and East Berlin separately. In both cases a fee of 25 DM per day was demanded. Additionally, the Finance Ministry, unlike in earlier regulations, now made obligatory a 7.5 DM per day payment for children between the ages of 6 and 15, and pensioners were required to pay the full sum.[133]

The central importance of the August protests of Polish workers in East Berlin's October 9 decision, which resulted in a shrinkage of Western travel into the GDR and East Berlin, was underscored by the East German leadership. The first reports of "the revanchist activities and demands from the FRG against the People's Republic of Poland,"[134] appeared in the September 4 issue of Neues Deutschland. Only three days before the currency exchange announcement, General Secretary Honecker criticized the Federal Republic and the Western media for "interference in the internal affairs of the GDR, the People's Republic of Poland, and the other socialist countries."[135] Although the East German leadership and media had levelled the charge of interference at the Federal Government on prior occasions, it had rarely appeared in direct pronouncements by Honecker. Nor was it characteristic of the latter to publicly and unambiguously list GDR demands on the West German Government for "further normalization" as was done four days after the currency exchange increase.[136]

The following discussion of the totals achieved in inner-German travel will address the five categories specified in the Basic Treaty: the travel of West Germans into the GDR and of East Germans into the Federal Republic, the border-district traffic, visits for urgent family matters, and family reunification. West German travel into the GDR was severely impaired in 1974, the first full year in which the Basic Treaty's travel-facilitation measures were in effect, primarily as a consequence of the November 1973 East German compulsory currency ruling. It recovered its numerical importance in 1975 and approximated the figure of 3 million through 1979, attaining a peak of 3.177 million in 1978. Travel to the GDR slumped to 2.7 million in 1980, again a result of the higher currency exchange requirement.[137]

The SED leadership thus succeeded in hindering a continuous expansion of West German visitation in the last half of the decade and markedly reduced it after 1979; the same tapering off in inner-German contacts was observable in faltering athletic cooperation in the late 1970's.[138] Nevertheless, SPD-FDP governments did prevail in doubling the annual travel totals over those registered for any year between 1958 and 1969.[139] The

intensification of this travel in 1975 and 1976 no
doubt originated in East Berlin's commitment to permit
travel into the entire area of the GDR and reflected
the impact of the somewhat-reduced currency payment.
One other development should be noted. Although GDR
authorities resorted to delays of the inner-German
traffic in late 1977 and early 1978, these policies
were not applied on a scale sufficient to appreciably
reduce the number of West German visits, particularly
in the peak year of 1978. The "throttling" of cross-
border travel was achieved instead through the indirect
method of increasing West Germans' and West Berliners'
currency obligations.

If one considers the relative vulnerability of the
SED leadership in the face of East German inhabitants'
new contacts with West Germans, it is hardly surprising
that East German travel to West Germany did not
increase as rapidly as visits in the opposite
direction. Whereas West German visits to the GDR were
158% more numerous in 1980 than in 1969, East German
travel to the FRG had increased by only 53% for the
same years. East German visits showed a gradual but
continuous increase, however, in the 1973-1980 period,
rising from 1.3 million in 1973 to approximately 1.6
million in 1980. The Federal Government continued to
press for a lowering of the ages of East Germans
permitted to travel to the FRG in preparation for the
December 1981 Schmidt-Honecker meeting. Such concern
was indicative of Bonn's recognition that non-
pensioners comprised less than one-third of East German
visitors in the 1973-1980 period and constituted barely
one-fourth by 1980.[140]

The fortunes of West German border-district travel
into the GDR followed those of the more general West
German travel into East Germany, peaking in 1978 and
declining noticeably in 1974 and 1980 after the 1973
and 1980 currency measures. Statistically, however,
the setbacks for the Federal Government in this
particular area have been even more serious. From a
high of 480,000 in 1978, border-district travel plunged
to only 392,000 in 1980. Clearly it had begun to
languish even before the October 1980 currency action,
since only approximately 416,000 West Germans made such
visits in 1979. Moreover, the September 1976 East
German grant of the full use of the automobile for this
traffic in no way improved future prospects
substantially, as traffic figures actually show a
decline in 1976 and 1977.[141] It cannot be ruled out
that the series of border incidents in the spring and
summer of 1976, culminating in the East German shooting
of the Italian truck driver Corghi along the inner-
German frontier, had a deterrent effect in this
respect.

The progress in East German visits to West Germany

for urgent family matters has also not developed in accordance with the Federal Government's fullest expectations. Approximately 340,000 such visits were permitted by East Berlin in this eight-year period,[142] the foundation of which was laid in two GDR "Directives on Regulations for Travel by GDR Citizens" in October 1972 and June 1973. The granting of an exit visa could arise in the case of births, marriages, silver and golden wedding anniversaries, critical sicknesses, and deaths as well as several other instances. SED curbs on such travel, which resulted simply from rejection of East German travel applications, began to be publicly deplored by West German spokespersons by early 1980; during this last year the visits declined by a further 9%.[143]

Finally, the West German Government has continued to pursue its efforts toward the reuniting of families separated by the division of Germany, especially parents and their children. As was emphasized earlier, exit visas granted to East Germans by the GDR leadership have been issued primarily to pensioners, but approximately 26,500 other permits were extended for the above reason from 1970 to 1979. Here one can view a considerable success by the Federal Government over earlier years, as the total number of such travel allowances for East Germans from 1964 to 1969 amounted to only 1,922, while 5,499 received such permission in 1975 alone.[144]

THE EXCHANGE OF MEDIA JOURNALISTS

The issue of West German journalistic activity in the GDR has occupied a prominent place in the day-to-day relations between the two governments. There is no other single problem that has resulted in as many official protests by Bonn as East Berlin's treatment of media representatives. The increase in East German inhabitants' reception of radio and television broadcasts from the Federal Republic has in many respects introduced a new factor into the relationship between the GDR population and its governing elite. Although the establishment of statistical precision is somewhat problematical here, it has been estimated that almost 90% of East German territory is accessible to Western radio and television transmissions.[145] In addition, since 1973 West German television correspondents have conducted on-the-spot interviews with East Germans, many of whom have offered critical comments on economic and political conditions in the GDR.[146] (These reports, of course, have also been restricted by East German authorities in a number of ways). Obviously, these changes could not help but dictate a re-thinking of the program of ideological

Abgrenzung on the part of the SED leadership.

The tendency of both German governments to avoid application of the Basic Treaty too comprehensively or literally finds expression once more in this aspect of the inner-German relationship. While Article 7 is the underlying foundation for the East and West German exchange of journalists, the Helsinki Final Act has come into play with greater regularity at times of friction arising from media activity. The basis for this assertion rests on the following observations: chronologically, the East German Government issued its most severe and frequent restrictions on FRG journalists in the years immediately after the Final Act was signed in August 1975, not in the 1973-1975 post-Basic Treaty period; Bonn's protests against the GDR's hampering of West German correspondents were more often based on the Final Act's "Basket Three" regarding the free flow of information,[147] and East Germans, particularly literary and artistic figures, began to rely upon this provision of the Helsinki Agreement in support of their own activities.

Although the Final Act intervened in this sphere at a number of points, the Bahr-Kohl exchange of letters in the Basic Treaty established the general conditions and principles for the regulation of journalistic activities. These, it will be recalled, provided for journalists' freedom of movement and access to information but only insofar as such privileges were granted to correspondents from other states: no reciprocity was required. Conversations between the two governments in February 1973 were followed later in the month by an East German "Decree on the Activities of Publication Organs of Other States in the GDR." This law formally confirmed a January 1972 decision by the SED leadership to empower the Foreign Ministry with the accreditation of foreign correspondents and approval for the opening of press offices. Central to this decree, especially in view of later East German actions, was the inclusion of a number of obligations to be observed by foreign news personnel, who were required

-- to observe the generally recognized norms of international law, -- to observe the laws and other legal provisions of the German Democratic Republic, -- to abstain from slander or defamation of the German Democratic Republic, its state organs and its leading personalities as well as states allied to the German Democratic Republic, -- to report truthfully, pertinently, and correctly as well as to permit no falsification of facts, -- to refrain from use of the granted working possibilities for actions which have nothing to do with the journalistic assignment.[148]

The East German announcement continued by stating that violation of the above principles would represent grounds for withdrawal of a correspondent's accreditation and thus of his working permission, or of operating permission for his office.[149] The GDR leadership therefore gave a broad definition to the "applicable modalities in the German Democratic Republic" to which, according to the November 1972 Kohl letter, West German journalists were to be subject. The Federal Government for its part enacted no comparable statute detailing specific regulations for East German journalists; the Bahr-Kohl arrangement was to serve as its point of origin along with the practice of registering GDR journalists with the Federal Press and Information Office. Government spokesman Ruediger von Wechmar left no doubt but that Bonn would consider the Bahr-Kohl letters as the future basis for its treatment of East German journalists.[150]

In spite of the potentially restrictive effect of the Decree on West German reporting opportunities, over half of the journalists permitted to work in the GDR through 1979 had received their accreditation by the end of the next month. Reporting rights were at that time granted to reporters from the major West German publications, including the newspapers Frankfurter Allgemeine Zeitung, Sueddeutsche Zeitung, and Frankfurter Rundschau, and to the periodicals Spiegel, Stern, and Konkret, all of them major West German publications. By 1979 the number of journalists from the Federal Republic had grown to 19, representing 17 publications.[151] Other news organs which have received permission to place permanent correspondents in East Berlin did not avail themselves of this possibility. Although the East German authorities ordered several expulsions of permanent correspondents, a topic for later discussion, the only case of a closing of a publication's East Berlin office took place with the January 1978 Spiegel closing. It has not been reopened up to the time of this writing. With respect to East German journalists in the Federal Republic, six have been dispatched to Bonn since 1973. Among these are to be counted the correspondents for the news agency ADN, the GDR State Committees for Radio and Television, and the dailies Neues Deutschland and Tribuene.[152]

With this background to the respective implementations in mind, it is possible to identify three distinct gradations of East German reactions to the reporting of West German correspondents. The first period spanned the time from the February 1973 GDR Decree through late 1975. During this first phase the Decree's provisions discouraging reporting judged inimical to the GDR remained formally in effect but were not applied so as to result in correspondents' expulsions or the closing of press offices. This state of affairs persisted through most of 1975, even though frictions over the use of the Berlin access routes, the unmasking of Guenter Guillaume, and the July 1974 East-West dispute over the opening of the FRG Environmental Federal Office in West Berlin all possessed a potential for intrusion into areas of inner-German cooperation. The second period, beginning in late 1975 and receiving its distinguishing marks in 1976, witnessed the inauguration of an East German campaign of reporter expulsions for news stories deemed "offensive" to the GDR and its leadership. This revised policy constituted the lending of practical effect to the 1973 Decree in the presence of the challenges posed by "Basket Three" of Helsinki and foreign reporting on GDR internal practices and on visible discontent within the East German population. The first expulsion of a West German correspondent in December 1975 is a case in point. Successive articles by Der Spiegel on the forced adoption of the children of East German parents captured during "flight from the republic" culminated in punitive action by the GDR elite. Spiegel correspondent Joerg Mettke was ordered to leave the GDR on December 16 "because of crude slander of the GDR" and, specifically, violation of the 1973 Decree.[153] A declaration by the GDR Foreign Ministry the next day asserted that the charge of forced adoption equalled "a slander which is pursued with provocative intentions. Its purpose is obviously to thwart the constructive peace policy of the GDR."[154]

The next year signalled that Mettke's expulsion augured the onset of a more rigid application of the 1973 measures. On March 16, three West German journalists were prohibited from attending the Leipzig Fair and the GDR leadership provided no explanation of the refusal. The Federal Government's protest of the Mettke incident as well as Economics Minister Hans Friedrich's criticism of the Leipzig action while at the Fair probably influenced East Berlin's decision to enter into force new practical alleviations for Western journalists, including eased cross-border travel practices for members of a journalist's family. The grant of journalists' direct access to the press agencies of GDR ministries, a concession formally extended by East Berlin in 1973, obviated the requirement that press personnel report to the Foreign Ministry.[155]

Only a year after the Mettke affair, a report by television correspondent Lothar Loewe resulted in the second expulsion of a West German correspondent. ADN justified Loewe's withdrawal of accreditation on the grounds of "the crudest defamation of the government and people of the GDR... crude interference in the internal affairs of the GDR," and "deliberate and malicious violation of the legal provisions of the

GDR."[156] Again the Federal Government protested this decision as a violation of the Helsinki Final Act.

East German actions against West German media representatives peaked in 1978; the preceding year saw the surfacing in the Western press of numerous reports depicting disturbances among GDR youth,[157] several of which reportedly produced anti-Soviet as well as anti-SED outbursts. A gradual escalation of punitive actions by the East German leadership resulted in January, beginning with an extended declaration by ADN. The statement asserted that reporters from the Federal Republic were covert employees of the West German intelligence service.[158] Once more Der Spiegel became the target of the SED leadership, as its reporter Karl-Heinz Vater was refused accreditation on January 3 and the periodical's office itself was closed one week later. The publication's two articles on disunity within the highest SED circles, which included a "dissident manifesto" of alleged middle- and higher-level party officials, once more drew the East German Government's rebuke of "continued and malicious slander of the GDR and its citizens."[159]

East Berlin also took steps to discourage unfavorable press reports short of the more controversial measure of formal expulsion. In both January and May of 1978, FRG correspondents received warnings from the GDR Foreign Ministry because of reports already publicized in West Germany, the second of which described riots at East German intershops. August 15, 1978 actually saw the first veto of a West German news piece by GDR authorities, as correspondent Lutz Lehmann was forbidden to publicly air a program on East German writers.[160]

The third stage in East German treatment of West German journalists dates from the April 11, 1979 announcement of an executive decision based on the February 1973 Decree. In considerable part, this decision represented a codification of East German practices already in effect. The key addition to the new regulation, however, struck at the journalistic practice of conducting on-the-spot interviews with GDR inhabitants. "Journalistic projects" in the state organs, cooperatives, factories, and other institutions "as well as interviews and inquiries of all types are subject to obligatory permission."[161] Past experiences with Western reporters plainly resulted in a targeting of correspondents such as Loewe who had maintained close contacts with East German writers openly chastised by the authorities for protesting the withdrawal of folk singer Wolf Biermann's citizenship. Accredited journalists were thus required to apply to the Foreign Ministry's Department of Journalistic Relations, and a legal justification for actions such as the Lehmann censorship was enshrined. The East

German authorities would consider travel correspondents' requests for reporting activity outside East Berlin only after application to the Department had been made: also obligatory was the reporter's announcement of the visit at least twenty-four hours in advance and the submission to the Foreign Ministry of precise information regarding the destination and purpose of the travel.[162]

The first fatality of the executive decision proved to be the Second German Television (ZDF) correspondent Peter van Loyen, who was expelled from the GDR on May 14, 1979 after providing for West German television a declaration by author Stefan Heym. The East German announcement of the action cited both the February 1973 and April 1979 decisions in explanation of the withdrawal of van Loyen's accreditation.[163] Bonn responded, as on past occasions, with a protest of the expulsion.[164]

East Berlin soon drafted a third instrument that was applied to the activities of foreign journalists in the GDR, a July 2, 1979 "Law for the Amending and Supplementing of Penal and Criminal Decisions,"[165] which entered into effect on August 1. The intent to curb physical communication between East German inhabitants and Western correspondents was reflected in the amending law, although media representatives were not directly referred to:

> Whoever collects, betrays, delivers or in any other manner makes accessible to a foreign power, its institutions or representatives or to an intelligence service or foreign organizations as well as their accomplices, news or items which are top-secret or to the disadvantage of the interests of the GDR will be punished with imprisonment of not less than five years... (2) Preparation and intent are punishable.[166]

Boelling declared the amending law to be "directed above all against critical intellectuals in the GDR and their contacts to Western journalists and media" and further interpreted the new regulation as a violation of the Final Act and the November 1972 letter exchange on journalists.[167] The GDR leadership nevertheless proceeded with the trial of a West German free-lance journalist on espionage charges later in the month despite the Boelling statement's warning against the prosecution of media representatives.

A distinction can therefore be drawn between the period between 1976 and early 1979, the point at which the executive decision to the 1973 Decree was introduced, and the period after April 1979. During the latter phase GDR treatment of journalists was geared specifically to obstructing all interviews with

East Germans, as the cumulative impact of earlier question-and-answer sessions led to preventive executive actions in 1979. While in the earlier period restrictive East German actions were enacted on the general grounds of "slander against the GDR," the later phase was characterized by the threat of prosecution of correspondents for alleged espionage activities as well as criminal rulings against East Germans in contact with foreign newspersons. In the face of growing labor unrest in neighboring Poland in August 1980, Western reporting in the GDR confronted renewed SED resistance. Warnings were issued to ZDF correspondents because of their earlier reports on the reaction of the East German population to the Polish events on August 29. On November 11, one month after East Berlin's increase in travel currency requirements, the GDR Foreign Ministry denied to several Western reporters coverage of the Synod meetings of the East German Evangelical Laender churches.[168]

THE FRONTIER COMMISSION

Aside from the activities of the Permanent Missions, the work of the delegations of the inner-German Frontier Commission has been the most continuous and produced the largest number of meetings of any such regular contact. From January 1973 to the end of 1979, for example, the delegations participated in fifty meetings aiming at the monitoring, renewal, and completion of the marking of the inner-German frontier as well as addressing "problems connected with the course of the frontier."[169] The Commission was formally authorized only to mark the frontier in correspondence with the agreements of the former occupation powers and could not undertake any further changes.[170] In addition to the Federal negotiators, representatives from the four West German Laender adjacent to the border took part in these talks.

Aside from the marking of the frontier, the Commission has been principally concerned with the negotiation of inner-German agreements on environmental protection. Although talks were initiated in November 1973 in pursuit of an environmental framework agreement, these discussions collapsed in 1974 largely because of the dispute over the FRG Environmental Federal Office in West Berlin. It was not until the May 1980 traffic agreement that the two sides committed themselves to negotiations on the chief environmental issue, the de-salination and purification of common rivers, especially the Werra, and other ecological problems.[171]

More limited environmental agreements were achieved in 1973, 1975, 1977, and 1978; however, the regulation of common waterways has been given the greatest attention in these understandings. On September 20, 1973, both governments agreed to exchange information toward the prevention of natural calamities such as floods, fires, and epidemics as well as air pollution. A second agreement signed the same day provided for the mutual maintenance and completion of border waterworks, the maintenance and use of dikes along the frontier and protective measures against soil erosion. Additionally, both governments signed approximately 500 technical provisions on the protection of waterways. A further declaration by both Commission delegations in December 1975 committed the water-level stations of both states to exchange information on the water level and its probable effects at designated points along a number of common waterways. An October 1977 declaration, on the other hand, resulted in East German allowance for a West German drawing of water from four border-proximate lakes, the Mechower, Lankower, Goldensee, and Dutzower, for the watering of cattle.[172]

Finally, in 1978 the Federal Government gained GDR assent to West German use of the Ecker Valley locks' drinking water, located adjacent to Lower Saxony, for which East Berlin received an annual lump-sum payment. It was also agreed that Bonn would maintain the Ecker water line lying in GDR territory and that there would be joint efforts toward preventing further damage to the waterways. Yet two of the most serious environmental problems in inner-German relations, the concentration of potash in the Weser and Werra rivers, remained unsolved in this period. (Practically all border-traversing rivers, including these two, flow from the GDR into the Federal Republic).[173]

Other accomplishments of the Commission relate to the marking of the coastal frontier between the FRG and GDR, an agreement providing for West German fishing in the Luebeck Brook, officially a part of East Germany, the regulation of the mining of border-traversing brown coal reserves in the vicinity of Helmstedt, and several provisions on the supply of drinking water to parts of the Federal Republic. The joint mining of the coal reserves, together with mutual use of natural gas reserves in the Wustrow-Salzwedel area, followed July 3, 1974 suggestions by the Commission that the matter be negotiated. For the water provisions, Bonn agreed to a lump sum payments of 4.2 million DM annually in exchange for the drawing of water from the GDR into the city of Duderstadt; similarly, a 650 million DM/year agreement was reached for water drawn from East Germany for use by the FRG border community of Herringen.[174] Both understandings were to be valid for the years from 1976 to 1980. Further technical agreements were concluded pertaining to the construction and

maintenance of a high-water basin in the East German
district of Coburg and the 1977 exchange of land-
register and surveying documents.[175]
The most important single result of the
Commission's activities consisted of a November 29,
1978 protocol which summarized its work up to that
point, entered into force ten of the agreements
described above that had only been provisionally
observed, and clarified the Commission's future work.
Central to this document was the detailed laying out of
the inner-German frontier and the technical
arrangements devised by each delegation between 1973
and 1976 toward the avoidance of territorial
infringements. This latter category included surveying
documents, maps and charts of the border area, and
agreed-upon indentification objects along the frontier
such as border markers and river buoys.[176]
Both delegations acknowledged that one troublesome
frontier-related problem remained: the marking of 94
kilometers of the Elbe River boundary as well as a 1.2
kilometer section near the West German city of
Braunlage. The Federal Government has supported the
position that the Elbe boundary should be drawn on the
eastern side of the river while East German
declarations called for its placement in the middle.
West German arguments were based on the May 25, 1950
transfer by the British occupation authorities of the
control functions on this section of the Elbe to the
Federal Government. The East German position relied on
the alternate drawing as an application of
international practices, given the GDR leadership's
decision to depict the frontier as a state boundary in
border negotiations in and after 1976.[177] In the
absence of a compromise arrangement, it was agreed that
both governments would proceed from the May 1972
Traffic Treaty and its "provisions for the guaranteeing
of a smooth internal shipping traffic as well as the
conceptions on the legal situation."[178] Although this
issue represented an important unresolved matter, the
delegations committed themselves to future discussion
of problems connected with the implementation of the
border-related agreements referred to earlier in
addition to the practical difficulties arising from the
November 1978 frontier accord.[179]

SPORTS

Inner-German sporting events showed a gradual
increase from the early 1970's through the year 1980,
but it should be noted that this slight expansion
proceeded from an abysmally low starting point in the
year 1973, with only 12 joint events taking place. In
1969, 88 such events were held in the GDR and Federal

Republic.[180] One of the paradoxes of the ·two states'
relations is thus an expansion of the areas of FRG-GDR
cooperation in the 1970's "detente" era but a decline
in athletic contacts following the 1950's, after which
such inner-German events did not even remotely approach
the level of the "Cold War" decade. The cumulative
total of 450 events held in the 1973-1980 period, for
example, compares with the total of 1,530 for only one
year in the 1950's, 1957.[181] Whereas the decline in
sporting activities in the 1960's can be explained in
large part by the nine-year hiatus in consultations
between the respective German sporting organizations
beginning in 1961, reasons for the modest pace of these
contacts in the 1970's must be sought elsewhere.

The impasse in inner-German athletic planning
ended in 1970 with the meeting of the West German DSB
and its East German counterpart, renamed the Federation
of German Gymnastics and Athletics (DTSB) in the East
German city of Halle. It was only with the conclusion
of the Basic Treaty, however, that a process of
momentum was inaugurated sufficient to give birth to an
athletic framework agreement between the two German
states. Prior to this understanding, the DTSB opposed
inclusion of the Berlin (West) Sports Federation in any
tentative agreement as a participating member of the
DSB, even though this municipal federation had been a
founding DSB member.

Discussions between the two organizations were not
actually finalized in an agreement until May 8, 1974,
when the DSB announced the concluding of the "Protocol
on the Regulation of Athletic Relations." The main
point of dispute was resolved to the Federal
Government's satisfaction through mutual agreement that
West Berlin's participation would be "regulated in
agreement with the regulations of the Quadripartite
Agreement of September 3, 1971.[182] The latter, of
course, provided for the joint participation of West
Berlin and West German residents in international
exchanges and exhibitions.[183] Nevertheless, East
Berlin's assent to the above had to first await
fulfillment of the preconditions of DSB
representatives' travel to East Berlin for two
negotiating sessions, where the Protocol was later
signed, as well as the West German federation's
agreement not to conduct DSB meetings in West Berlin.
DSB-DTSB agreement to meet annually toward the
formulation of a plan for sporting events in each
upcoming year coincided with the Federal Government's
aim of creating regular inner-German contacts. 33
athletic events were approved the same day.[184]

Two other features of the agreement are of note.
Each German government was to carry the costs of its
athletes' transportation during their stay in the
neighboring state, while the host state was required to

finance hotel and meal accommodations for visiting
athletes, an application of the principle of
reciprocity that has usually not been possible in other
areas of mutual activity. On the other hand, the two
organizations' commitment to regulate relations "in
accordance with the regulations and practices of the
International Olympic Committee and international
sporting organizations"[185] does not appear surprising
in view of Brandt's notion of inner-German "treaties
with international validity."

One immediate consequence of the initiation of an
institutionalized FRG-GDR athletic link was the
"information visit" of a DSB delegation to East Germany
in October 1975, headed by DSB President Willi Weyer;
DTSB President Ewald then travelled to the Federal
Republic in March 1977. Neither visit resulted in
tangible evidence of possiblities for future expansion
of athletic activities, although the SPD-FDP coalition
did thereby provide support for the principle of
"dialogue enhancement."

In accounting for the modest level of inner-German
sporting activities, which rose from 12 in 1973 to a
peak of 75 in 1979,[186] it is at first apparent that
international athletic events in which separate German
teams compete have to some degree displaced the earlier
bilateral East-West German competitions. In 1978, for
example, 516 West German and 351 East German athletes
took part in such events, compared to 124 of the former
and only 2 of the latter in 1973.[187] Such
participation, of course, is related to the GDR's
intended projection of an international presence and is
consciously reinforced through East Berlin's additional
practice of inviting a number of foreign athletic teams
to events in East Germany in which West German teams
also participate. Consequently, of the 305 sporting
events jointly planned by the DSB and DTSB between 1974
and 1978, only 127, or 41.6 percent, were exclusively
inner-German affairs. In 1980, these events equalled
less than one-third of planned competitions.[188] Seen in
retrospect, it cannot be denied that with the
conspicuous rise of East Germany to a pinnacle of
international athletic performance, the GDR leadership
undoubtedly found less incentive to favor bilateral
undertakings with West German teams.

The international dimension to the sports-politics
connection was reflected in Ewald's cancellation of 21
of the 76 tentatively scheduled sporting events for
1980, which the DTSB President justified on the grounds
of the Federal Republic's boycott of the 1980 Moscow
Olympics.[189] On the other hand, the Berlin question,
upon which both sides had apparently reached a modus
vivendi in 1974, continued to intrude into the athletic
area. Frictions arose particularly after the GDR's
post-1976 steps to renounce the validity of Four Power

authority in East Berlin. The DSB was clearly unable to gain acceptance for its efforts to include West Berlin athletes in scheduled events, as only four competitions between 1978 and 1980 allowed for their participation.[190]

The failure of inner-German sports to develop beyond a narrow range of activities became a reality that DSB officialdom could scarcely conceal. The year 1978 provides an illustration of the athletic expectations of both sides: the West German organization's January suggestions to the DTSB envisioned a sports calendar of 223 purely bilateral events but was answered with Ewald's counter-proposal of 73 events, only 25 of which were solely FRG-GDR affairs. (In fact, the actual numbers for that year coincided almost exactly with this latter plan).[191] DSB President Weyer failed to sign but instead "confirmed" the Ewald calendar in a return letter, unlike earlier years, and the DSB proclaimed that joint athletic efforts "still give no evidence of normal relations between our neighboring athletic organizations."[192] In addition to the later practical absence of West Berliners in bilateral events, the East German Government throughout the 1973-1980 period continually refused to permit use of the border-district traffic for athletic events, the participation of youth clubs or organizations in sporting activities, or the holding of events for athletes performing at a lower level of athletic skill. In addition, sports such as hockey, riding, and tennis were excluded as possibilities.[193]

One can identify historical reasons why inner-German sports flourished in the 1950's but languished in the 1960's and 1970's. The existence of a stable agreement which provided for the inclusion of Berlin athletes after 1952 greatly simplified athletic endeavors which after the building of the Berlin Wall were complicated by the question of the former German capital's status. Certain other "symbolic" differences that spilled over into the athletic area were not hindrances in the 1950's: the absence of an East German flag until 1959 simplified a common national athletic participation. More fundamentally, however, SED athletic policy in the 1950's bore a close resemblance to an overall All-German program that had been reversed by the 1970's-- the pursuance of "Confederation" proposals and active courting of the West German SPD and labor movement.[194] Alongside such documents as the 1957 Confederation proposal and "National Front" manifestoes, the promotion of inner-German athletic events could be presented as East Berlin's (and Moscow's) visible commitment to overcoming Germany's division, an impression that East German leaders later abandoned after a doctrine of national de-limitation was demanded.

SPECIAL ARRANGEMENTS FOR THE RELEASE OF EAST GERMAN PRISONERS

An evaluation of West German attempts to "purchase" the release of Germans from GDR prisons remains problematical even in the post-Basic Treaty period. As the inner-German Ministry's documentation Zehn Jahre Deutschlandpolitik declares:

> The Federal Government, also acknowledging the experiences of earlier Federal Governments, represents the standpoint that the public treatment of individual humanitarian cases is not useful for those directly as well as indirectly concerned.[195]

Since the Federal Government makes no official statistics available to the public and inner-German agreements in this area are highly confidential, a reliance on ever-increasing newspaper accounts and articles is necessary in order to gauge Bonn's success in the so-called "human trade." This approach will allow some rough estimates of the numbers of prisoners involved in the transactions, although there are no block figures for the 1973-1980 period.

Both the newspaper Die Welt and Michel Meyer's Des hommes contre des marks place the number of arrested Germans permitted to emigrate or return to the FRG between 1969 and 1975 at 5,000, although the latter's estimate of the payment, $166 million, exceeds the former's figure of $80 million.[196] The Inner-German Ministry, on the other hand, reported that $42 million alone had been expended for releases in 1975 and that this sum resembled those agreed upon between the FRG and GDR for previous years.[197] With regard to the price paid by Bonn for each prisoner, the absence of exact figures once more makes conclusions tentative. It will be recalled that Meyer determined an average transaction of 50,000 DM for each release in the mid-1960's, and public sources assert payments of approximately 40,000 DM for 1974, a year in which 2,000 were released for settlement in the FRG.[198]

Thereafter, intermittent reports disclose some information on the scale of this activity. A December 1976 arrangement reportedly ensured the release of a number of prisoners and this time carried a minimum transaction cost of $20,000 per person.[199] The agreement was intended to aid East Berlin in the acquisition of food and consumer items. Reports of mass applications for emigration at this time[200] were indicative of the SED's post-1975 dilemma. The presumed quid pro quo for Bonn was to consist of a more restrained East German Government policy towards political dissidents. To the extent that this desired end was achieved, the Federal Government effected a deferral rather than a cessation of government actions against the East German creative intelligentsia.[201] Overall, the Inner-German Ministry has announced the release of over 13,000 prisoners from 1970 to 1979,[202] although it provided no year-by-year breakdown of the totals nor of payments.

Two GDR amnesties of political prisoners in October 1972 and December 1979 should be singled out in this discussion both because of the unusual publicity given to the events by the SED leadership and because they serve to contrast the changes in this important area of inner-German activity in these seven years. In the first case, 2,000 prisoners were granted an early release from prison and allowed to take up residence in West Germany. In the second instance, an amnesty of approximately 22,000 prisoners by the GDR Council of State followed an earlier report that East Berlin decided to terminate future "Menschenhandel" at the behest of fellow Warsaw Pact members. In contrast to the 1972 amnesty, only four of the released East Germans were permitted to reside in the Federal Republic, although 149 foreign prisoners, the majority of which were actually West Germans or West Berliners, returned to their home residences.[203]

Despite Egon Franke's characterization of media accounts of the GDR suspension of the secret exchanges as "sensationalistic journalism,"[204] few notable successes emerged into view in 1980, as evidenced by the low total of East Germans actually emigrating during the amnesty. (This nadir also corresponded with disappointing developments in Bonn's efforts to promote cross-border family meetings in urgent cases). In this connection, it must be strongly suspected that Chancellor Schmidt's June 1980 visit to Moscow was impelled not only by considerations of Soviet-American conflict, which assumed significant proportions at the time, but also by a desire to stimulate cooperation in a number of immobile inner-German areas.[205]

In addition to the quantitative and qualitative results of the "human trade" transactions, it should be stressed that both German governments consistently utilized the Evangelical Church of Germany (EKD) as the operational conduit for these exchanges. While the details relating to the transportation of prisoners, the choice of those to be transported, and the sum of money paid for each prisoner continued to be settled by Vogel and Juergen Stange, the West German churches have served as the "go-between" in receiving East German lists of goods to be delivered to the GDR in fulfillment of the bargain. The West German Government pays for such goods, rather than transferring money directly to East Berlin, by routing the necessary amounts through the EKD's Bonn Office and authorizing the Church's representative to pay for requested

products. The EKD has also funded numerous deliveries
of items sent to the East German Evangelical Church for
the purpose of humanitarian assistance.[206]

MAIL AND TELECOMMUNICATIONS

The September 1971 Postal Protocol, according to which
the Federal Government paid an annual lump-sum of 30
million DM for East German postal assistance, formed
the basis for inner-German postal transactions until
1976. It was not until March of that year that a
framework agreement similar in scale to those already
concluded in the areas of health and sports was
finalized by FRG and GDR negotiators. More than three
years and twenty-four rounds of discussions preceded
this eventual outcome, with the initial talks beginning
two weeks prior to the signing of the Basic Treaty.
Although the Protocol remained in force in this period,
its stipulation that the telephone connections between
the two German states be fully automated by the end of
1974 could not be fulfilled by GDR authorities because
of technical and economic difficulties in
installation.[207] The 1976 accord became valid on July
1, 1976; it included a government-to-government
agreement on the general principles of future postal
and telecommunications cooperation as well as three
administrative agreements relating to postal
deliveries, telecommunication link-ups, and the
calculation of payment for services performed in the
first two areas.[208]
    If one approaches this agreement with an eye to
the inner-German symbolism contained, the tendency to
"split the difference" is observable along the same
lines of the often ambiguous Basic Treaty. The former
confirmed what had existed as a declaration of
intention in the latter, namely, that the document "has
been concluded on the basis of the statute of the
Universal Postal Union (UPU) and the International
Telecommunications Treaty."[209] Three other
international postal agreements were also cited as
having established norms to be followed in the inner-
German exchanges. This adoption of international
practices for a joint East-West German undertaking,
however, was to be qualified somewhat by the
simultaneous validity of several special procedures
such as the non-enactment of foreign postal fees or
customs declarations of the contents of mailings by the
two governments.[210] The actual postal transactions were
in practice to be conducted largely devoid of the
customary formalities and complicated regulations of
the UPU and International Telecommunications Union, and
both states formally acknowledged the binding effect of
the two organizations' statutes.[211]

The agreement on postal deliveries expanded somewhat the possibilities for future mail flows and introduced several new practices. In addition to the usual mail deliveries by way of the West German border city of Helmstedt, new rail routes were made available at the border-crossing points of Bebra, Hof, and Buechen. The two states also agreed that roads between the Federal Republic and West Berlin could be used for postal deliveries in addition to the Helmstedt traffic. With regard to the technical mailing procedures, FRG and GDR postal authorities were now required to report to their counterparts information on mailings lost or mishandled as well as to specify the mailing laws violated in the case of mail returned to its sender.[212]

The negotiators of the postal agreement, as before, calculated West German payment for East German postal services on the basis of the April 1970 agreement, which fixed the annual lump-sum payment at 30 million DM in the absence of a demonstrable change in the volume of mail handled. This practice was to apply to the year 1976, and the two governments also established the principle of future unscheduled meetings between the FRG and GDR postal ministries toward harmonizing the interpretations and applications of the agreement.[213]

An October 19, 1977 exchange of letters between the Ministerial Director of the West German Postal Ministry and the High Director of the GDR Postal Ministry determined the annual lump-sum payment from 1977 until 1982. This sum was raised to 85 million DM per year. In order to further improve telephone communication, the letter committed the East and West German Governments to connect a total of 216 and 486 new telephones through 1982, respectively.[214]

An appraisal of the quantitative impact of post-1972 inner-German postal agreements is subject to the limitation that the Inner-German Ministry supplies no annual numerical breakdown of mail deliveries during the 1973-1980 period with the exception of the year 1978. Rather, available statistics disclose that from 1969 to 1981, approximately 2.77 million letters and 573 million packages and parcels crossed the inner-German frontier in both directions.[215] Beyond these totals, the publication Zehn Jahre Deutschlandpolitik offers the general comments that the volume of letters delivered to the GDR "has periodically decreased" while those sent to the Federal Republic "are still very great." Package and parcel exchanges, on the other hand, showed "a slightly diminishing tendency."[216] The one category of postal transactions for which year-by-year figures do exist, that of confiscated and returned packages, indicates a visible improvement in the degree of FRG-GDR cooperation in the 1970's. Announcements of packages confiscated by East German authorities dropped

by three-quarters from 1970 to 1973 and stabilized at
about 20,000 per year. Mail returned to its West
German sender declined even more strikingly, as the
average of 400,000 refusals each year in the early
1970's was reduced to only 44,000 in 1978.[217]
Although the uneveness of the data made public by
the Federal Government tends to disqualify postal
cooperation as an expanding inner-German activity, it
should not be overlooked that increased travel
opportunities, which allow for the carrying of a
certain number of gifts, and telephone communication
have undoubtedly reduced the need for cross-border
mailings. Regarding development of the latter, SPD-FDP
governments have pointed to the increase in FRG-GDR
telephone lines from 34 to 1,061 between 1970 and 1979.
Automation of telephone conversations also gradually
became a reality, although the foreseen goal of
complete direct dialing possibilities between the two
German states remained unfulfilled in this period. The
Inner-German Ministry estimated that 80% of all calls
from West Germany to the GDR could be placed directly,
permitting approximately 45,000 such calls each day.[218]
No statistics have been forthcoming for calls from the
GDR, where a smaller proportion of dialing is
automated. On the other hand, East-West German
telegram transmissions were fully automated by the end
of 1971, making possible immediate reception, whereas
the number of lines put in operation for this purpose
rose from 24 to 88. In addition, these years saw an
increase in telex lines of almost threefold.[219]

HEALTH

In the area of health, the Federal Government
initiated two successful undertakings with the GDR.
The first was a health agreement signed by
representatives of the two German states on April 25,
1974 which became effective on January 1, 1976. A
later accord signed December 21, 1979 contained
provisions for veterinary cooperation committing both
sides to efforts to prevent the spread of contagious
animal diseases.[220]
The most significant single result of the Health
Agreement was the extension of legal entitlement to
free ambulatory or stationary medical assistance by
authorities in the host German state for visitors from
the neighboring German state. Such assistance would be
forthcoming "in cases of all acute sicknesses and
accidents as well as acute deterioration of recurrent
sicknesses."[221] Repeat examinations were also provided
for according to the patient's degree of sickness. The
actual medical assistance extended free of cost
encompassed such items as pharmaceuticals, seeing and

hearing aids, and dental work as well as the overall hospital and doctor's care and ambulatory transportation. In cases of the life-endangering sicknesses of cross-border travellers, both treaty partners obligated themselves to make medical announcements "in a manner customary in the other state" and inform the neighboring state's Permanent Mission "within the framework of their possibilities."[222]

Other sections of the agreement were completed with an eye to special types of medical assistance and an exchange of information.[223] This aim was reflected in the allowance for inhabitants from one German state to obtain special treatment or cures in the other state when such assistance could not be sufficiently offered in their own. The carrying of pharmaceuticals was now permissible in the cross-border traffic in cases of personal need or, in certain cases, the sending of drugs to needy patients. With respect to the exchange of medical information, both sides agreed to especially focus on contagious diseases, pharmaceuticals, and the misuse of drugs and narcotics. A letter exchange between FRG and GDR health officials the day of the agreement's signing foresaw later negotiation over the exchange of organ transplants and medical-scientific information. Here, it should be pointed out, some cooperation had already been evident in the past in the form of technical meetings between medical-scientific societies in both states.[224]

Both governments also agreed to name representatives "whose task it is to find more appropriate regulations on the measures necessary for the implementation of this agreement as well as to settle difficulties and differences of opinion on the use and interpretation of this agreement through consultations."[225] This practical step toward further inner-German dialogue led to eight conversations between the East and West German representatives. Finally, Berlin was to be included in the agreement in accordance with the provisions of the Quadripartite Agreement, as was the case in the FRG-GDR sports agreement.

The 1979 agreement on veterinary cooperation attempted to create a foundation for technical information exchanges and official contacts for the prevention and control of contagious animal diseases. This problem was finally addressed for reasons of the extensive transportation of animals and animal products between the Federal Republic and GDR. In addition to providing information to the partner state on specific instances of animal diseases (the border information points created by the Frontier Commission could be utilized for this purpose), the agreement also set the goal of expanding the veterinary information flow in all areas and maintaining the links between East and West German health agencies for disease prevention. West Berlin received the same inclusion in this agreement as in the earlier Health Agreement.[226]

NON-COMMERCIAL PAYMENTS AND BANK ACCOUNT TRANSFERS

No appreciable monetary transfers from bank accounts in the GDR to West Germany had been permitted after the currency reforms of June 1948. East German policy provided only for limited withdrawals from such accounts to be expended solely in East Germany during visits by FRG inhabitants, with 15 DM per day as the upper spending limit. The Basic Treaty proclaimed both states' intention to undertake negotiations in this field, however, and a modus vivendi was reached through the conclusion of two partial agreements on April 25, 1974. The first regulated the transfer of alimony payments between the FRG and GDR,[227] while the second allowed several categories of holders of blocked accounts to transfer funds across the inner-German border.[228]

The alimony agreement mainly affected children, spouses, and parents legally entitled to payments. It resulted in 93,000 payments of 107.2 million DM to claimants in the GDR by West Germans and 265,000 payments of 29.7 million DM in the opposite direction through mid-1979. The agreement also guaranteed the transfer of payments for compensatory damages according to legal liability provisions.[229]

The second agreement on the transfer of money from blocked accounts affected a greater number of Germans (pensioners, recipients of social assistance, young orphans). Under this document's regulations, Germans in either state were permitted to draw 200 DM or GDR marks from their accounts in the neighboring state monthly, with the currency exchange ratio set at 1:1. A limiting factor to these transactions was introduced, however, insofar as it was also required that "the remittances from one state cannot be higher than remittances from the other state altogether."[230] Since East German inhabitants have not utilized this transfer process as frequently as FRG residents, this condition created waiting periods for completion of the latter's transfers and even a temporary stop on West German transfers. Yet the agreement's provisions did allow for the transfer of 42 million DM in both directions by the end of 1978.[231]

A December 16, 1978 protocol to the agreement was signed which stipulated that the East German Government would pay 50 million DM annually into a clearing account with the FRG Bundesbank within the framework of the April 1974 agreement.[232] These payments, which were to continue through the year 1982, had the purpose of facilitating West German utilization of the account transfer privileges which before had been subject to the balancing obstacle.

CULTURE, SCIENCE AND TECHNOLOGY, AND LEGAL ASSISTANCE

Both German governments began negotiations in 1973 toward the attainment of framework agreements in the practical areas of culture and science and technology. Agreements were also to be the goal of talks begun in August 1973 that aimed at simplifying inner-German legal assistance. An impasse soon developed in the cultural negotiations as a controversy over the Prussian Cultural Foundation, a collection of art and historical museum objects that were moved from East to West Berlin after 1945, produced an East German charge that the Federal Government would not return these objects to East Berlin.[233] The talks were not resumed again in this period. Nor was an agreement on science and technology concluded; here no compromise formula proved workable on the question of West Berlin's inclusion. Moreover, Minister Franke represented the position that simultaneous science negotiations with the Soviet Union could not be "prejudiced" by a prior inner-German document.[234]

In spite of the failure of both German states to achieve an overall regulation of these activities, several cultural exchanges developed after the breaking off of discussions in 1975. The first West German cultural exhibition to be viewed in the GDR, presented with the theme "Photography in Science and Technology," appeared in East Berlin in January and February of 1977. A second such event was the presentation of the East German exhibit "Photography in the German Democratic Republic" in Cologne in September and October of 1979. Again in October of 1980, despite considerable inner-German fallout after East Berlin's October 9 travel measures, East and West German "film weeks" were held, respectively, by the FRG and GDR leaderships.[235]

Although no science agreement was reached in this period, the two authorized delegations had met twenty-four times for this purpose by the end of 1979. The main forum for meetings of East and West German scientists proved to be international scientific conferences and congresses. In the absence of regularized cooperation between FRG and GDR scientific institutions, contacts between scientists resulted only from private initiative and in particular cases. Requests by East German scientists for meetings with their colleagues in the Federal Republic were frequently not granted by the GDR leadership although

they were not excluded in all cases. The possibility
of the mutual attendance of lectures by German students
in the neighboring state was severely restricted. In
addition, the acquisition of technical literature
essentially represented a one-sided affair, as only
East German access to West German scientific journals
and publications was secured on a general basis.[236]
    Little has changed in regard to the practice
employed in inner-German legal assistance since the
SPD-FDP accession to office. A January 1, 1976 GDR
"Regulation of Civil Cases" preserved the former East
German policy of directing West German and West Berlin
courts' petitions for legal assistance from GDR courts
successively through the FRG Land Justice
administrations, the East German Ministry of Justice
and, finally, the intended GDR court. The completed
inquiry was returned through the GDR Ministry to the
FRG Minister of Justice and then directed to the
original petitioning court by way of the Land Justice
administrations.[237] This complicated procedure was once
more executed by GDR authorities to emphasize East
German regulation in the "foreign treaty" area by
involving the central authorities. East Berlin has
continued to require that legal requests from the
Federal Republic's Prosecuting Attorney be sent to the
East German General Prosecutor, and the reverse
transmission of requests was also imposed.
Negotiations conducted between the West German State
Secretary in the Federal Justice Ministry and the GDR
State Secretary of Justice have not led to agreement
due to differences over the citizenship and Berlin
questions.[238]

THE ACCREDITATION AND ROLE OF THE PERMANENT MISSIONS

    The question of the status accorded to the East
and West German Permanent Missions by both governments
is a central one because of its bearing on the nature
of the states' relations and because the Missions
potentially serve as an important mechanism in inner-
German consultation. A November 16, 1973 Bundestag law
granted to the GDR Permanent Mission all the
conveniences, privileges, and exemptions normally
extended to the diplomatic missions of states under the
1961 Vienna Convention on Diplomatic Relations. This
statute was followed by a joint FRG-GDR "Protocol on
the Institution of the Permanent Missions" four months
later.[239]
    This document, which entered into effect on May 2,
was so crafted as to promote the political purposes and
national conceptions of each leadership chiefly in the
passage designating the agencies empowered to serve as
the formal communication channel for the Missions. The

East German standard of "two sovereign states" found
its expression in a Protocol regulation: "The Ministry
of Foreign Affairs is responsible for the affairs of
the Permanent Mission of the Federal Republic of
Germany."[240] On the other hand, Bonn's promotion of the
thesis of "special" inner-German relations determined
the nature of the GDR Mission's link with the Federal
Government: the Chancellor's office was declared
responsible for the affairs of the East German
Permanent Mission.[241] The two Missions were assigned
the task of

> representing the interests of the dispatching state
> in the host country, including aid and assistance
> for persons as well as promoting normal, good-
> neighborly relations between the FRG and GDR in the
> political, economic, and cultural area as well as
> in other areas.[242]

The only other inner-German particularities in the
Protocol were contained in two additional notes. A
former GDR "Office of the Ministry of Foreign Trade" in
Duesseldorf was to be reorganized as an agency of the
East German Permanent Mission's Commercial Department.
Additionally, the two leaderships repeated the earlier
Basic Treaty pledge that Bonn's Permanent Mission could
"represent the interests of Berlin (West) in agreement
with the Quadripartite Agreement of September 3,
1971."[243]

Once these specifications have been recognized,
there is little to be found in the Federal Government's
further regulation of the East German Mission that
distinguishes it markedly from the embassies and
diplomatic missions of third states. With the April
24, 1974 passage of a "Decree on the Granting of
Conveniences, Privileges, and Exemptions to the
Permanent Mission of the GDR," Bonn declared the
Mission to be fully subject to diplomatic extra-
territoriality and entitled to display both the GDR
flag and coat-of-arms. This policy further included
exemption from all taxes "insofar as these are not
imposed as compensation for certain services
performed," GDR use of all suitable means for the free
transmission of mail as well as a Mission radio
installation, and the immunity of all the Mission's
members from civil and administrative prosecution.[244]
The Basic Treaty provisions regarding both states'
autonomy "in internal and external affairs" thus had
definite consequences that departed radically from
postwar practices.

The Directors of both the East and West German
Permanent Missions, Michael Kohl and Guenter Gaus,
presented their letters of credentials on June 20,
1974. In agreement with the March 1974 Protocol, Kohl

was received by the FRG President, while Gaus submitted
his letter to Council of State Chairman Honecker.
Thereafter each government availed itself of the
Missions to different degrees. The main tasks of the
Federal Mission consisted generally of the continued
promotion of special German relations and narrowly of
the maintenance of the Mission as a contact place for
assisting East Germans, as a vehicle for obtaining
agreements with the East German Government,
particularly on West Berlin, and as a consultative
channel in times of GDR travel hindrances. The Mission
has also undertaken the role of observer and benefactor
of East German prisoners and those tried by GDR
courts.[245] The activities of Gaus, however, have given
the most lasting imprint to the Mission; this entailed
the negotiation of seventeen agreements with the GDR
leadership between 1974 and 1981. The most notable of
these agreements, the November 1978 Berlin traffic and
transit payment agreement, reflects the geographical
importance of the Federal Mission in East Berlin as a
safeguard for the protection of West Berlin's
interests. Gaus' regular contact with Assistant
Foreign Minister Kurt Nier developed into a regular
institutional link that was utilized especially during
inner-German disputes and for the purpose of travel
facilitation.[246]

Neither the East nor West German Permanent Mission
has escaped controversy in this eight-year period.
Various incidents involving threats and acts against
the GDR Mission in Bonn have surfaced, the most
publicized of which was the throwing of a gas device
into the Mission building on January 23, 1977. ADN
attributed the event to "the massive anti-GDR campaign
of incitement by certain political forces and mass
media."[247] On the other hand, SED opposition to the
choice of the FRG Mission as a rallying point for East
Germans wishing to avail themselves of its assistance
in January 1977 revealed itself in the form of the East
German requirement that permission for entry into the
Mission could only follow the acquisition of a pass
from the GDR Foreign Ministry.[248] Thus the GDR
leadership once more attempted to portray the Mission
as the representation of a foreign state.

Regarding the Federal Government's own bestowal of
status on the GDR Permanent Mission, several West
German practices have been in evidence that are
somewhat at variance with Bonn's depiction of the
Mission in the joint inner-German protocol. Although
the latter formally empowered the Chancellor's Office
with responsibility for the Mission's affairs, Kohl's
successor, Ewald Moldt, has met on a number of
occasions with officials of the FRG Foreign Office.
This entailed, for example, conversations with State
Secretary van Well in October 1979 and March 1980, the

first of which reportedly initiated an exchange of
views on disarmament questions. General discussions
were also pursued between Moldt and Foreign Minister
Genscher on April 1, 1980, although the latter insisted
that he was conducting the talks in his capacity as
Chairman of the Free Democratic Party.[249] Bonn's fear
of creating an impression of "foreign relations"
through an upgrading of the GDR Mission apparently
subsided to the extent that it was willing to maintain
inner-German consultations in a number of forums short
of a GDR-FRG Foreign Office institutional channel.

POLITICAL CONSULTATION

The most regularly used transmission belts for
inner-German communication are undoubtedly the two
Permanent Missions; in the case of the West German
Director, significant negotiating authority was
bestowed as well toward the completion of numerous
agreements. Nevertheless, the extensive activity of
this institution in FRG-GDR relations does not
constitute policymaking autonomy, as the Mission was
clearly subordinated to the Chancellor's Office.[250]
Aside from the participation of the Missions and
representatives in ongoing negotiations, such as the
Frontier Commission, the inner-German dialogue has been
pursued principally through ministerial consultations
in which certain officials have emerged as "trouble-
shooters" or as architects of proposed projects. The
East and West German heads of state have communicated
mainly by way of telephone or letters rather than
through face-to-face meetings.

It is sufficient to note that there were two
gatherings during which Chancellor Schmidt and Council
of State Chairman Honecker conferred directly: the
July-August 1975 Helsinki Conference and the May 1980
funeral of Yugoslav President Josef Broz Tito.
Inasmuch as these high-level meetings took place on
occasions when both German statesmen were present for
reasons other than inner-German consultation, it is
evident that the political conditions for an East-West
German "summit" were not forthcoming in the 1973-1980
period. Undoubtedly the need for each leadership to
attach its own preconditions to any prospective
meeting, also observable in the preparation for the
1970 Erfurt meeting,[251] played a role in the
cancellation of envisioned discussions. Yet it was the
impact of extra-German developments, particularly the
December 1979 Soviet invasion of Afghanistan and the
Polish crisis of August 1980, that proved decisive in
postponing Schmidt-Honecker meetings.[252]

Although it is not possible to reconstruct the
content of the two leaders' Helsinki conversations, it

was reported that both committed themselves in general
terms to avoiding complications in the observance of
the Quadripartite Agreement's sections relating to
Berlin.[253] Treatment of this theme could not have been
neglected, given the past year's crisis over Bonn's
establishment of the Environmental Federal Office in
West Berlin and the continuing quarrel over the range
of the Federal Republic's admissible ties with the
city. Other subjects concerned the progress in family
reunification and West German lump-sum payments for
travel to the GDR and Berlin; the talks were
supplemented by an exchange of opinion between Foreign
Ministers Genscher and Oskar Fischer.[254]

Concerning the 1980 Belgrade meeting, public
accounts do not reveal any extensive discussion of
bilateral German problems. Schmidt and Honecker
generally shared the hope that the two states'
relations would be maintained at an acceptably high
level in the presence of a deteriorating international
climate. Reportedly they also supported the view that
a prospective future meeting between the two in East
Germany should be postponed no longer than necessary,
although no date could be announced for a Schmidt
visit.[255] Council of State Chairman Honecker also
conversed with FRG President Karl Carstens. Once more,
the inner-German political picture prior to the meeting
mirrored the ambiguous nature of the two states'
relations. A visit to the FRG by SED Central Committee
member Guenter Mittag one month earlier symbolized a
renewed determination to consolidate economic cooperation with Bonn, an aim that was largely shared within
the West German Government, but the attempt coincided
with a marked cutback in the number of family-related
border crossings permitted by East Berlin.[256]

Of the types of consultation under discussion
here, it has been the ministerial meetings which have
occurred with the greatest regularity. Such meetings
fall into two categories: those planned in advance to
promote further cooperation in technical areas or
exchange views and those arranged in an attempt to de-
fuse periodic inner-German crises. The prime object of
contacts in the first category, particularly if one
takes account of the government departments involved,
is readily identifiable as economic cooperation. Both
the Hannover and Leipzig Trade Fairs, symbolically,
have been frequently selected as the sites for
countless FRG-GDR conversations; each year since 1973
trade talks were arranged between the State Secretary
of the FRG Ministry of Economics and the GDR Ministry
of Foreign Trade, thus displacing some of the tasks
performed earlier by the Inter-zonal Trade Trusteeship.
At the 1979 Leipzig Fair, it was the West German
Economics Minister Otto Graf Lambsdorff who for the
first time discussed trade and economic relations with

his counterpart in the GDR Foreign Trade Ministry, Horst Soelle.[257] It should not be assumed, of course, that the two governments succeeded in insulating the above discussions from periodic disputes. The absence of linkage would have run counter to Bonn's intentions; since trade was the intended topic for each meeting, it was of practical importance that the East German desire that inner-German economic relations develop apart from other considerations be contested publicly. Such a motivation came into play in Federal Minister Friedrichs' protest of an East German exclusion of three West German journalists from the 1976 Leipzig Fair. In similar fashion, Lambsdorff responded to East Berlin's 1979 imposition of restrictions on the activities of Western journalists in the GDR with cancellation of his scheduled visit to an East German exhibit at the Hannover Fair.[258]

Just as the FRG Economics Minister was the cabinet minister most often called upon to pursue discussions with GDR officials on a regular basis, Secretary Mittag emerged as the appropriate East German "talking partner." Mittag counted as one of the key participants in the September 1978 visit of FRG Building Minister Wolfgang Junker to East Berlin. Furthermore, it was Mittag who met with Lambsdorff and Chancellor Schmidt in April 1980, an event which was noteworthy both because it represented the highest-level visit of any East German official since the 1970 Kassel meeting and because it occurred at a time of heightened East-West tension. Despite the proposed American economic sanctions against the Soviet Union, Mittag, who also consulted with representatives of the West German business concerns Hoechst and Krupp, reportedly gave evidence of a "loosened attitude" towards the prospect of future GDR dealings with such firms. The Mittag visit capped Krupp's completion of a chemical installation in the East German city of Halle and, even more significantly, the Federal Government's announcement of a possible Schmidt-Honecker meeting in East Germany in May.[259]

Other meetings arranged in advance can be concisely referred to here: a September 1974 meeting between the East and West German Ministers of Agriculture, 1978 and 1979 conversations of the respective Building Ministers Junker and Dieter Haack, and a March 1979 information visit by the West German Minister of Education and Science to his East German opposite, State Secretary Werner Lorenz.[260] Such meetings occurred with little regularity, as they were not part of ongoing negotiations, although discussions continued in the area of science and technology and were impeded only by disagreement over the question of West Berlin's inclusion. A fundamental motive behind

these contacts resided in the West German commitment to
continue the inner-German dialogue even if no tangible
result could be promised. This purpose can certainly
be detected in the FRG-GDR disarmament talks, the goal
of which, according to the Office of the West German
Permanent Mission, is to "contribute to an atmosphere
of mutual predictability on both sides."[261]

This "dialogue maintenance" aspect of the
disarmament talks was given added emphasis through the
Federal Government's insistence that the conversations
did not constitute negotiations and could yield no
settlements on armament issues.[262] Rather, the two
chief discussants, FRG Special Ambassador for
Disarmament Affairs Friedrich Ruth and GDR
representative Ernst Krabatsch, conducted talks on the
East-West military balance and the possibilities for
the reduction of medium-range nuclear weapons in
Europe. Annual meetings were held between 1977 and
1980.

The other common form of ministerial activity in
East-West German relations, that of "trouble-shooter,"
has been much in evidence during this period; as was
noted in the previous section, the Directors of both
Permanent Missions have played central roles. The most
important ministerial participant on the West German
side, however, has clearly been Wischnewski, a former
Minister of Development Assistance in the "Grand
Coalition" who gained increasing influence in SPD
circles as an important architect of the party's 1969
campaign victory.[263] In particular, his channel of
communication with GDR Permanent Mission Director Kohl
in Bonn was utilized during several periods of tension
in 1977. At that time State Minister in the
Chancellor's Office, Wischnewski met with the latter
during the January 1977 interdiction of East Germans
seeking to enter the FRG Permanent Mission in East
Berlin as well as during the peak of inner-German
border incidents in the summer of 1977. (These last
developments, together with the GDR leadership's
refusal to allow a CSU delegation to visit Potsdam,
necessitated two rounds of Wischnewski-Kohl talks in
August). The GDR leadership's actions in 1978,
including the closing of the Spiegel office and the
refusal to allow CDU leader Helmut Kohl's entry into
East Berlin, also led to Wischnewski's discussions with
Hermann Axen and Foreign Minister Fischer in East
Berlin.[264] A second meeting of the State Minister with
Fischer followed in January 1979.

145

A SUMMATION OF THE BASIC TREATY'S IMPLEMENTATION

The Basic Treaty could not and did not provide the blueprint for FRG or GDR inner-German policies in the 1973-1980 period. It was employed only selectively by SPD-FDP governments, in part because of the treaty's existence within a larger framework of multilateral policy, because the citing of East German violations of specific articles was deemed counterproductive, and because the treaty's area of applicability is limited. East Berlin has also adopted the above approach, at times utilizing Articles 2, 4, and 6 to defend GDR citizenship policy and internal and external autonomy.

In line with Chancellor Brandt's "two states in one German nation" standard, the West German Government basically observed East German autonomy, although not to the exclusion of its All-German consular authority or its pursuance of one German citizenship. Such a course was necessitated in view of the floor of "recognition" granted to East Germany in the Basic Treaty and because it can be seen as the quid pro quo for the increase in West German visits to the GDR and related contacts. The application of an intermediate status to the GDR in legal and legislative practice (e.g., a state considered to possess an autonomous jurisdiction but not a foreign land with respect to the Federal Republic) formally left the door open for future steps in support of the reunification imperative and allowed Bonn a flexible inner-German policy through its very ambiguity. "Sovereign jurisdiction" remained the prized principle of SED spokesmen, on the other hand, and East German opposition to the "Karlsruhe Decision" logically followed from the doctrine of ideological and national de-limitation. The polarities ascribed to the East-West German relationship by the GDR elite therefore resembled those advanced in the days of Ulbricht. Disagreement here, however, did not noticeably impair practical cooperation.

The emergence of the two German leaderships as genuine "talking partners" contrasts markedly with the frequent polemics of the 1950's and 1960's, when East-West German conversations were in considerable part confined to regulating several technical areas. The SPD-FDP avoidance of remarks or terminology considered offensive by the GDR leadership necessarily accompanied Bonn's program for expanded practical contacts, since this program was in many respects far more dangerous for East Berlin. Yet the rhetorical approximation of "good neighbourly relations" must also be attributed to a dawning recognition by the SED leadership. Ulbricht's departure from power in 1971, apparently due to Soviet pressure, confirmed that excessive East German "Abgrenzung" would not be permitted to run athwart of Soviet relaxation measures aimed at the Federal

Republic. Consequently, General Secretary Honecker's style of discourse toward the West German leadership reflected a policy readjustment, particularly in his praise for inner-German economic contacts and a soft-pedalling of the citizenship dispute. The "Polish events" of 1980, of course, suspended many of these positive expressions and recurrent border incidents as well as the Guillaume affair testified anew to the tensions endemic to the division of Germany.

The course of inner-German practical and humanitarian cooperation also evinced a West German disinclination to resort to the momentary reprisal, although the resulting policy did not ensure an intensification of all activities nor did it markedly differ from frequent West German practices of the 1960's. Trade underwent constant absolute increases, but, mainly due to higher inflation rates, did not compare favorably with the level of the 1960's. Like their immediate predecessors, Brandt and Schmidt did not counter GDR travel restrictions with curbs on trade or on trade credits. Both nevertheless took pains to publicly sustain the impression that inner-German trade could not develop in isolation from other activities; these efforts were reflected in the 1974 "swing" negotiation and Minister Friedrich's March 1976 protest at the Leipzig Fair.

With the exception of sports and the problematical areas of the "human trade" and postal communication, the remaining practical areas show a clear upswing in the level of FRG-GDR cooperation over the years prior to the 1969-1972 period. West German travel to the GDR had been cut from its 1978 peak by 1980, but annual visits were still twice the number of those in the 1960's, with East German visits to the FRG rising gradually. Moreover, Bonn's extension of long-term lump-sum payments to East Berlin for West German motorists' use of East German streets made it more difficult for the SED leadership to arbitrarily impose on-the-spot toll increases on travellers, a source of friction in the past. The Federal Government was far less effective in guaranteeing even-handed East German treatment of Western media correspondents, as GDR punitive actions targeted journalistic contacts with critical intellectuals in the aftermath of the 1975 Helsinki Agreement.

Despite persisting complications in day-to-day relations, both German states achieved agreements in areas not regulated before, such as the exchange of journalists, the marking of the inner-German frontier, environmental protection, and health. Where practical and humanitarian successes were impeded, this was less the result of technical or doctrinal differences than it was attributable to "spillover" from the Berlin question. Disagreement on the latter obstructed the

securing · of framework agreements in science and
technology and legal assistance, provoked the
cancellation of environmental negotiations in 1974, and
contributed to the stagnation in East-West German
athletic undertakings. However, the impact of
doctrinal conflicts on practical cooperation was more
limited in the 1973-1980 period than during Ulbricht's
tenure as head of state. Divergent national conceptions could be detected in the failure to obtain
regulations for legal assistance and the drawing of the
Elbe boundary, but in all other areas the operative
assumptions of the Basic Treaty, where international
practices were sometimes observed, permitted an
insulation of technical arrangements from status
disputes.

[1]"... der Vertrag, der einen wichtigen Bestandteil
des gesamten Vertragswerkes der sozialistischen Staaten
mit der BRD darstellt." Neues Deutschland, 21 June
1974.

[2]"'Fuenf Jahre Grundlagenvertrag' von
Bundesminister Egon Franke, 20 Dezember 1979," Zehn
Jahre Deutschlandpolitik, p. 323.

[3]See, for example, Brandt's February 1972 and
January 1973 reports to the Bundestsag as well as a
similar report by Schmidt. Zehn Jahre
Deutschlandpolitik, pp. 407, 411, 415.

[4]Frankfurter Allgemeine Zeitung, 9 November 1973.

[5]Ibid., 13 October 1980.

[6]Frankfurter Allgemeine Zeitung, 2 May 1980.

[7]Zehn Jahre Deutschlandpolitik, p. 325.

[8]Ibid. "Die Bundesregierung ist sich bewusst,
dass Ihre Bemuehungen gemessen am Ideal der
Freizuegigkeit unzureichend sind."

[9]This past characterization of the GDR leadership,
which actually refers to the SED residential district,
was intentionally employed to emphasize the
exclusivist, undemocratic nature of the East German
state.

[10]"Bundeskanzler Schmidt: Regierungserklaerung zur
Lage der Nation," Texte 3 (January-December 1975): 11.

[11]Deutschland Archiv 10 (April 1977): 427.

[12]"... in bezug auf seine raeumliche Ausdehnung allerdings teilidentisch," so dass insoweit die Identitaet keine Ausschliesslichkeit beansprucht." Bundesverfassungsgericht, "Urteil des Bundesverfassungsgerichts vom 31. Juli 1973," Seminarmaterial des Gesamtdeutschen Instituts (date not given), pp. 8-9.

[13]"in dem Schuetzbereich der staatlichen Ordnung der Bundesrepublik Deutschland," ibid., p. 3.

[14]"... zwei Staaten, die Teile eines noch immer existierenden, wenn auch handlungsunfaehigen, weil noch nicht reorganisierten umfassenden Staates Gesamtdeutschland mit einem einheitlichen Staatsvolk sind...," ibid., p. 11.

[15]"eine staatsrechtliche Grenze... aehnlich denen, die zwischen den Laendern der Bundesrepublik Deutschland verlaufen." Ibid., p. 12.

[16]Ibid., p. 9.

[17]Texte 12: 22. "Die Erhaltung des Friedens rangiert noch vor der Frage der Nation... Nur der lange und muehsame Weg von Nebeneinander zum Miteinander der beiden Staaten bietet der Nation ihre Chance."

[18]Frankfurter Allgemeine Zeitung, 18 June 1974.

[19]"Ueber Parteigrenzen und sonst unterschiedlichen Auffassungen hinweg sollten wir diesen Tag in seiner Bedeutung erkennen und uns an die Opfer errinern, die er gefordert hat. Jedenfalls sollte er nicht degradiert werden zum Anlass fast beziehungsloser, gewissermassend musealer Feierstunden." Texte 12: 757.

[20]Ibid.

[21]As a rule, West German authorities have not required GDR inhabitants to accept these slips during trips to the Federal Republic but have permitted them the option of acquiring them for visits. New York Times, 23 February 1977.

[22]Deutschland Archiv 7 (November 1974): 1188.

[23]Dokumente zur Aussenpolitik der DDR 15: 817, 952, 1037. "... die friedliche Regelung der deutschen Frage... die Herbeifuehrung eines einheitlichen friedliebenden und demokratischen deutschen Staates."

[24]BFIB, Dokumente zur Deutschlandpolitik 10 (1980): 717-720.

[25]"Der neue Freundschafts- und Beistandsvertrag zwischen UdSSR und DDR," Deutschland Archiv 8 (November 1975) : 1204-1206.

[26]Die Welt, 12 January 1977.

[27]"Hermann Axen: Zwei Staaten-- zwei Nationen. Deutsche Frage existiert nicht mehr." Deutschland Archiv 6 (April 1973): 415.

[28]"Wir sind im Vergleich zur Bundesrepublik Deutschland schon eine historische Epoche weitergegangen. Wir repraesentieren, um es kurz auszudruecken, im Gegensatz zur Bundesrepublik Deutschland das sozialistische Deutschland... Dieser Unterschied ist der entscheidende. Unser sozialistische Staat heisst Deutsche Demokratische Republik, weil ihre Staatsbuerger der Nationalitaet nach in der uebergrossen Mehrheit Deutsche sind... Die Antwort auf diesbezuegliche Fragen lautet schlicht und klar und ohne jede Zweideutigkeiten: Staatsbuergerschaft-- DDR, Nationalitaet-- deutsch. So liegen die Dinge." "Die 13. Tagung des Zentralkomitees der SED," Neues Deutschland, 13 December 1974.

[29]"Interview der 'New York Times' mit Erich Honecker," Deutschland Archiv 6 (January 1973): 97.

[30]One Neues Deutschland article even emphasized that Chancellor Schmidt "interfered in East German internal affairs" through his statement that the two states had special relations. New York Times, 23 December 1976.

[31]"Zwei deutschen Nationalstaaten," p. 417.

[32]"Hermann Axen zur nationalen Frage," Deutschland Archiv 7 (February 1974): 201.

[33]Deutschland Archiv 6 (February 1973): 213.

[34]"Die Leninschen Prinzipien der friedlichen Koexistenz setzen sich immer mehr als die allgemeine Normen der Beziehungen zwischen den sozialistischen Staaten, darunter der DDR, auf der einen Seite und den kapitalistischen Staaten auf der anderen Seite durch... Friedliche Koexistenz schlieest jedoch gesetzmaessig die sich weiter vollziehende Abgrenzung der sozialistischen DDR und der kapitalistischen BRD ein." "Axen: Zwei Staaten," p. 415.

[35]Neues Deutschland, 16 August 1973.

[36]New York Times, 23 February 1977.

150

[37]Neues Deutschland, 14 Oktober 1980.

[38]"Denkschrift der Bundesregierung zum Entwurf eines Gesetzes zum Beitritt der Bundesrepublik Deutschland zur Charta der Vereinten Nationen," Bundesratdrucksache 650/72: 40, quoted in Ress, Die Rechtslage Deutschlands, p. 313. "...die gleichzeitige Mitgliedschaft der beiden Staaten in Deutschland in den VN... die besondere Lage in Deutschland nicht (praejudiziert)."

[39]See this chapter's later section on trade.

[40]Zehn Jahre Deutschlandpolitik, p. 21.

[41]"Die Bundesregierung resigniert nicht angesichts der Wirklichkeit einer Grenze an der auf der anderen Seite noch in juengster Zeit Schuesse fallen." Frankfurter Allgemeine Zeitung, 29 October 1976.

[42]"Antwort der Bundesregierung auf die Grosse Anfrage der Fraktion der CDU/CSU: Wirtschaftliche, soziale, und kulturelle Rechte in der DDR; Selbstbestimmungsrecht des deutschen Volkes sowie buergerliche und politische Rechte in der DDR," Zehn Jahre Deutschlandpolitik, p. 382.

[43]Sueddeutsche Zeitung, 20 January 1978.

[44]Frankfurter Allgemeine Zeitung, 20 December 1980.

[45]"Bundestag Presse- und Informationszentrum, Deutschlandpolitik: Oeffentliche Anhoerungen des Ausschusses fuer innerdeutsche Beziehungen 1977 (Bonn: Druckhaus Bayreuth, 1977), p. 30.

[46]"Note der DDR-Regierung," Deutschland Archiv 8 (March 1975): 332-333; Frankfurter Allgemeine Zeitung, 18, 22 January 1975)

[47]Bundesrepublik Deutschland, Deutscher Bundestag, Verhandlungen des Deutschen Bundestages III, 8 Wahlperiode, 166 Sitzung, 1979: 13310.

[48]"Als Ausland im Sinne dieses Gesetzes gelten die Gebiete, die weder zum Geltungsbereich dieses Gesetzes noch zu den Waehrungsgebieten der Mark der Deutschen Demokratischen Republik gehoeren." Ibid.

[49]"unter Erhebungsgebiet im Sinne dieses Gesetzes ist der Geltungsbereich des Gesetzes mit Ausnahme der Zollausschluesse und der Zollfreigebiete zu verstehen. Aussengebiet im Sinne dieses Gesetzes ist das Gebiet,

das weder zum Erhebungsgebiet noch zum Gebiet der Deutschen Demokratischen Republik und von Berlin (Ost) gehoert." Verhandlungen 112: 14434.

[50]Verhandlungen 111: 13310; Verhandlungen 112: 14434.

[51]Frankfurter Allgemeine Zeitung, 27 November 1980.

[52]Ibid.

[53]"Gesetz zur Regelung von Fragen der Staatsbuergerschaft," Zehn Jahre Deutschlandpolitik, pp. 198-199.

[54]Koelner Stadtanzeiger, 29 July 1976.

[55]Sueddeutsche Zeitung, 26 July 1976; Neues Deutschland, 9 August 1976.

[56]Sueddeutsche Zeitung, 16 June 1976.

[57]"Interview mit Erich Honecker zu den Parteiwahlen 1973/74," Deutschland Archiv 6 (December 1973): 1327.

[58]"Erklaerung von Bundesminister Egon Franke zum Missbrauch der Transitwege, RIAS-Kommentar," Zehn Jahre Deutschlandpolitik, pp. 374-375.

[59]"dass Entspannungspolitik nur moeglich ist, wenn beide Partner stabil sind." Deutschland Archiv 10 (April 1977): 428.

[60]"Wir haben ganz deutlich erklaert, dass, wie auch immer Sie die Absender firmieren, die Bundesregierung damit nichts zu tun hat. Fuer mich ist nur die politische Reaktion der SED- und DDR-Fuehrung von Bedeutung." Der Spiegel 32 (9 January 1978): 29. Schmidt's reference to "the so-called manifesto," which advocated both the fulfillment of individual rights in the GDR and German reunification, reflected his disinclination to heighten SED suspicions or provide a pretext for further East German retaliation after the punitive actions of that month.

[61]"Interview des Generalsekretaers des ZK der SED und Staatsratsvorsitzenden der DDR, E. Honecker, mit der 'Saarbruecker Zeitung,'" Zehn Jahre Deutschlandpolitik, p. 335.

[62]Conference on Security and Cooperation in Europe Final Act (Ottawa: Information Canada, 1975), p. 6.

[63] See, for example, the SED Politburo's report on the Seventh Plenum of the Central Committee. _Deutschland_ _Archiv_ 11 (January 1978): 101.

[64] An August 1976 _Neues_ _Deutschland_ article alleged the Federal Government's violation of Article 6 through its condemnation of the East German role in various border incidents. _Neues_ _Deutschland_, 9 August 1976.

[65] _New_ _York_ _Times_, 23 December 1976.

[66] _Frankfurter_ _Allgemeine_ _Zeitung_, 11 October 1980.

[67] "Chronik," _Deutschland_ _Archiv_ 7 (August 1974): 896; _Neues_ _Deutschland_, 14 October 1980.

[68] Staatliche Zentralverwaltung fuer Statistik der DDR, _Statistisches_ _Jahrbuch_ _der_ _DDR_ _1977_ (Berlin: Staatsverlag der DDR, 1977), pp. 257-258 and _Statistisches_ _Taschenbuch_ _der_ _DDR_ _1978_ (Berlin: Staatsverlag der DDR, 1978), pp. 91-92.

[69] Lambrecht, "Entwicklung der Wirtschaftsbeziehungen," p. 460.

[70] See Chapter 1 and U.S., Department of State, _General_ _Agreement_ _on_ _Tariffs_ _and_ _Trade_: _Torquay_ _Protocol_ _and_ _Schedules_, vol. 1 (Washington, D.C.: Government Printing Office, 1951), p. 13.

[71] The practical changes resulting from this decision were the application of the Community's Common External Tariff to East German exports destined for the non-German members of the EEC and the appropriation of Community export rebates for delivery of the latter's products to the GDR. Reinhold Biskup, _Deutschland's_ _offene_ _Handelsgrenze_ (Berlin: Verlag Ullstein GmbH, 1976), pp. 98-99.

[72] The measure stands in contrast to such earlier Community regulations as the May 1966 decision not to invoke a third-state status for East Germany in applying EEC agricultural provisions. Rudolf Morawitz, "Der innerdeutsche Handel und die EWG nach dem Grundvertrag," _Europa_ _Archiv_ 28 (25 May 1973): 360.

[73] Lambrecht, "Entwicklung der Wirtschaftsbeziehungen," p. 459.

[74] _Zehn_ _Jahre_ _Deutschlandpolitik_, p. 29.

[75] Lambrecht, "Entwicklung der Wirtschaftsbeziehungen," p. 458.

[76]Zehn Jahre Deutschlandpolitik, p. 29.

[77]Ibid.

[78]Bundesrepublik Deutschland, Statistisches Bundesamt Wiesbaden, Warenverkehr mit der Deutschen Demokratischen Republik und Berlin (Ost) 1981 (Stuttgart und Maynz: W. Kohlhammer GmbH, 1981): 11.

[79]Zehn Jahre Deutschlandpolitik, p. 29.

[80]Lambrecht, "Entwicklung der Wirtschaftsbeziehungen," p. 459.

[81]Frankfurter Allgemeine Zeitung, 19 November 1981.

[82]Frankfurter Allgemeine Zeitung, 21 September 1974.

[83]Frankfurter Allgemeine Zeitung, 16 October 1980.

[84]Wilhelm Bruns, Deutsch-deutsche Beziehungen Praemissen, Probleme, Perspektiven (Opladen: Leske Verlag, 1979), p. 70.

[85]It has been estimated that as many as 100,000 West German jobs are dependent on inner-German trade. Ibid., pp. 73-74.

[86]Frankfurter Allgemeine Zeitung, 17 December 1981; Neues Deutschland, 25 November 1972; New York Times, 19 July 1978.

[87]Frankfurter Allgemeine Zeitung, 14 March 1977.

[88]Franklyn D. Holzman and Robert Levgold, "The Economics and Politics of East-West Relations," in: C. Fred Bergsten and Lawrence B. Krause, ed., World Politics and International Economics (Washington, D.C.: The Brookings Institution, 1975), p. 285.

[89]Lambrecht, "Entwicklungen der Wirtschaftsbeziehungen, pp. 462-463.

[90]This aim was given its earliest direct expression in a much-celebrated July 1963 speech by Egon Bahr at the Evangelical Academy of Tutzing and was lent practical effect through such actions as Bahr's negotiation of a commercial agreement with Prague in August 1967. See BFIB, Dokumente zur Deutschlandpolitik 9 (1978): 572-575, and New York Times, 4 August 1967.

[91]Der Fischer Weltalmanach-- Zahlen, Akten, Fakten, Hintergruenden/82 (Frankfurt: Fischer Verlag, 1981), p. 927; Zehn Jahre Deutschlandpolitik, p. 29.

[92]Zehn Jahre Deutschlandpolitik, p. 29.

[93]Ibid; Fischer Weltalmanach, p. 927.

[94]Deutsche Bundesbank, "Monthly Reports of the Deutsche Bundesbank," February 1983, p. 72; Zehn Jahre Deutschlandpolitik, p. 29. It should be emphasized that due to the absence of any available statistics on the annual price rises in East German exports, the real rate of increase for East German deliveries was determined by dividing the absolute increase by the percentage increase in the price of FRG overall imports.

[95]Ibid; Fischer Weltalmanach, p. 927.

[96]Ibid.

[97]Statistisches Jahrbuch der DDR 1978, pp. 232-233. As might be expected, GDR figures for the goods trade with the FRG and West Berlin (services are not included in East German statistics) are consistently lower than those published by the Federal Government. Computed on the basis of the former, inner-German trade dwindled to only 8.0% of GDR external trade in 1979, while according to the latter calculations an 8.5% share was registered. In any case, these results represent a slight downturn from the level of the early 1970's. Statistisches Bundesamt, Warenverkehr mit der DDR 1981, pp. 12-13; Statistisches Jahrbuch der DDR 1980, pp. 234-235.

[98]Statistisches Jahrbuch der DDR 1978, p. 232.

[99]Statistisches Jahrbuch der DDR 1971, p. 291.

[100]Thus East German debt to the FRG is not included in Bank for International Settlements figures. Wall Street Journal, 7 December 1982.

[101]"Denn nicht die absolute Debet- oder Kreditposition ist entscheidend, sondern das jeweilige Verhaeltnis von Lieferungen und Gegenlieferungen (sog. Deckungsquote) oder die Relation von kumuliertem Saldo zu Jahreslieferungen." Lambrecht, p. 469.

[102]Hans-Dieter Schulz, "Scheinbar ohne Swing und Zwang," Deutschland Archiv 14 (September 1981): 1021.

[103]Fischer Weltalmanach, p. 927.

[104]Europa Yearbook 1982, vol. 1 (London: Europa Publications Ltd., 1982), pp. 661, 1205.

[105]Europa Yearbook 1976, vol. 1, p. 699; Europa Yearbook 1979, vol. 1, p. 710; Europa Yearbook 1982, vol. 1, p. 701.

[106]Europa Yearbook 1976, 1979, 1982 Schulz, "Ohne Swing und Zwang," p. 1021.

[107]Statistisches Bundesamt, Warenverkehr mit der DDR 1973, Reihe 6, p. 11; Warenverkehr mit der DDR 1977, p. 12; Warenverkehr mit der DDR 1981, p. 10

[108]Ibid.

[109]Warenverkehr mit der DDR 1974, Reihe 6, p. 13; Warenverkehr mit der DDR 1974, (December 1974), Reihe 6, p. 15.

[110]Warenverkehr mit der DDR 1974, Reihe 6, p. 10; Warenverkehr mit der DDR 1981, p. 11.

[111]Ibid.

[112]Lambrecht, "Entwicklung der Wirtschaftsbeziehungen, p.465.

[113]Warenverkehr mit der DDR 1974, Reihe 6, p. 10; Warenverkehr mit der DDR 1977, p. 13; Warenverkehr mit der DDR 1981, p. 11.

[114]Lambrecht, "Entwicklung der Wirtschaftsbeziehungen," p. 465. This contribution has in the past equalled nine-tenths of all GDR investment goods exports.

[115]Fischer Weltalmanach, p. 927.

[116]Ibid., pp. 43, 226-232.

[117]See, in particular, Neues Deutschland, 1 November 1973.

[118]"Anordnung ueber die Durchfuehrung," Zehn Jahre Deutschlandpolitik, pp. 286-289.

[119]Such West German visits were less numerous in 1974 than 1973 even though the travel facilitation regulations were only in effect for six months in the latter year. Ibid., pp. 279-280.

[120]"Vereinbarung ueber den Swing," Deutschland Archiv 8 (January 1975): 82-83.

[121]"Anordnung des Ministers der Finanzen der DDR ueber die Befreiung vom Mindestumtausch fuer Jugendliche und Rentner," Zehn Jahre Deutschlandpolitik, p. 283.

[122]Neues Deutschland, 7 December 1974.

[123]"Erklaerung der Bundesregierung zu Verbesserungen im Reise- und Besucherverkehr sowie zu Fragen einer Swing-Regelung mit der DDR," Zehn Jahre Deutschlandpolitik, p. 280.

[124]"Vorschlaege der Regierung der DDR an die Regierung der BRD," ibid., p. 281.

[125]"Vorschlaege der Regierung der DDR," ibid., p. 281.

[126]"Mitteilung der Bundesregierung ueber Erleichterungen, ibid., p. 310.

[127]New York Times, 5 November 1976, 5 December 1976, 12 January 1977.

[128]Frankfurter Allgemeine Zeitung, 17 March 1977.

[129]"Die Bundesregierung hat fuer derartige noch zu vereinbarende Baumassnahmen und Leistungen fuer die Zeit nach 1981 eine Kostenbeteiligung bis zu 500 Millionen DM in Aussicht genommen." Ibid., p. 342. The two governments also committed themselves to the completion of work on the border crossing Wartha/Herleshausen. Ibid.

[130]Zehn Jahre Deutschlandpolitik, p. 379.

[131]"Protokoll ueber die Vereinbarung einer Pauschalabgeltung von Strassenbenutzungsgebuehren fuer Personenkraftzeuge im Verkehr in und durch das Gebiet der Deutschen Demokratischen Republik, 31 Oktober 1979," ibid., pp. 385-386.

[132]"Briefwechsel ueber den Autobahnbau bei Wartha und Eisenach, ueber Eisenbahnmassnahmen sowie ueber Gewaesserschuetzfragen," in: Presse- und Informationsbuero der Bundesregierung, Dokumente zur Entspannungspolitik der Bundesregierung (Hamburg: Hanseatische Druckanstalt GmbH, 1981), pp. 159-175.

[133]Frankfurter Allgemeine Zeitung, 11 October 1980.

[134]Neues Deutschland, 4 September 1980.

[135]"Einmischung in die inneren Angelegenheiten der DDR, Volkspolen, und der anderen sozialistischen Laender." "Chronik," Deutschland Archiv 13 (November 1980): 1231.

[136]Neues Deutschland, 14 October 1980.

[137]BFIB, "Angaben zum Reiseverkehr zwischen der Bundesrepublik Deutschland und der DDR seit 1953 (ohne Berlin)," (date not given).

[138]See the later section on inner-German sports.

[139]No statisiics are available for the years 1961-1966, however. Ibid.

[140]BFIB, "Angaben zum Reiseverkehr"; Frankfurter Allgemeine Zeitung, 5 July 1980.

[141]BFIB, "Angaben zum Reiseverkehr."

[142]BFIB, "Angaben zum Reiseverkehr."

[143]Ibid.

[144]Peter Christian Ludz, ed., DDR Handbuch (Koeln: Verlag Wissenschaft und Politik, 1979), p. 1089; Zehn Jahre Deutschlandpolitik, p. 52.

[145]David A. Andelman, "The Road to Madrid," Foreign Policy, Nr. 39 (Summer 1980), p. 161; Bruns, Deutsch-deutsche Beziehungen, p. 56.

[146]Melvin Croan, "New Country, Old Nationality," Foreign Policy, Nr. 37 (Winter 1979-80), p. 148.

[147]Invocation of the Helsinki Agreement had the advantage of supporting the FRG position with a specific provision that promoted the enhancement of communication, but it is also important to recognize that this document essentially represents an international, as opposed to a purely inner-German, understanding. Bonn's citation of it is therefore not altogether consistent with the notion of "special German relations" that can be inferred from the Basic Treaty.

[148]"... die allgemeine anerkannten Normen des Voelkerrechts einzuhalten... die Gesetze und anderen Rechtsvorschriften der Deutschen Demokratischen Republik einzuhalten... Verleumdungen oder Diffamierungen der Deutschen Demokratischen Republik, ihre staatlichen Organe und ihrer fuehrenden Persoenlichkeiten sowie der mit der Deutschen

Demokratischen Republik verbuendeten Staaten zu
unterlassen... wahrheitsgetreu, sachbezogen und korrekt
zu berichten sowie keine boeswillige Verfaelschung von
Tatsachen zuzulassen... die gewaehrten
Arbeitsmoeglichkeiten nicht fuer Handlungen zu
missbrauchen, die mit dem journalistischen Auftrag
nichts zu tun haben." Ibid., p. 217.

[149]Ibid.

[150]Frankfurter Allgemeine Zeitung, 7 March 1973.

[151]Frankfurter Allgemeine Zeitung, 8 March 1973;
Zehn Jahre Deutschlandpolitik, p. 56.

[152]Zehn Jahre Deutschlandpolitik, p. 56.

[153]Sueddeutsche Zeitung, 17 December 1975.

[154]"Chronik," Deutschland Archiv 9 (January 1976):
110. "... eine Verleumdung, mit der provokatorische
Absichte verfolgt werden. Ihr Zweck ist
offensichtlich, der konstruktiven Friedenspolitik der
DDR entgegenzuwirken."

[155]Zehn Jahre Deutschlandpolitik, p. 56.

[156]Frankfurter Allgemeine Zeitung, 23 December
1976.

[157]See, for example, the Times (London), 10
October 1977, 14 November 1977; Sueddeutsche Zeitung,
13 October 1977.

[158]Neues Deutschland, 2 January 1978.

[159]"'Spiegel' Buero in Ost-Berlin geschlossen,"
Deutschland Archiv 11 (February 1978): 216.

[160]Zehn Jahre Deutschlandpolitik, p. 20.

[161]"Journalistische Vorhaben und staatlichen und
wirtschaftsleitenden Organen, Einrichtungen,
volkseigenen Kombinaten und Betrieben, Genossenschaften
und gesellschaftlichen Einrichtungen und Institutionen
sowie Interviews und Befragungen jeder Art sind
genehmigungspflichtig." Ibid., p. 376.

[162]Zehn Jahre Deutschlandpolitik, p. 376.

[163]Ibid.

[164]"Erklaerung von Staatsseketaer Boelling zur
Ausweisung des ZDF-Korrespondenten van Loyen aus der

DDR," Zehn Jahre Deutschlandpolitik, p. 377. GDR
authorities had declared that the van Loyen broadcast
constituted an interview with the dissident Heym, hence
punishable under the April 1979 executive decision
because the journalist had not received prior
permission from the GDR Foreign Ministry. The Federal
Government proceeded from the assumption that since
Heym had not responded to questions from van Loyen but
issued a declaration, no interview had taken place.
"Chronik," Deutschland Archiv 12 (2 July 1979): 670.

[165]Gesetzblatt der Deutschen Demokratischen
Republik, Teil I (2 July 1979): 139-146.

[166]Ibid., p. 141.

[167]"Sie richten sich in erster Linie gegen
kritische Intellektuelle in der DDR und ihre Kontakte
zu westlichen Journalisten und Medien," "Chronik,"
Deutschland Archiv 12 (September 1979): 1006.

[168]Frankfurter Allgemeine Zeitung, 12 November
1980.

[169]FRG Press and Information Office, The Bulletin
20, Nr. 38 (14 November 1972), p. 295.

[170]"Erklaerung zu Protokoll ueber die Aufgaben der
Grenzkommission durch die beiden Delegationsleiter,"
Zehn Jahre Deutschlandpolitik, p. 211.

[171]Frankfurter Allgemeine Zeitung, 2 May 1980.

[172]Zehn Jahre Deutschlandpolitik, pp. 26, 245,
247-248, 290, 320.

[173]Zehn Jahre Deutschlandpolitik, pp. 331,
335-336; Frankfurter Allgemeine Zeitung, 21 December
1982; Hansjuergen Schierbaum, Intra-German Relations
(Munich: Tuduv Verlagsgesellschaft, 1980), p. 55.

[174]Ibid., pp. 272-276, 295-297.

[175]"Vereinbarung zwischen der Regierung der
Bundesrepublik Deutschland und der Regierung der
Deutschen Demokratischen Republik ueber die Regelung
von Fragen, die mit der Errichtung und dem Betrieb
eines Hochwasserrueckhaltebeckens an der Itz
zusammenhaengen," ibid., pp. 373-374;
"Protokollvermerk der Grenzkommission, 6 Dezember
1973," Ibid., pp. 250-251.

[176]"Protokoll zwischen der Regierung der
Bundesrepublik Deutschland und der Regierung der

Deutschen Demokratischen Republik ueber die
Ueberpruefung, Erneuerung, und Ergaenzung der
Markierung der zwischen der Bundesrepublik und der
Deutschen Demokratischen Republik bestehenden Grenzen,"
Ibid., pp. 353-372.

[177]Frankfurter Allgemeine Zeitung, 19 December
1975, 27 February 1978.

[178]"im Rahmen des Vertrages vom 26 Mai 1972...
getroffenen Regelungen zur Gewaehrleistung eines
reibungslosen Binnenschiffsverkehr sowie die
Auffassungen zur Rechtslage," Zehn Jahre
Deutschlandpolitik, p. 355.

[179]Ibid., pp. 362-363.

[180]Frankfurter Allgemeine Zeitung, 31 January
1981; DSB, "Gesamtdeutscher Sportverkehr," quoted in
Lemke, Sport und Politik, p. 37.

[181]Frankfurter Allgemeine Zeitung, 31 January
1981.

[182]Zehn Jahre Deutschlandpolitik, p. 270.

[183]"Viermaechte Abkommen," ibid., p. 161.

[184]Ibid., pp. 271-272.

[185]"Beide Seiten werden ihre sportlichen
Beziehungen entsprechend den Bestimmungen und
Gepflogenheiten des Internationalen Olympischen
Komitees und der internationalen
Sportsorganisationen... regeln." Ibid, p. 270.

[186]Frankfurter Allgemeine Zeitung, 31 January
1981. This latter figure is to be compared with the
over 100 Soviet-West German bilateral athletic events
for the same year. Zehn Jahre Deutschlandpolitik, p.
66.

[187]Zehn Jahre Deutschlandpolitik, p. 65.

[188]Knecht, "Unveraendert Stagnation im deutsch-
deutschen Sportverkehr," Deutschland Archiv 11 (March
1978): 233; Frankfurter Allgemeine Zeitung, 31 January
1981.

[189]Frankfurter Allgemeine Zeitung, 31 January
1981.

[190]Ibid.

[191]Ibid., 31 January 1978; Zehn Jahre Deutschlandpolitik, p. 65.

[192]Frankfurter Allgemeine Zeitung, 31 January 1978. "... weisst noch keine normale Verhaeltnisse zwischen unseren nachbaren Sportsorganisationen."

[193]Knecht, "Unveraendert Stagnation," p. 231.

[194]Siegfried Kupper, "Politische Beziehungen zur Bundesrepublik Deutschland, 1955-1977," in: Jacobsen, ed., Drei Jahrzehnte Aussenpolitik, pp. 409, 415.

[195]"vertritt die Bundesregierung unter Berufung auf die Erfahrung nach frueherer Bundesregierungen den Standpunkt, dass die oeffentliche Behandlung von humanitaeren Einzelfaellen im Interesse der unmittelbar wie der mittelbar Betroffenen nicht zweckmaessig ist." Zehn Jahre Deutschlandpolitik, p. 53

[196]The majority of those freed from imprisonment in these cases have been East Germans apprehended after unsuccessful escape attempts or West Germans who assisted during such attempts. New York Times, 6 October 1975, 6 May 1978; Meyer, Des hommes, p. 225.

[197]New York Times, 4 April 1976.

[198]"Lieber im verborgenen," Der Spiegel 29 (1 September 1975): 29.

[199]New York Times, 4 December 1976.

[200]The total of such petitions in 1976 was estimated at between 100,000 and 200,000. Ibid., 12 January 1977.

[201]Incidents such as the apprehension of regime critic Rudolf Bahro and the house arrest of physicist Robert Havemann resumed in the summer of 1977. "Chronik," Deutschland Archiv 9 (August 1977): 1007-1008.

[202]Zehn Jahre Deutschlandpolitik, p. 53.

[203]Ibid.; Frankfurter Allgemeine Zeitung, 28 October 1979, 18 December 1979.

[204]Ibid., 29 October 1979. The Federal Government reportedly succeeded in "purchasing" 700 prisoners at a cost of approximately $200 million in 1979. New York Times, 28 October 1979.

[205]This would hold true despite the fact that the

desire for practical joint efforts was at the time expressed by both German leaderships. Frankfurter Allgemeine Zeitung, 2 February 1980.

[206]New York Times, 4 April 1976.

[207]Zehn Jahre Deutschlandpolitik, p. 35; Sueddeutsche Zeitung, 8 December 1972, 8 November 1974.

[208]"Abkommen zwischen der Regierung der Bundesrepublik Deutschland und der Regierung der Deutschen Demokratischen Republik auf dem Gebiet des Post-Fernmeldewesens," Zehn Jahre Deutschlandpolitik, pp. 302-308.

[209]Ibid., p. 302.

[210]Ibid.

[211]Frankfurter Allgemeine Zeitung, 31 March 1976.

[212]Ibid., p. 305.

[213]Ibid., pp. 303, 304.

[214]"Briefwechsel zwischen dem Bundesminister fuer das Post- und Fernmeldewesen und dem Ministerium fuer Post- und Fernmeldewesen der DDR ueber die Postpauschale 1977-1982," ibid., pp. 319-320.

[215]BFIB, "Statistiken im innerdeutschen Postverkehr," 10 June 1983.

[216]Zehn Jahre Deutschlandpolitik, p. 36.

[217]Ibid.

[218]Ibid., pp. 36-37.

[219]Ibid.

[220]"Abkommen zwischen der Regierung der Bundesrepublik Deutschland und der Regierung der Deutschen Demokratischen Republik auf dem Gebiet des Gesundheitswesen," Zehn Jahre Deutschlandpolitik, pp. 264-270; "Abkommen zwischen der Regierung der Bundesrepublik Deutschland und der Regierung der Deutschen Demokratischen Republik auf dem Gebiet des Veterinaerswesen," ibid., pp. 387-388.

[221]Ibid., p. 265.

[222]Ibid.

[223]Fulfillment of the latter was accomplished in September 1977 with the exchange of information and medical opinions on rehabilitation of the handicapped; these conversations included representatives of the FRG Ministry of Labor and Welfare and the GDR Ministry of Health. Ibid., p. 49.

[224]Ibid., pp. 64, 265, 267.

[225]Ibid., p. 266.

[226]Ibid., pp. 387-388, 400.

[227]"Vereinbarung zwischen dem Bundesminister der Finanzen der Bundesrepublik Deutschland und dem Minister der Finanzen der Deutschen Demokratischen Republik ueber den Transfer von Unterhaltszahlungen," Ibid., pp. 261-262.

[228]"Vereinbarung zwischen dem Bundesminister der Finanzen der Bundesrepublik Deutschland und dem Minister der Finanzen der Deutschen Demokratischen Republik ueber den Transfer aus Guthaben in bestimmten Faellen," p. 33.

[229]Ibid., pp. 33, 261.

[230]"Insgesamt koennen die Ueberweisungen aus dem einen Staat nicht hoeher sein als die Ueberweisungen aus dem anderen Staat." Ibid., p. 262.

[231]Ibid., p. 33.

[232]"Nichtkommerzieller Zahlungsverkehr: Protokoll," ibid., p. 349.

[233]Sueddeutsche Zeitung, 7 March 1975.

[234]Frankfurter Allgemeine Zeitung, 29 October, 1979.

[235]"Chronik," Deutschland Archiv 13 (November 1980): 1232. Publishers from both states have displayed contemporary publications at the Frankfurt and Leipzig Book Fairs each year, although cooperation between the two literary associations was confined to international forums. Zehn Jahre Deutschlandpolitik, pp. 50, 62.

[236]Zehn Jahre Deutschlandpolitik, p. 51.

[237]"Gesetz ueber das gerichtliche Verfahren in Zivil-, Familien- und Arbeitsrechtssachen-- Zivilprozessordnung," Gesetzblatt der Deutschen

Demokratischen Republik, Teil I (11 July 1975):
533-564; Zehn Jahre Deutschlandpolitik, pp. 51-52.

[238]Zehn Jahre Deutschlandpolitik, p. 52;
Frankfurter Allgemeine Zeitung, 27 October 1979.

[239]"Gesetz ueber die Gewaehrung von
Erleichterungen, Vorrechten, und Befreiungen an die
Staendige Vertretung der DDR," Zehn Jahre
Deutschlandpolitik, p. 249.

[240]Ibid., p. 257.

[241]Ibid.

[242]"... die Interessen des Entsendestaates im
Gastland zu vertreten, einschliesslich Hilfe und
Beistand fuer Personen, sowie normale gutnachbarliche
Beziehungen zwischen der Bundesrepublik Deutschland und
der Deutschen Demokratischen Republik auf politischem,
wirtschaftlichem, und kulturellem Gebiet wie auch auf
anderen Gebieten zu foerdern und auszubauen." Ibid.

[243]Ibid.

[244]Ibid., pp. 258-261.

[245]Zehn Jahre Deutschlandpolitik, pp. 24-25.

[246]The Federal Government made use of the Gaus-
Nier channel, for example, during both the January 1977
incident centering on East Germans' access to the FRG
Permanent Mission and the aftermath of the eviction of
a West German television correspondent three weeks
earlier. "Chronik," Deutschland Archiv 10 (January
1977): 110; "Chronik," (February 1977): 222.

[247]Panorama DDR, "Attack on the GDR's
Representation at Bonn," (Dresden: Verlag Zeit im Bild,
1977), p. 3.

[248]Sueddeutsche Zeitung, 12 January 1977.

[249]Frankfurter Allgemeine Zeitung, 29 October
1985, 2 April 1980.

[250]Zehn Jahre Deutschlandpolitik, p. 24.

[251]See Chapter 2.

[252]New York Times, 31 January 1980; Die Welt, 23
August 1980.

[253]Frankfurter Allgemeine Zeitung, 1 August 1975.

[254]Ibid.; Zehn Jahre Deutschlandpolitik, p. 21. The only regular conversations between the two foreign ministers were pursued once annually at the United Nations.

[255]Sueddeutsche Zeitung, 9 May 1980. Three months later, however, Director Moldt delivered an invitation to Schmidt from the SED General Secretary for a "working visit" by the Chancellor to the GDR. Schmidt called off the intended meeting eleven days later. Die Welt, 12, 23 August 1980.

[256]Frankfurter Allgemeine Zeitung, 18 April 1980.

[257]Zehn Jahre Deutschlandpolitik, p. 21.

[258]Die Welt, 17 March 1976; Zehn Jahre Deutschlandpolitik, p. 21.

[259]Frankfurter Allgemeine Zeitung, 14, 18 April 1980, 29 May 1980.

[260]In his return visit to the Federal Republic, Junker also consulted with several West German cabinet as well as parliamentary leaders. Zehn Jahre Deutschlandpolitik, p. 21.

[261]Federal Republic of Germany, Press and Information Office, The Week in Germany, vol. 11, Nr. 26 (10 July 1981), p. 2.

[262]Ibid.

[263]Brandt, Begegnungen und Einsichten, p. 181.

[264]Frankfurter Allgemeine Zeitung, 12 January 1977, 13 August 1977, 17 September 1977; Sueddeutsche Zeitung, 30 January 1978. The State Minister's failure to secure the reopening of the Spiegel office testified once more to the fragility of post-Basic Treaty cooperation in practical areas, especially in view of the West German periodical's publication of the maligning dissident manifesto with its portrayal of fragmentation within the SED.

4
Inner-German Problems

Having explored the implementation of the Basic Treaty's inner-German provisions, attention will now be devoted to the most salient problems of the 1973-1980 period. Because of the necessary interweaving of West German Deutschlandpolitik into the larger framework of Ostpolitik, the chapter will first investigate the progress and differences in Soviet-East German and Soviet-West German relations. One purpose in doing so is to identify the multilateral as opposed to the purely bilateral dimension of inner-German relations in an effort to explain the resolution or continuation of problems. A second aim is to arrive at a judgment on the impact of West German travel into and media reporting from the GDR, the two most important elements of the West German presence. The concluding section of the chapter will assess changes in the pattern of behavior of the two states toward one another, also accounting for the intrusion of international disputes into the inner-German arena.

SOVIET-EAST GERMAN RELATIONS

Before investigating the impact of Soviet-East German affairs on post-1973 cooperation, several features of the relationship must be emphasized. First, the position of the Soviet Union as the dominant influence on the East German ruling elite's outlook and GDR foreign policy alignment is not open to question. This primacy emanated above all from the presence of approximately 400,000 Soviet troops on the soil of East Germany,[1] the ultimate guarantor of SED domestic authority. The Soviet Union's larger population and military capability, its leading position in the Warsaw Pact alliance, and its founding role as patron of the

East German state all provide Moscow with considerable leverage over the GDR when the ledger-sheet of mutual influences is considered. The issue of actual SED autonomy from Moscow is formulating policy is admittedly handicapped by the absence of reliable information relating to specific Soviet-East German consultations and thus the GDR leadership's success in bargaining per issue. However, one can safely assert that the Kremlin and the SED share a fundamental political aim to degrees that are for all practical purposes identical: each has and will continue to regard the existence and basic viability of the GDR as a non-negotiable item in international politics.

Second, while the scope of Soviet interests as well as Soviet power demand a sensitivity and attentiveness to foreign developments outside Central Europe, GDR capabilities, geographical vulnerabilities, and national competition with the Federal Republic have consigned this area to the foreground as the domain and object of SED external policy. This asymmetry of interests has sometimes provided a basis for significantly divergent perspectives in foreign policy; the necessity for the containment of Western penetration of WTO states in the proximity of East Germany has therefore been even more acutely felt by the GDR leadership than Moscow.[2] In this context, both the Quadripartite Agreement and Basic Treaty process, while unsettling to East Berlin in a number of respects, corresponded to an immediate Soviet desire to extend the quid pro quo necessary for the preparation of the Helsinki Conference.

A third observation is that, the above differences notwithstanding, the two states generally possess overlapping interests regarding the political stability of Warsaw Pact members. The Kremlin and the SED are to be counted among the most outspoken WTO signatories in opposition to Western attempts to expand the breadth of information and popular contacts with East European Communist states through a reliance on the Helsinki Final Act. A necessary complement of this basic interest was also disclosed in Soviet and GDR support for the full harmonization of WTO strategy toward outside states and regions reflected, for example, in the 1974 East German constitution and the 1975 Soviet-East German Friendship Treaty. SED perception of the fragility of its popular acceptance, given the unresolved national question and persistent attempts at "flight from the republic,"[3] compelled the leadership to advocate preventive measures against autonomous currents that often exceeded even those contemplated by Moscow. Thus it was the Ulbricht leadership that strongly urged the use of military force against Dubcek's reforms in Czechoslovakia in mid-1968, a time when the Kremlin was exploring possible diplomatic avenues to resolve the crisis and Bonn was pursuing an active East European policy.[4] The eventual Soviet adoption of the East German solution once more gave evidence of a recurrent pattern of USSR-GDR identity of interests at times of severe confrontation with the West, as in 1958, compared with some ostensible dissension between the two in the face of Soviet detente probings, as in Khrushchev's August 1964 West German overtures and Brezhnev's 1969-1972 "Westpolitik." Soviet security apprehensions can therefore be expected to equal those of East Berlin at moments of popular unrest in the Eastern camp. The GDR leadership's narrow definition of security and its support for the Soviet role in Eastern and Central Europe, on the other hand, explain its own adherence to the "Brezhnev Doctrine." The execution of ideological and physical "Abgrenzung" vis-a-vis the Federal Republic is, of course, of more urgency to SED than Soviet decisionmakers, in view of the former's pursuance of insulation from the West that reached unparalleled levels in the years just prior to Ulbricht's removal. Soviet security apprehensions would prove hardly less pronounced, however, at moments of unrest in the Eastern camp, notably during the "Polish events" of June 1976 and August 1980 and the post-Helsinki formation of dissident groups in Eastern Europe. Under such conditions, there is little reason to suppose that Soviet-East German disputes over inner-German policy would find strong expression.

With this background to Soviet-East German relations in mind, it is now possible to examine the particular aspects or phases of the relationship in the 1973-1980 period that left their mark on inner-German relations. First, the Kremlin leadership was at pains to closely monitor its primary German concern once it had achieved its goal of ratification of the Moscow Treaty and initiation of the CSCE process. Maintaining a reliable SED ally and preserving the stability of the GDR itself with the appearance of some closer FRG-GDR popular contacts retained their high priority. The replacement of Ulbricht had reminded the SED leadership of the former, and a pragmatic, centrist-oriented Erich Honecker now occupied the two most important positions in the GDR with the third, chairmanship of the Council of State, to be added in October 1976 during a reshuffling of the party leadership. The reapportionment of positions at the Eighth SED Party Congress, the occasion of Ulbricht's departure as General Secretary, strikingly reflected the shift of the party balance of power in favor of those supporting an ideological but flexible, "scientific" and "strategic" interpretation of Marxism-Leninism.[5] This occurred despite the retention in leading positions of the so-called "Old Guard" party dogmatists such as

Politburo member Albert Norden and Friedrich Ebert of
the Volkskammer Presidium. In particular, two
newcomers to the Politburo, Honecker associates Werner
Lamberz and Werner Krolikowski, embodied the dual
approach of practical cooperation but continued
ideological "Abgrenzung" toward the FRG sanctioned at
the Twenty Fourth Party Congress in 1971. The
emergence of the "Honecker functionary" was given added
expression in the formation of the new SED Central
Committee in June 1971; almost none of the nineteen
appointed members had formerly held posts in GDR
economic agencies, where Honecker's personal
associations were more limited.[6]

As far as can be determined from public
statements, realignments of the SED hierarchy, and
Soviet policy measures, Moscow's support for the
general course of GDR policy under Honecker was never
withdrawn during this period. With regard to the
person of Erich Honecker, it was noted that on the
occasion of the October 28, 1976 reorganization of the
SED Central Committee his standing in the leadership
was rounded out with assumption of the Council of State
chairmanship. Despite the fact that the Council was
largely a body with formal powers such as receiving
diplomatic letters of accreditation and ratifying
treaties,[7] the collective impact of its prestige when
added to that of the offices of SED General Secretary
and Defence Council Chairman was to confirm Honecker's
authority as the dominant figure in the ruling elite.
Clearly much of his base of support gained through past
leading roles in the Free German Youth (FDJ) and
security apparatus[8] remained intact.

It must be emphasized, of course, that attempts to
identify domestic impulses as opposed to the direct
role of the Kremlin in internal regroupings of the SED
are usually problematical. Conclusive judgments on the
internal politics of the SED as well as Moscow's
intervention on behalf of or in opposition to certain
candidates or factions can only be inferred, not
pinpointed with certainty. In addition, arguably the
two most important SED officials after Honecker, Willi
Stoph and Guenter Mittag, received the key posts of
Council of Ministers Chairman and SED Economics
Secretary as a result of the October 1976 decision, the
first of which has reportedly gained in influence since
1972.[9] Neither of these two is indebted to Honecker for
past promotions or their cultivation of a party base of
support, as Mittag was actually demoted from the
position of SED Economics Secretary to the office of
First Assistant to the Chairman of the Council of
Ministers in 1973. Therefore, to some degree
Honecker's autonomous room for maneuver within the SED
must be said to have been held in check: it certainly
does not approximate the authority enjoyed by Ulbricht

in the 1960's, since the former East German leader had eliminated all significant opposition by 1957. Nevertheless, although perceptible challenges to the stability of the GDR might be translated into Soviet reservations about East German policy under Honecker, the General Secretary proved adaptable to changing conditions. Two instances are of particular note in this regard. With the return of Pyotr Abrassimov as Soviet ambassador to the GDR in 1975, an inner-German specialist quite committed to forestalling any autonomist currents in Warsaw Pact leaderships, the belief was strengthened that Moscow would now set more strict limits to inner-German cooperation that had intensified noticeably under Honecker's aegis, particularly after trade relations had been capped with the December 1974 "swing" package and travel improvements. The Kremlin's reported displeasure with the East German role in the "swing" negotiations,[10] however, gave way to a situation in which Soviet and East German policies increasingly converged. In the aftermath of the Helsinki Agreement, both East German actions against the Western press and alleged West German border violations in 1976, the second of which produced a lengthy Soviet as well as East German condemnation of the Federal Republic, precluded further inner-German rapprochement.[11] Honecker's acquisition of the Council of State chairmanship in October could hardly be read as a sign of Moscow's dissatisfaction with prevailing policies.

A second "crisis" in Soviet-East German relations encompassed the late 1977-1978 period. An entire series of episodes, including reports of anti-Soviet incidents in East Berlin and the Spiegel publication of the alleged "dissident manifesto," stimulated press reports of a loss of Soviet confidence in Honecker and "intershop socialism." Moscow, for its part, had to be as concerned as the SED leadership over the sometimes incalculable results of a more open East German internal policy. At the end of the same month, warnings by two Soviet generals in the East German press as well as increasing patrols by the Soviet military in West Berlin attempted to discredit the impression of an unstable GDR.[12] The East German expulsion of all Spiegel personnel, however, was a swift and decisive short-term action through which East Berlin assured the Soviet leadership of its will to prevent a public undermining of the regime. Regarding the long-term resolution, the GDR leadership introduced the April and June 1979 restrictions on journalistic activity and contacts with foreigners.

The SED's retention of Soviet confidence in the face of such problems is based on several considerations. First, it should be emphasized that Honecker, unlike his deposed predecessor, has resisted the temptation to trumpet the virtues of a unique (and superior) East German variant of established communism. Unnecessary frictions and Soviet pique over questions of prestige were thus avoided. Second, the post-1971 leadership emphasized anew its eternal fealty to the Soviet Union and has aligned its official foreign policy more closely with the Kremlin, as evidenced by the 1974 constitution and the 1975 Friendship Treaty.[13] Third, the Honecker leadership, having learned the lessons of Ulbricht's political demise, adhered to the "dual approach" to Bonn necessitated by Moscow's interest in securing West German political cooperation in defined areas. Therefore SED "Abgrenzung," whether in the form of recounting the two German states' ideological opposition or militarily reinforcing the inner-German frontier, coexisted with practical agreements and even Honecker's lofty praise for FRG-GDR economic contacts.

It would be inaccurate, of course, to suggest that Soviet confidence in the SED leadership and GDR stability was unwavering or unproblematical in this period. Nor is there reason to suppose that the historical SED fear of a possible Soviet sacrifice of "the socialist achievements of the GDR" in fulfillment of Moscow's other interests will ever be completely allayed.[14] The return of Abrassimov in 1975 can be seen as a signal to East Berlin that it could not enjoy exclusive benefits from any relationship with the Federal Republic. Differences in the Soviet and East German tactical approaches to the Berlin question as well as to the continued legal existence of "Germany as a whole" could be detected in periodic statements.[15]

Yet the readiness of the Soviet leadership to withdraw support for Ulbricht's unconditional "Abgrenzung" contrasts with its perception of the ultimate reliability of Honecker's differentiated approach to the Federal Republic. It is also probably true to say that, rather than an SED "fall from grace," the Kremlin was instead unsettled by the post-1975 developments in Eastern Europe: the formation of the Polish Workers' Committee and "Charter 77" in Czechoslovakia provided new justification for Soviet vigilance toward popular contacts with the West.

SOVIET-WEST GERMAN RELATIONS

The revised Deutschlandpolitik formulated by Willy Brandt and Egon Bahr was predicated on the assumption that "the road to East Berlin leads through Moscow," a premise validated by the Basic Treaty's conclusion only after West German ratification of the Moscow Treaty. Given the reality of a dominant Soviet influence in GDR external policy, the hopes for changes in SED behavior foreseen in Article 7 might be accomplished against the Honecker leadership's wishes, but not without Soviet assistance. The securing of such assistance did not appear impossible in the early 1970's; Kremlin pressures had apparently produced Ulbricht's ouster in 1971 specifically for his opposition to concessions to the Federal Republic and implementation of an "Abgrenzung" unsuited to the needs of the moment. The Soviet desire for Western, particularly West German, technology and trade benefits could be detected in a number of Soviet statements and has been observed by by countless authors.[16] Beyond purely economic benefits, however, General Secretary Brezhnev's utterances indicated that the Soviet leader saw some utility in making use of Bonn as a "talking partner" in Europe through the maintenance of a continuous dialogue on intimate concerns, including both global issues and European military security.[17] To the degree that such a new relationship could contribute to the loosening of the Federal Republic's ties with the United States, Soviet interests would also be served.

The realization of these mutual aims, of course, depended in large part not simply on the two states' bilateral relations but on the overall course of East-West political conflict and cooperation. Soviet pressure on the SED regime on behalf of Bonn could not be counted on even when the equivalent trade-offs existed if a simultaneous domestic unrest in the Eastern camp compelled the Kremlin to reinstate bloc discipline. East Germany, by virtue of its vulnerable position at the periphery of the FRG and its exposure to a variety of West German influences, could then expect a Soviet-imposed de-limitation and inner-German contacts would at best remain immobile, at worst contract. Another potential disturbance factor was that of West Berlin, which had by no means been resolved through the Quadripartite Agreement. While Moscow increasingly insisted that the latter understanding required Bonn to reduce all forms of "state-political links" with the city,[18] the Federal Government and Bundestag parties maintained a policy promoting official government "ties" with West Berlin.[19] Moscow's and East Berlin's doctrinal interpretations of the exact legal status of the city's western half had differed slightly in the past,[20] but both once more saw its western orientation as a security challenge to the East German state and united in objecting to a number of specific West German as well as West European ties, especially after 1975.[21]

SPD-FDP Deutschlandpolitik was also affected by one additional element, namely, the question of whether the Soviet Union or GDR was responsible for given acts of "Abgrenzung." Now that Bonn had itself established relations with East Berlin, credence was lent to Soviet suggestions that the Federal Government take up the matter of inner-German traffic, for example, with the SED leadership. In such a case, the appearance of an obstinate East German leadership could conceivably serve to improve the Soviet bargaining position vis-a-vis Bonn, or Moscow might at the least avoid accepting culpability for damaging detente with the Federal Republic.

Inner-German relations were thus no less complicated by the problem of Soviet interests in the German question than was the case prior to the Basic Treaty. Kremlin policy continued to display a deliberate ambiguity on the question of ultimate authority on the Berlin access routes even after the conclusion of the Quadripartite Agreement.[22] Because the 1971 agreement could not alter the precarious location of West Berlin 110 miles inside East German territory, West German officials exerted themselves to support the viability of the city. Given the crucial nature of this question, the Federal Government of necessity oriented its attitude toward Moscow on the basis of Soviet observance of the Berlin settlement broadly speaking. Future dispute could not be avoided in view of the continuing argument over West German ties; for Bonn the main task was to preserve physical access which had been cut in earlier East-West crises. Additionally, a serious conflict over Berlin could have prompted a resurgence of SED delimitation and a freeze or reduction of inner-German contacts, resulting also in an erosion of the domestic bases of support for the revised policy towards the GDR.

On the other hand, the West German promotion of ties with West Berlin made clear to the Kremlin that Bonn did not intend to regard this question as an "insoluble" problem which the Federal Government would no longer seriously contest, as the Soviet leadership had hoped. It is not implausible to suggest that some of the more conspicuous West German Berlin measures prior to 1977, including the 1974 opening of the Environmental Federal Office and the decision to initiate West Berlin's participation in elections to the European Parliament, allowed the SED leadership to easily gain Soviet support for "Abgrenzung" countermeasures. Among these is to be counted the January 1977 abolition of military control points between East Berlin and the outlying GDR, a move that notified Bonn that its German counterpart could also effect an interpretation of Berlin's status to its advantage. The additional deployment of police controls around the West German Permanent Mission ten days later, while more directly related to East Germans' applications for emigration and GDR charges of "internal interference," was undoubtedly facilitated by the Soviet-West German dispute over Berlin which intensified in 1976.[23]

Such developments testify to the degree to which East-West German relations were inevitably a function of the management of the Berlin problem, with both subject to the changing fortunes of East-West relations. It should be noted that travel to West Berlin and the GDR in general was not physically obstructed, as in earlier periods, but was reduced through two currency increases for travellers in 1973 and 1980. The first, as was explained earlier, was partially withdrawn in 1974. In the presence of a deterioration of Soviet-American relations after the December 1979 Soviet invasion of Afghanistan, travel to Berlin remained stable up to the announced currency increase in October 1980. The security of Berlin was thus in practice de-coupled from a potential U.S.-Soviet conflict in the Persian Gulf and an American campaign supporting economic sanctions against Moscow. Foreign Minister Genscher, of course, declared, "We expect solidarity from the United States on the Berlin question, and we shall not deny them our solidarity in the question of the Olympic Games,"[24] implying that a potentially troublesome Soviet linkage on Berlin could not be dismissed. Yet the Schmidt Government's desire to obtain a "divisibility of detente" because of its geopolitical disadvantage on the Berlin problem and the broader aims of FRG Ostpolitik had been largely fulfilled by early 1980. In light of this result, Bonn decisionmakers balanced the negative event of the Moscow-supported currency measure against relative Soviet caution toward Berlin, where the Federal Republic was also partially at a legal disadvantage.[25] It is therefore not surprising that Klaus Boelling's public enunciation of the West German refusal to cut the amount of the "swing" credit justified the decision out of a concern for the well-being of Berlin.[26]

TRAVEL AND JOURNALISTS' ACTIVITIES

Inner-German travel in the 1970's represented a genuine problem for both the East and West German leaderships. For East Berlin, the re-establishment of ties between relatives and acquaintances across the frontier could over time dilute the effectiveness of SED appeals to a separate GDR national consciousness, a program that was from the beginning handicapped by the common German heritage of those in both states. The flooding of the GDR with inhabitants from the Federal Republic would in any case have proven incompatible with East German security requirements, since the revised FRG German policy had largely removed inner-German competition from the international plane but continually reaffirmed the goal of "change through rapprochement." For the Brandt and Schmidt

Governments, travel constituted a problem in that the very success of West German policy in this area created the further public expectation that such intimacy could be sustained or even expanded. As was observed earlier, the Federal Government attributed the value of the Basic Treaty to its provision for practical cooperation based on Article 7, thus it was most vulnerable to opposition criticism that drew attention to palpable setbacks in this area.[27] Such disappointments could be identified with little difficulty due to eventful GDR travel payment increases and the Inner-German Ministry's publication of annual travel statistics. Additionally, if only a "stable" East German state would possess the confidence for a more relaxed inner-German policy, as Schmidt proposed, then SPD-FDP governments were compelled to satisfy domestic expectations at the same time that they could ill afford over-reaction to East German travel-limiting policies in an area of extreme SED sensitivity. In particular, political unrest in other Warsaw Pact states could not be openly supported by Bonn without risking abrupt East German reprisals in the inner-German traffic.

The previous chapter recorded the observation that the SPD-FDP coalition succeeded in obtaining a doubling of the number of West German travellers to East Germany, although the end of the decade saw marked declines in the totals for three of the five travel categories. While travel restrictions were gradually eased by GDR authorities, with most regular hindrances being removed by 1976, the November 1973 and October 1980 travellers' payment increases were of key importance in discouraging West German travel. In addition to their numerical impact, it is instructive to examine these two measures because they allow one to compare the Soviet as opposed to the East German interest in implementing practical de-limitation. Such an examination can also point out the unique conditions in each case that produced the actions and influenced the Federal Government's response.

To understand the background to the November 1973 decision, an evaluation of the balance sheet of Ostpolitik is demanded in addition to a survey of the inner-German relationship. Regarding the first, it should be emphasized that Soviet "Westpolitik" had seen substantial progress in already securing most of its objectives by the latter part of 1973. The successful conclusion of the 1970 Moscow Treaty, the ratification of which required the Kremlin's assent to treaty-based inner-German contacts as well as a Berlin settlement, was one such aim. The taking up of preliminary East-West talks on European security and cooperation in November 1972, an event linked to Soviet readiness to participate in Mutual and Balanced Force Reduction talks, represented a second realization of long-range Soviet policy in Europe. With respect to East Germany, the Brezhnev leadership had decisively moved against SED "chicanery" toward the Federal Republic during the last two years of Ulbricht's tenure in anticipation of Soviet-West German treaty cooperation. Once the above wider assignments were fulfilled, however, it was no longer in Soviet interests to oppose East German obstructionist measures that stopped short of making future West German flexibility impossible and which, after all, corresponded to Moscow's own policy of East European demarcation toward Western Europe.[28]

The November 1973 currency action must be understood in this context. Once the two German states had themselves signed agreements regulating inner-German travel not covered by the Quadripartite Agreement, it now followed that the Federal Government would deal more frequently, although not exclusively, with East Berlin when travel curbs were imposed by the latter. On the inner-German horizon, a number of problems had arisen in 1973 concerning travel along the Berlin-FRG access routes and West German representation of Berlin, the first of which particularly impinged on SED security perceptions. The East German Government had on September 22 threatened to re-impose controls on the transit routes following numerous incidents in which West German "escape contractors" assisted fleeing East Germans.[29] Moreover, the total amount of East German escapes in 1973, notably doctors, scientists, and professional specialists, exceeded the numbers registered for any year after the building of the Berlin Wall. This increase in "flight from the republic" was reportedly based on the belief that the Federal Government would return such East Germans to the GDR once both states were accepted for U.N. membership,[30] but it was also spurred by a somewhat more relaxed East German regulation of traffic after the December 1971 FRG-GDR traffic agreement. Four days before the GDR Foreign Ministry's announcement of the payment increases, General Secretary Honecker cited "the officially tolerated and even promoted misuse of the transit routes between the FRG and West Berlin"[31] as a particular instance of the Federal Government's failure to observe concluded treaties.

No less evident were SED reproaches against Bonn's outward maintenance and development of ties with West Berlin. East German objections peaked in the three months preceding November, although escapes along the transit routes presented a more immediate security problem for the SED regime. For example, Neues Deutschland published an August 31 commentary which condemned the foreseen West German construction of the Environmental Federal Office in West Berlin as "a crude violation of the Quadripartite Agreement,"[32] and the

GDR Foreign Ministry formally protested the plan to the West German Foreign Office two months later. In addition, Erich Honecker revived a demand formerly advanced by Ulbricht calling for "a dismantling of the Federal presence" in West Berlin in an interview four days before the currency increase.[33]

East German explanations of the travellers' payment increase, however, justified the action on the grounds of the illegal carrying of East German marks into the GDR by Westerners, the higher amount of marks needed by tourists to defray the costs of their visits, and the need to offset traveller purchases of East German goods that the GDR imported. This statement of justification also condemned the GDR mark's "swindle rate" supported by Western banks that exchanged the marks for other currencies,[34] a rate which was partially affected by the East German ban on Western travellers' transporting of additional "East marks" into East Germany. The political rationale for the action could be seen in the fall-off of visitors to the GDR and East Berlin in the months thereafter. Bonn for its part protested the action but did not permit its disappointment to disturb the convening of inner-German negotiations on environmental protection, culture, and science and technology later in the month. Indeed, the exemption of Western pensioners from the compulsory payment in November 1974 and the elimination of the greater part of the currency increase was forthcoming in December 1974, coinciding in time with the "swing" regulation and verifying that the GDR leadership's financial motivation in effecting the increase was not inconsiderable.

In the period between the November 1973 and October 1980 travellers' payment increases, the SED leadership chose to implement certain other travel restrictions; these did not prove as decisive in their impact as the above two actions, but they were applied more systematically than the usual random refusals of travel applications. One can see that the "Charter 77" movement in Czechoslovakia, which became the object of increasing Western media attention in January 1977, had an apparent East German counterpart in a movement supporting the right of citizens to emigrate.[35] GDR authorities had already by the end of 1976 moved to contain political dissent and restore cultural orthodoxy with the withdrawal of Wolf Biermann's citizenship and the house arrest of physicist Robert Havemann.[36] Following the December 1976 Bucharest meeting of the Political Advisory Committee of the Warsaw Pact, the Honecker leadership also introduced the dismantling of control points between East Berlin and the GDR and the placing of police controls around the FRG Permanent Mission.

It was in this setting that a wave of travel

curbs, first reported in December 1976, emerged into
view. Approximately 1,000 West Germans and West
Berliners were prohibited from entering the GDR and
East Berlin between January and March 14 of 1977
according to the Federal Government.[37] A clue as to SED
motivations in this matter was provided by the East
German Representative for Berlin Travel Joachim
Mitdank: of the three categories of travellers denied
permission to visit at that time, two were comprised of
former GDR inhabitants who sought reunification with
family members still in East Germany and those who had
legally resettled in the FRG but who, prior to leaving,
had "incited unrest against the state."[38] The SED thus
selectively pursued efforts to counter the emigration
movement by refusing entry permission to former East
German residents who through their example might make
emigration appear more attractive. The GDR
leadership's restrictions served both SED and Soviet
goals: both alliance obligations, in view of East
European post-Helsinki stirrings, and internal security
needs spoke for these actions. Moreover, the scale of
the curbs did not risk a breakdown in relations with
Bonn. Director of the West German Permanent Mission
Gaus, for example, at the time described the inner-
German relationship as "characterized by the attempt to
produce an equilibrium of interests through many
individual steps, an interweaving of equilibriums of
interests which neither side can rupture to its
advantage."[39]

The second increase of travellers' payments in
October 1980, as was noted earlier, also attempted to
meet both Soviet and East German concerns, this time
anticipation of the disruptive effects of the Polish
union movement. Bonn's responses to the two East
German actions are of note. From November 1973 to
November 1974, the Federal Government took no apparent
counter-action against the East German regime and
Secretary Bahr stated that "it is not sensible to
negotiate with the GDR over a modification of the
measure."[40] In the second instance, Bonn reacted with
more specificity. Again, trade sanctions were ruled
out, as West German spokesman Boelling declared that
"the unity of the nation... is not served if the
Federal Republic now counters the 'Abgrenzung' policy
of East Berlin with its own 'Abgrenzung' policy."[41]
More to the point, Boelling, in connection with a West
German response, declared that "one may do nothing
which brings additional pressure on citizens in both
German states and Berlin." He added that "existing
inner-German agreements would not be encumbered"
because of the travel measures.[42]

Nevertheless, government officials left little
doubt that progress in the FRG-GDR dialogue would
depend upon corrective policies by the GDR leadership.

It was announced that the Federal Government saw "no
reason to negotiate with the GDR over the 'swing,'"
scheduled for the spring of 1981.[43] In orienting Bonn's
future attitude towards the credit and two other
planned projects, involving the construction of brown
coal works and the electrification of GDR rail tracks,
Boelling stated that the Federal Government would "test
how the inner-German climate is then."[44] The FRG
leadership could thereby exhibit a graduated response
based on general East German accommodation; rather than
a direct issue linkage, Bonn established a "total
connection" regarding future policy toward the GDR. By
not insisting that the currency increase be fully
withdrawn for a return to normalization, it was implied
that a combination of East German steps similar to
those undertaken in late 1974 might suffice to restore
the inner-German business basis. Specific demands
were thus not made on East Berlin at a time when
developments in Poland required that the GDR elite both
show solidarity with the Soviet Union and limit the
potential for domestic disturbances.

As was indicated previously, the reaction of East
German authorities to the reporting of Western
journalists in the GDR has led to numerous official
protests by Bonn, a result to be contrasted somewhat
with SPD-FDP governments' more restrained attitude with
regard to public criticism of perceived GDR violations
of human rights standards. That East Berlin sees this
area of inner-German activity as a troublesome one is
not surprising, given the fact that since the
overwhelming majority of GDR territory can receive West
German television transmissions, one can view this as
the FRG-GDR contact over which the SED leadership has
the least control.[45] General Secretary Honecker's May
1973 statement that "frankly speaking, one can
certainly turn on or off (Western television) according
to his preference,"[46] signalled the leadership's
practical decision not to interfere with FRG
television; such interference, in any case, had proven
unsuccessful in the past.[47]

Inner-German communication is therefore probably
the weakest link in the chain of ideological
"Abgrenzung." Aside from the crucial point that East
Germans obtain Western accounts of political
developments quite at variance with those advanced in
the GDR news media, SED officials have also thereby
been compelled to comment on events that might
otherwise have been omitted from public discussion or,
as in the case of a much-publicized October 1977 youth
disturbance in East Berlin, which could have been
declared to be isolated incidents. More generally, a
lasting impact is registered on GDR television viewers
who are exposed to West German reports often quite
critical of the Federal Government, an exposure which

tends to place the GDR media in a more unfavorable light due to their unreservedly supportive attitude toward East German governmental policies. To the extent that such a comparison enhances a public impression of SED weakness, the often fragile foundation of the party's legitimacy is further called into question.

If, then, one recognizes the degree of influence that the GDR leadership relinquishes in terms of its ability to nurture citizens' identification with "the state GDR" because of unimpeded Western broadcasts, restrictive actions against FRG journalists and efforts to influence their reports are even less surprising. West German governments, acting in accordance with Schmidt's earlier-stated supposition regarding GDR stability, also took account of the formidable internal problem faced by the GDR elite in shaping their reactions to East German punitive actions against the press. Although Bonn issued formal protests and otherwise objected to press restrictions, available evidence does not suggest that the Federal Government's inner-German diplomacy substantially aimed at changing specific GDR policies in this area through the use of a "carrot" or a "stick." As State Secretary in the Chancellor's Office Boelling explained two days after the expulsion of ZDF correspondent van Loyen:

> The present development observable in the GDR touches on basic principles of freedon of the press, over which there are deep differences of opinion between East and West. We cannot solve this ideologically constrained conflict. Even countermeasures... could not change any of this. And for political and humanitarian reasons we must also consider that the working possibilities of our journalists are not the only factor that can determine our relations with the GDR. The Federal Government is obliged to perceive and to protect the totality of interests of the Federal Republic of Germany toward the GDR.[48]

Evidently, Bonn was quite concerned that such frictions should not hinder the promotion of practical inner-German cooperation. Three days after the expulsion of Spiegel correspondent Mettke, for example, the two governments signed the transportation agreement establishing a new level of lump-sum traffic payments by the FRG and the completion of transit routes between West Germany and Berlin. In another case, West German protests against the exclusion of several correspondents from the Leipzig Fair in March 1976 did not prevent the signing of a regulation of border waterways three days later. Clearly no amount of West German revulsion at these East German internal

182

practices would be allowed to stand in the way of
practical accommodation.
     East German media restrictions served to cloud the
inner-German landscape, particularly in 1979 when the
April executive decision and the July penal code opened
the possibility of surpassing ad hoc expulsions and
broadly preventing journalistic interviews. It would
nevertheless be incorrect to conclude that the Honecker
leadership always behaved in an entirely arbitrary
manner with maximum obstruction of West German
journalistic efforts in the 1973-1980 period. First,
it bears stating that the vast majority of West German
broadcasts and reporter access to public gatherings,
such as the Leipzig Fair, were not hindered by East
German authorities but were curtailed with a certain
degree of selectivity. The 1976 Leipzig Fair action,
for example, evidenced an SED refusal to admit
correspondents of the radio stations "Deutsche Welle"
and "Deutschlandfunk," an event for which reporter
permission had largely been a formality. The two
stations, together with Der Spiegel, could be
considered the East German elite's bete noire by virtue
of reporting that the SED considered excessively
critical and offensive. Since the GDR leadership had
constantly singled out these two stations in its
criticisms prior to March 1976,[49] it can be supposed
that the former was surprised at the intensity of the
Federal Government's objection to the Fair hindrance;
the introduction of further alleviations for the
Western media later in the year offers some support for
this interpretation. In addition, a "Deutschlandfunk"
correspondent was permitted to attend the next two
major political gatherings in East Germany, the May SED
Congress and the June conference of European Communist
parties.
     Second, a number of other incidents involving
journalists reflected an SED disinclination to effect a
complete deterioration of East-West German relations,
East German charges of "malicious distortions"
notwithstanding. In connection with the 1975 Spiegel
article on forced adoption, Neues Deutschland exclaimed
that "it should not be assumed that one intends to
promote the (inner-German) visitors' traffic with this
hysterical campaign against the GDR."[50] This veiled
warning was not followed by East German measures
against travellers, however. Some semblance of
restraint could even be observed in the May 1979
expulsion of Peter van Loyen. Although GDR authorities
moved swiftly against van Loyen after the Heym
"interview," the leadership took care not to expel a
more prominent member of the media. Van Loyen, who had
spent only several weeks in East Germany,[51] clearly did
not fall into this category.
     Third, East German actions against the Western

media were often excessive but were in the vast
majority of cases directly related to press reports
themselves. East Berlin generally did not seize upon
severe inner-German crises unrelated to media activity
as a pretext for sudden restrictions on media
representatives. Thus no hindrances were forthcoming
in the presence of FRG-GDR disputes over the misuse of
the Berlin access routes throughout 1973,[52] the July
1974 Environmental Federal Office controversy, or the
series of border incidents in the summer of 1976.
Inner-German travel, as was noted, could not be
insulated from such points of conflict. In particular,
the two most precipitous curtailments by the SED
leadership, the Spiegel closing and the April 1979
executive decision, resulted from the publication of
the unsettling "dissident manifesto" and the
journalistic practice of on-the-spot interviewing in
the GDR, respectively.

Finally, there is some reason to doubt the
supposition that East Berlin removed the primary
disturbance potential of Western television broadcasts
by introducing the formal limitations of 1979.
Certainly the impact of "political" events, among which
may be included interviews with dissident authors,
televised accounts of singular occurrences such as the
August 1976 self-immolation of the pastor Bruesewitz,[53]
or disturbances at East German intershops, could be
more easily contained by GDR authorities through the
enforcement of the 1979 provisions specifying
government permission. By requiring that journalists
announce in advance the destination and purpose of
visits outside East Berlin, the SED leadership gained
time for GDR security organs to arrange more sedate
surroundings from which television correspondents could
report. Nevertheless, the intangible effects of the
new East German regulations, according to ARD
television correspondent Fritz Pleitgen,[54] translated
the press restrictions into "a Pyrrhic victory" for the
GDR leadership:

> The April 1979 executive decision restricted and
> limited the possibilities to collect more authentic
> material, but the situation changed less than I had
> feared... It turned out to be more a loss of
> prestige for the GDR because we often had to say
> 'we cannot show you this event'... When I look at
> my reporting material, I am still amazed at what we
> were able to do."[55]

The shift to "a new kind of reporting... reporting the
everyday life of the people," still allowed the West
German media journalist to report on aspects of
economic life in East Germany, while a public event,
such as SED party congresses or the Leipzig Fair, could

be used "as a background illustration to get one's
message across."[56] There is reason to believe that
aired reports in which the correspondent was forbidden
to confirm a story through interviews and stated this
fact in his report still enjoyed a high degree of
credibility among the East German population. In the
words of Pleitgen, "our job was neither to stabilize
nor destabilize the GDR, but to show the reality."[57]
The West German television reporter's disinclination to
simply target the weaknesses of the East German state
together with his readiness to offer critical
assessments of West German as well as East German policies compared favorably in East German inhabitants'
eyes with the GDR media's presentation of
information.[58]

The East German leadership's refusal to provoke a
total freeze in inner-German relations through its
practices, noted earlier, could also be discerned in
its occasional post-April 1979 granting of interviews
to FRG news personnel, although this concession proved
more the exception than the rule. ARD's Pleitgen thus
produced six reports in which interviewing was
permitted after April 1979. On the other hand, "the
control was on political issues like the GDR
population's reaction to the invasion of Afghanistan or
the uproar in Poland."[59] Even in the case of the
latter, however, the April 1979 executive decision
proved insufficient to prevent August 1980 broadcasts
by ZDF on popular East German reactions to the Polish
events, giving rise to new SED apprehensions.[60] East
German efforts to alter the content of West German
television transmissions could not modify the scale of
East German popular reception of broadcasts nor, more
importantly, the long-term attractive power of a media
whose raison d'etre did not correspond to supporting
the policies of Bonn or East Berlin.

In the same way that it is difficult to judge
whether inner-German relations generally stagnated or
advanced in the 1973-1980 period, one has to exercise
caution in making the categorical statement that the
GDR was more "unstable" because of increased West
German transportation and journalistic activity at the
end of these eight years than at the outset. To begin
with, direct West German press access to events that
reflected East German popular unrest was strictly a
phenomenon of the post-Basic Treaty period; accounts of
incidents disquieting to the Ulbricht regime were
acquired mainly from secondary sources such as
emigrants to the Federal Republic or travellers to the
GDR. The greater Western information on the GDR in the
1970's might thus prompt the invalid inference that
since more such incidents were reported, their number
had increased over those in the 1960's. It should also
be recalled that due to the tenuous nature of popular

identification with the East German regime and its policies, a by far greater instability was in evidence in the earlier years of 1953 and 1961. On these occasions SED economic and social policies[1] were followed by a broadly-based uprising in the first case and a massive flight fron the GDR in the second. It may therefore be argued that the leadership's internal policies would continue to create a strong impetus for dissatisfaction with or without a high level of inner-German contacts, although the latter surely contributes to popular comparisons of the two German states and the Honecker leadership did not preside over the draconian social and economic restructuring imposed under Ulbricht.

Despite the difficulty of drawing a defensible conclusion on this question, one may be arrived at by viewing the perceptions of the GDR and Soviet leaderships as they can be detected in government actions. That the GDR elite saw an excessive risk in permitting Western-style television reporting from East Germany, especially interviewing, was confirmed by the April 1979 executive decision; the magnitude of its success in thereby containing the FRG media's independent influence is open to question. However, in order not to overstate the Honecker leadership's vulnerability to inner-German contacts, it must be stated that the irreversible October 1980 setback in East-West German travel did not result from the cumulative impact of annual travel unsettling the SED. As was explained earlier, East Berlin had successfully limited and even reduced visits by young East Germans to the Federal Republic, urgent family visits, and the border-district traffic. As West German statements testified, this did not diminish the eagerness of the FRG leadership for a Schmidt-Honecker meeting. Rather than perceiving an East German state destabilized by West German visitors by 1980, the Honecker leadership evidently acted in concert with the Kremlin to remove the possibility of ripple effects from the Polish labor movement. Not surprisingly, the October travellers' payment increase was accompanied by a severe curtailment of East German-Polish border travel.[2]

From these observations, it is clear that the potential instability of the GDR was even greater than during the "Prague Spring" of 1968 because of the additional element of intensified East-West German contacts and the Helsinki Agreement; the contacts themselves were nevertheless insufficient to provoke the SED measures against West German and West Berlin travellers until the "Polish events." Moreover, the problem of GDR popular unrest had not assumed such proportions that Moscow would risk the relationship with the FRG, whose assistance was desired all the more after new U.S. attempts to restrict exports to the

Soviet Union.[63] On the basis of past Soviet military interventions in East Germany, Hungary, and Czechoslovakia as well as the Kremlin's often-expressed doctrine of "limited sovereignty,"[64] there is little doubt but that a genuine undermining of the GDR regime after 1973 would have been followed by a similar Soviet and East European military action. Short of this event, however, Soviet assessments of GDR stability were necessarily related to other concerns. While the Kremlin clearly perceived post-Helsinki stirrings in East Germany and either devised or supported SED "Abgrenzung" measures, internal unrest had not manifested itself to a degree that would dictate reversing the progress in all inner-German cooperative areas. The need to continue a dialogue with Bonn in the area of security and trade, a policy personally pursued by Brezhnev, contributed to Moscow's forbearance.

The Kremlin could also be reassured that Honecker, unlike Ulbricht, exhibited an agile adjustment to the turns in Soviet policy. While "intershop socialism" may have departed slightly from the prototype of established Soviet communism, the fact that it was initiated in the GDR was testimony to a Soviet preference for sacrificing socialist orthodoxy where, by doing so, popular approval of the Warsaw Pact client regimes might be enhanced.[65]

TRADE AND LINKAGE

In the preceding chapter, it was observed that West German governments under Brandt and Schmidt refrained from the cutting of a considerable inner-German trade to counter objectionable East German practices. The GDR continued to benefit from the interest-free credit of 850 million DM per year established in late 1974 as well as the Federal Government's taxing incentives for the trade discussed earlier.

Nevertheless, the real rate of increase of inner-German trade declined in the 1970's over the 1960's, attributable to higher inflation rates in the later decade, West German budgetary limitations and trade controls, and an East German avoidance of unnecessary reliance on Bonn. At second glance, it is apparent that there were some additional political motivations for the containment of the trade on the West German side. Several of these surfaced during Economics Minister Lambsdorff's visit to the Leipzig Fair in March 1979, where both Lambsdorff and GDR Foreign Trade Minister Soelle proposed long-term inner-German trade agreements. The West German Minister later indicated to reporters that the 1951 Berlin Agreement "must

continue to be the basis for inner-German economic
relations."⁶⁶ Although Lambsdorff had himself suggested
a FRG-GDR trade pact similar to the 25-year treaty
concluded between the Federal Republic and Soviet Union
a year earlier, the Berlin framework has not been
deviated from to this day.

Two primary West German interests have clearly
inhibited movement on this front. The Basic Treaty's
specification that the trade would continue "on the
basis of the existing agreements" had given priority to
the Federal conception of "special" East-West German
relations. In retrospect, a new inner-German
"framework agreement" for trade might not have been
easily distinguishable from those concluded with other
COMECON states and therefore could have lent credence
to the notion that the GDR was being treated as a
foreign land. Just as critical a factor in the West
German decision, however, was the probability that the
inclusion of West Berlin would not have been automatic
as in the 1951 agreement, particularly in view of the
numerous post-1974 Soviet and East German protests
against continued Federal ties with the city.

Other dampening influences on the trade consisted
of a shortage of GDR units of account due to a lack of
hard currency⁶⁷ as well as the fact that the trade's
volume was also determined by private West German
firms' calculations of benefit. The Federal Government
could stimulate inner-German exchanges through tax and
credit incentives but individual arrangements depended
on the responsiveness of business.⁶⁸ As for East
Germany, both private consumption and payments for
Soviet oil and Polish coal, made primarily through East
German exports of machinery, have limited SED
possibilities for additional imports from the FRG
without creating a trade imbalance.⁶⁹

There is considerable support for the argument
that the total psychological connection between West
German trade credits and East German alleviations in
travel was tacitly observed by both German governments.
This mutual understanding not only was reflected in the
expanded "swing" regulation of December 1974,
intentionally announced a week after GDR exemption of
West German pensioners and youth from travel payment
requirements, but persisted in the post-1974 period.
The Federal Government continued to bestow the "swing"
at its 1975 level while East Berlin imposed only
selective travel restrictions until the October 1980
currency measure. Bonn thus abstained from retaliating
economically against GDR cutbacks in East Germans'
border-district travel and urgent family meetings,
since the general travel payments remained the same, in
the same way that the Erhard Government ruled out the
cancellation of inner-German trade short of a complete
interruption of West German access to Berlin. Periodic

travel curbs, such as the August 1976 East German
transit ban on CDU/CSU youth busses headed for Berlin,
were also not grounds for economic sanctions, although
some members of the West German opposition contemplated
this type of counter-measure.[70]

At the same time, it cannot be excluded that the
West German leadership's continuation of the "swing"
was geared to the broad range of SED behavior toward
the FRG rather than the single issue of travel. As
Boelling confirmed in October 1980, the Federal
Government was inclined to consider future trade
prospects in line with the overall inner-German
"climate." It is important to recognize that although
the trade credit was not once cut in this period, nor
was it adjusted according to the often steep inflation
increases of the 1974-1980 period that impacted
directly on the GDR economy.[71] Indeed, if one employs
the more liberal formula granted by Bonn in 1968 for
calculating its extension of the "swing," namely, 25%
of East German deliveries to the FRG for the previous
year, the credit would have risen to approximately 980
million DM in 1977 and 1.2 billion DM in 1980. Instead
the fixed December 1974 rate was maintained for the
entire period, even in the presence of indications that
East Berlin was displeased with this ceiling and
attempted to negotiate a larger annual amount.[72]

The SED elite nevertheless had reason to be
pleased with the unfolding of the trade, given the
"special" concessions extended as well as Bonn's
unwillingness to exert outright economic pressure in
pursuance of political objectives. Moreover, the
balancing of its trade with the Federal Republic by
1980 aided in the management of GDR debt, which in this
last year could still be covered by approximately two-
thirds of East German deliveries.[73]

DIPLOMATIC STATUS AND REPRESENTATION OF GERMANS

Wilhelm Kewenig, a noted commentator on legal
aspects of the German question, observed that while the
Brandt Government perceived the Basic Treaty as
possessing "instrumental" value in pursuance of
intensified practical inner-Germam contacts, for East
Berlin it contained primarily "exchange" value in
securing West German acknowledgment of the GDR's
existence as an independent state.[74] Having attained
less than an unqualified FRG recognition of the latter,
however, it followed that the treaty was assigned an
instrumental function for the East German leadership as
well in that it could be utilized as a platform for
Bonn's eventual cession of full or "lasting
recognition." In the absence of such an upgrading of
status, some East German purposes could be fulfilled

through third states' recognition of the GDR.
In addition, it has been widely remarked that the
GDR leadership's program for the attainment of
international recognition in the 1970's was motivated
in part by a belief that SED attempts to foster an
authentic East German national consciousness, and thus
GDR stability, could be served through such a policy.[75]
In line with this assertion, it must also be supposed
that East Berlin was no less interested in employing
the improvement of its international position for
maximum effect upon the external policy of the Federal
Republic. As was noted earlier, East and West German
governments continued to support the notions of
"international" and "special" inner-German relations,
respectively, a dichotomy which was already
foreshadowed in the Basic Treaty's open-ended reference
to "the national question." The "Karlsruhe Decision"
provided a workable, if legally inconsistent, policy
framework within which Bonn could deal with the GDR as
a state but one without all the attributes of statehood
under international law, notably citizenship. Erich
Honecker, on the other hand, continued to advance the
separate East German citizenship and, despite the Basic
Treaty's designation of the inner-German
representatives as "Directors" of the Permanent
Missions, East German pronouncements often referred to
the GDR Director as "Ambassador Moldt."[76]
However, there is less evidence that the SED
leadership presented its demands for a full upgrading
of the Missions into embassies as an item for serious
negotiation with Bonn. To be sure, the avowed desire
to wrest a change in the West German position could be
found in several East German declarations, the most
forceful of which was Honecker's October 1980 Gera
speech. Yet East German leaders were made aware of
non-negotiable West German requirements in this
matter.[77] An exchange of embassies would have
represented an evident breach of the Basic Law's
reunification imperative, in contrast to the Basic
Treaty formula which could be defended on the grounds
of its protection of a number of West German legal
provisos. It is also true that the treaty, by virtue
of its ambiguity, has already provided the SED with
arguments to the effect that Bonn has adopted
international relations with the GDR for internal
consumption. While the GDR leadership clearly
perceived gains in securing "lasting" recognition from
the Federal Republic, it would also have to reckon with
the negative effects arising from the loss of its
status as a silent member of the EEC. Since the Rome
Treaty's characterization of FRG-GDR trade as "internal
German trade" would surely disappear with an inner-
German exchange of embassies, the East German state
would thereby forfeit its exemption from EEC import

levies and the application of the high Community internal agricultural price to GDR commodities.[78]

Closely related to the issue of international recognition is the SED's demand for the recognition or "respecting" of a GDR citizenship, another issue which was not subject to East or West German trade-offs. Indeed, in 1977 the SED General Secretary stated, "For us the question of citizenship is not fundamentally a question for negotiation," and Federal Minister Franke expressed an identical West German position.[79] The fact that no legal assistance agreement could be reached due to the impasse in this area testified to the limited room for concessions on both sides. In a sense, Bonn had by 1973 already moved in the direction of "respecting" an East German citizenship by setting limits to the Federal Republic's sovereign jurisdiction. East Germans, who were still considered Germans within the meaning of Articles 16 and 116 of the Basic Law, could only pursue West German legal rights "when in the protective area of the FRG."[80]

Aside from the desire to continue to promote German national unity, an essential consideration that militated against a modification of Federal citizenship policy was support for the concept of durable ties between the FRG and West Berlin. Occasional suggestions for the creation of separate East and West German citizenships under the "roof" of a still-existing All-German citizenship[81] obviously could not be envisioned without also assessing the likely effects of such a measure on the East German population, for whom FRG governments have never abandoned their pledges of solicitude. Equally, the Brandt and Schmidt Governments could not ignore the possibility that separate citizenships would further blur the visibility of West German ties to West Berlin, which were based on a delegation of the Western Powers' rights and responsibilities and possessed little legal existence aside from that. It is also doubtful that direct recognition of a GDR citizenship would have been viewed as any less of a transgression of the reunification imperative than an East-West German exchange of embassies.

East German pronouncements also provide support for the contention that East Berlin neither anticipated nor made strenuous efforts to force an alteration of West German policy here. A more likely conclusion is that the GDR leadership submitted its claim simply to avoid extending concessions to Bonn at times of extreme SED insecurity. During the August 1980 Polish upheaval, for example, Erich Honecker declared that the GDR would only lower the travel age for East German visits to the FRG upon West German recognition of the GDR citizenship. The General Secretary added, however, that Bonn's refusal to do so"does not hinder the GDR from behaving generously in humanitarian matters."[82] (emphasis added). West German agreement was thus not portrayed as an indispensable East German desideratum, rather, the East Berlin leadership was drawing attention to its inability or unwillingness to permit travel alleviations in the presence of political unrest in a neighboring WTO state. Similarly, an earlier linkage of travel improvements to FRG recognition of the GDR citizenship in early 1977 coincided in time with reports of numerous applications for emigration from East Germany and a surfacing of dissident protest.[83] In short, East German calls for an upgrading of status did not produce tangible consequences in the aftermath of the Basic Treaty; since this was "not a question for negotiation," demands were issued instead as an intentional stumbling block to SED concessions.

A related aspect of this question did, however, give rise to a more concrete policy dispute between the two German states. Attempts by West German Foreign Minister Genscher to prevent the signing of an Austrian-East German consular treaty that recognized a GDR citizenship ultimately failed, not least of all because of issues at stake that were vital to Vienna.[84] The problem was in its essence less a question of citizenship than, as an East German protest of Bonn's action proclaimed, one relating to the interference of one German state in the external affairs of the other. East Berlin claimed with some plausibility that the Federal Government had violated Basic Treaty Articles 2, 4, and 6 through its active opposition to the treaty.[85]

Austrian Chancellor Bruno Kreisky's blunt refusal to drop his government's recognition of the East German citizenship from the concluded treaty was followed three months later by a Finnish-GDR consular treaty with a similar citizenship provision. In addition, continued East German opposition to the West German extension of legal and consular assistance to East Germans, a priority reflected in Honecker's Gera speech, underscored the disinclination of both governments to compromise on this application of Article 4. Yet the Federal Government obtained a workable, albeit not ideal, validation of its position after the 1975 events. Austrian officials provided assurances that they would continue to observe U.N. regulations regarding the granting of asylum and would not hinder anyone seeking assistance in the West German Vienna embassy. No comparable West German dispute with a third state on this issue emerged after Genscher's intervention in the Austrian capital; West European states, in particular, have upheld the West German right to represent East Germans in Western capitals, although Bonn has not universally succeeded in acquiring the formal affirmation of this prerogative such as that announced by the British Government in 1976. Rather, it has quietly pursued the representation of GDR inhabitants without involving the host country in inner-German quarrels.

In conclusion, it is evident that since Bonn no longer opposed third states' adoption of diplomatic relations with East Berlin nor East German membership in international organizations, international attempts to fortify the notion of All-German unity expressed in the Basic Law have largely been confined to the consular sphere. The SED leadership's drive to gain international recognition of a GDR citizenship via consular treaties and lend practical effect to national "Abgrenzung" produced ambiguous results. The citizenship was in fact recognized by Western states but without a GDR monopoly on representation of its citizens when the latter sought the assistance of the Federal Republic.

BORDER DISPUTES

In the presence of some quite significant changes in inner-German relations after Willy Brandt's accession to the chancellorship, the continued physical "Abgrenzung" of the FRG-GDR border represents the aspect of the relationship that has changed the least since Ulbricht's removal as General Secretary. Indeed, due to the potentially attractive power of Brandt's "unity of the nation" thesis as well as the de facto expansion of contacts of GDR inhabitants with West Germans, the perfection of East German defense fortifications and policing methods emerged as an even more urgent priority, lest the porous tendencies of the East German state so visible in 1960-1961 reappear. Inasmuch as the SPD-FDP's more receptive policy toward East Berlin encumbered the SED leadership's attempts to portray the Federal Republic as a hostile capitalist state, periodic border incidents provided the latter with convenient opportunities to proclaim intentional West German violations of GDR sovereign rights. East German decisionmakers thereby hoped that such a representation of events could be a long-term spur to GDR national cohesion. A fundamental precept of SED postwar internal policy was this sustained attempt to mold a separate East German identity by emphasizing the external pressures on the GDR from the West, an allegation of hostility that was intimately connected with the leadership's declaration of the ideological oppositions of capitalism and socialism.

The problems relating to the inner-German frontier, however, must also be seen in the broader context of the legal character of the postwar European boundaries as well as Soviet and East German definitions of security, the last of which is based on a number of psychological perceptions. Article 3 of the Basic Treaty confirmed the "inviolability" of the FRG-GDR border and Article 6 limited the sovereign jurisdiction of each to its "state territory," although it should be noted that the treaty omitted the reference to "state frontiers" that was included in the 1969 Ulbricht draft treaty. The Helsinki Agreement, additionally, produced a wider international recognition of the inviolability of post-1945 European frontiers. Yet the resolution of differences on this matter was obviously not viewed with total satisfaction by Moscow as well as East Berlin, given West German provisos concerning the status of the border and post-Helsinki developments in Eastern Europe.

It is instructive to observe that perhaps the most extended Soviet article on inner-German relations appearing in the East German press, a January 1974 entry by J. Rshewski in the journal _Mezhdunarodnaja Zhizn_,[86] attacked in some detail the "Karlsruhe Decision's" characterization of the inner-German frontier as similar to those running between the West German Laender. After citing Basic Treaty Articles 2 and 3, the first of which invokes the aims of the U.N. Charter, the article reads:

> Thus the FRG has undertaken the obligation to respect the non-infringement of the border with the GDR within the meaning of the fundamental aims and principles of international law. In opposition to these, the domestic law of the FRG is completely irrelevant."[87]

The use of the term "non-infringement" instead of "inviolability" (Unverletztlichkeit), the literal designation in the Basic Treaty, was further justified by the author by reference to Bonn's respecting of borders and commitment to conclude a treaty with East Germany contained in the Moscow Treaty. After remarking that the West German attempt to expand contacts between inhabitants of the two states equalled a policy to overcome the "common frontier... in a reorganization of Germany," Rshewski asserted that

> The Federal judges have the presumption to support the government of the FRG right down to the end... in its claim to change the existing order of protection of the frontier of the GDR. Nothing further needs to be said."[88]

The author's rejection of the concept of "special" inner-German relations and espousal of the concept of "two sovereign German states" later in the article rebutted the July 1973 judicial decision and formed a unified whole in the sense that a fully sovereign East German state could not possess less than sovereign borders.

Subsequent Soviet reactions to border incidents were quite consistent with Rshewski's rejoinder to the "Karlsruhe Decision." In the summer of 1976, a series of gradually escalating inner-German border incidents surfaced in July as mutual East and West German recriminations appeared with unusual sharpness and regularity. On July 24, three West German tourists were apprehended by East German border guards near the frontier and a Hamburg resident was shot and apprehended by guards after unknowingly crossing into GDR territory. (He was returned to West Germany two days later). As was the practice during instances of GDR press curbs, the Director of the FRG Permanent Mission delivered a protest to the GDR Foreign Ministry over these developments, which promptly occasioned an East German counter-protest "against the increasingly provocative violations of the state frontier of the GDR from the territory of the FRG."[89]

In August, however, the Soviet news media began to exhibit a lively interest in these inner-German developments, an event noteworthy in view of the fact that scant attention had customarily been paid to the two German states' relations in the 1973-1980 period.[90] On August 1, both Pravda and Moscow Radio supported the East German criticisms of the Federal Government's role in the border disputes. Significantly, the Soviet publication New Times in condemning West German border "provocations" echoed Rshewski's condemnation of the "Karlsruhe Decision"; the "nationalistic slogans" in the Federal Republic for "making the frontier to the GDR penetrable" were linked with the Karlsruhe judges' portrayal of the frontier as a Laender boundary.[91]

With reference to one particular incident, the article continued:

> However, there is nothing accidental in the West German border violations. They represent a logical consequence of attempts to present the FRG-GDR border as an 'inner-German border' in violation of treaty obligations and, based on this deceitful pretext, to bring into doubt the right of the GDR to protection of the non-infringement of its territory."[92]

On August 6, New Times this time accused "West German reactionaries" of "discrediting the positive gains that have been achieved in the relations between the Federal Republic of Germany and the GDR,"[93] with similar press criticisms of West German border hostility on August 11 and 12. Finally, both the Moscow radio station "Peace and Progress" and the Soviet ambassador to East Germany offered lengthy support for the earlier East German turning back of CDU/CSU youth busses headed for Berlin on August 21 and August 28.

Such Soviet interest tended to reinforce the impression that this was not simply a matter of GDR sovereign rights in regulating affairs internally, although the principle was certainly underscored in the Soviet declarations and has gained sustained Soviet support. Moscow's concern for guarantees of the Warsaw Pact states' external security, of which a key element is the recognition of state frontiers, had obviously deepened in the face of labor upheaval in neighboring Poland during these months. The June 25 rescinding of food price increases by the Gierek Government after strikes by Polish workers mirrored the precarious state of political conditions that might see their impact in the GDR'[4] As late as September 18, press reports still depicted an uneasy resolution of the crisis in the aftermath of the workers' actions.'[5] Soviet support for the "state quality" of the inner-German frontier therefore had to be registered at this moment in view of Bonn's alternate conception which did not view the border as immutable.

East Berlin, which reprinted each of the Soviet criticisms of West German "provocations" in GDR dailies, once more found its external policy converging with the Kremlin's at a time of some tension within the Eastern camp. The domestic objective of presenting the image of a "revanchist" Federal Republic to East German inhabitants was also to be served through ADN's announcements regarding intentional West German incursions. In addition, both the Kremlin and the SED showed little concern that activities such as GDR border guards' apprehension of West Germans might mobilize national sentiments in the FRG that could benefit the CDU/CSU in the upcoming election; it became obvious that the sensitivity of security issues prevailed over any desire to support a particular West German "talking partner."

East German priorities were clearly defined with respect to inevitable incidents along the inner-German border. Hand in hand with reliance on the Soviet Union in the external sphere was the perceived need to deter East German escapes, ward off unexpected intrusions by West German inhabitants into GDR territory, and maintain and strengthen the effectiveness and loyalty of the approximately 160,000 troops of the National People's Army. In fulfillment of these three complementary objectives, the GDR ruling elite did not wait for the attractive power of Brandt's inner-German program to take effect but adopted immediate steps along the common frontier in an effort to reduce the number of uncontrollable elements in East German life. One of these initial measures reportedly consisted of a

fundamental reorganization of the East German border
troops toward greater centralization of authority in
the summer of 1973. Four operational commands were now
to supervise the work of the eleven frontier brigades,
with a corresponding major-general for each command and
the placing of a lieutenant general in charge of the
entire force. The two independent units responsible
for the borders with Poland and Czechoslovakia remained
separate from this organizational structure.[96]
    With regard to the physical penetrability of the
inner-German frontier, the beginning of 1974 saw the
levelling of buildings in its vicinity which had
visually obstructed the border guard's line of fire.
GDR demolition crews, according to the conservative
daily <u>Die Welt</u>, were set to work along a 140-kilometer
stretch of the Mecklenburg border; several villages in
this region were reported to be dismantled altogether
in order to prevent concealment of those fleeing East
Germany.[97] Simultaneously, border fortifications were
constructed anew in other border-proximate areas and,
in areas of Lower Saxony, were continued through the
summer of 1974. GDR authorities introduced new
electronic monitoring devices, cement observation
points, and "forward command points" to facilitate the
insertion of GDR alert troops at times of unauthorized
border crossings. Broader measures for instilling a
miltary consciousness in the East German population
included a September 1978 conscription regulation which
for the first time obligated ninth and tenth grade
students to participate in military training as well as
GDR passage the next month of a "Law for the Defense of
the GDR." The latter contained provisions for
exercises in civil defense and assigned to the National
Defense Council "the central direction of defense and
security measures." Hitherto existing directives had
empowered the Council of State with this authority.[98]
    The intent of these preventive measures
corresponded to the SED desire to neutralize the
effects of expanded West German travel into the GDR as
well as the results of a "creeping detente" that might
thwart attempts to portray the West German state to
East German inhabitants as a hostile counterpart. The
somewhat more relaxed East German travel policy on the
Berlin access routes, as was noted earlier, also
undoubtedly gave rise to East Berlin's apprehensions
regarding the flight of younger, skilled East Germans
from the GDR. The augmentation of double barbed-wire
fences, guard dogs, and automatic shooting devices did
not end in the 1973-1974 period but continued apace,
with annual increases from 5-20% in such categories in
1978 over 1977, for example.[99]
    Although Bonn condemned the increasing perfection
and deadliness of this policy,[100] which still resulted
in the deaths of some Germans yearly, one irony of this

state of affairs was that the very success of such SED measures removed some points of friction from the East-West German agenda. GDR border guards, because of intensified surveillance and physical obstructions to escape, increasingly apprehended those fleeing the state before they had reached the actual frontier.[101] By the late 1970's the more dramatic instances of wounded or slain East Germans had been reduced mainly through unilateral SED "Abgrenzung," since the East German leadership refused to discuss border incidents in the Frontier Commission. It was reported that between August 1976, the month of a fatal shooting of an Italian truck driver, and mid-1980, no shots had been fired across the entire inner-German frontier.[102] In fact, the later GDR "frontier law" of March 25, 1982 explicitly forebade the firing of shots into a neighboring state by guards.[103] There is little question but that the formidable dimensions of escape across the inner-German border were a clear deterrent factor, reflected in the realization that in the first four months of 1980, less than 10% of those "illegally" fleeing the GDR utilized this escape route.[104] Also of some consequence was the reduced probability of accidental border intrusions from the West German side, given the November 1978 Frontier Protocol between the two German states which initiated the use of more visible land and water border markers.

That the ambiguous treaty and judicial provisions regarding the inner-German border had not removed some of the traditional vestiges of jurisdictional differences was verified by the persisting problem of the West German "Central Survey Agency" in Salzgitter. The work of the Agency, which has operated as an office of the Justice Ministry of Lower Saxony, consisted of collecting information on such events as escape attempts in East German border areas, the apprehension and trial of those targeted by the GDR leadership for political reasons, and acts of violence committed against East German inhabitants by GDR security personnel. A more far-reaching aspect of its work has also been the one most objected to by East Berlin, namely, the introduction into East German courts of preliminary judicial inquiries against GDR agencies for harsh rulings against East Germans, especially those convicted on political grounds. 16,000 such inquiries were introduced by the Agency between 1961 and 1974, and in two cases West German court actions were initiated against East German convictions.[105]

The GDR leadership has protested the activities of the Agency in a number of cases and constantly called for its elimination, the most recent of which was General Secretary Honecker's 1980 Gera speech. The institution was criticized for "open encouragement of the misuse of the transit routes of the GDR" through its intercession on behalf of West German "escape contractors," but the central objection was that its judicial inquiries represented the attempt to apply the jurisdiction of the Federal Republic to the GDR, since the Agency's activities were based on the FRG penal book. Protests of the East German Foreign Ministry charged West German officials with violation of the Basic Treaty and the Helsinki Final Act, specifically for its "presumption" of the applicability of FRG jurisdiction, "a crude interference in the internal affairs of the GDR," and demanded its disbandment.[106]

The frequency and timing of the East German charges give some indication of SED motivations here. In the face of controversial issues that touched GDR security interests, the inner-German frontier became a special point of vulnerability and thus of SED demands that West German "interference" there be removed. This could be seen in the fact that on two of the four occasions when the Agency's border activities were condemned, other urgent East German and Soviet concerns were at issue: the July 1974 Environmental Federal Office dispute and the Polish labor upheaval in late 1980. Perceived or possible West German border practices that grated on the Honecker's leadership's sensitivities and claims to state autonomy thus had to be countered. Yet during the two periods of less direct confrontation in early 1975 and 1976, East German protests were direct responses to statements or actions by Agency officials; the latter either published documents to be submitted as legal inquiries, or, as in the second case, announced the intention to pursue additional inquiries.[107] Although East German attacks on the Agency did appear in the 1973-1980 period, there were large gaps in time between each protest and little reason to suspect that this controversy, also partially a doctrinal question,[108] developed into an issue to be negotiated. Honecker's designation of the abolition of the Agency as a "Gera demand" was, not surprisingly, packaged with other items that were non-negotiable for Bonn, such as recognition of a GDR citizenship and an exchange of embassies.

A CONCLUDING ASSESSMENT OF THE POST-BASIC TREATY PERIOD

One who takes a careful look at the East-West German relationship over this eight-year period faces a sometimes bewildering patchwork of high-level consultations and agreements that often coincide with intense espionage campaigns, charges of internal and external interference, and sustained border disputes. The 1973-1975 period, the "take-off" stage for most of the practical agreements achieved, also saw an

arbitrary increase in payments for Western visitors to
the GDR as well as the uncovering of an East German spy
whose activities would contribute to Willy Brandt's
resignation. GDR retaliation against the destabilizing
effects of the Helsinki Final Act and FRG Berlin policy
contributed to an inner-German impasse from 1976 to
1979, but West German travel to East Germany peaked in
1978 along with the concluding of significant inner-
German frontier and transportation agreements. The
absence of a seamless web in bilateral relations
together with the intrusion of East-West developments
into the inner-German picture frustrate attempts to
identify distinct phases in the evolution of the
relationship with extreme precision.

However, to begin to understand the actions and
programs of the two leaderships, one must proceed from
postwar "givens." With respect to the Soviet Union and
its East German ally, the harmonization of foreign
policies in the post-Basic Treaty period underscored
the fundamental continuity of the relationship. This
was reflected not only in outward symbolic measures,
such as the 1975 Friendship Treaty and intensive joint
institutionalized contacts between the two states, but
also in their respective approaches to the Federal
Republic. SED measures continued to promote the
ideological as well as physical "Abgrenzung" of the two
German states but also accommodated Soviet cultivation
of the West German "talking partner" through frequent
verbal praise for FRG-GDR relations and receptivity to
some mutual inner-German undertakings that were of some
economic value to East Germany. The support of this
"dual track" by East German decisionmakers clearly
suited Soviet requirements and was forthcoming even
though East Berlin had a far more single-minded
apprehension over West German penetration of the GDR
than the Kremlin; it therefore did not always gain
Soviet assistance in its periodic maximal threats to,
for example, disrupt the West German-Berlin traffic.

This slightly divergent perspective
notwithstanding, the Soviet leadership was compelled to
recognize that the GDR leadership's grip could become
less secure not only through inner-German contacts that
might regenerate All-German sentiments but also through
prolonged economic stagnation. This reality introduced
an inherent tension into Soviet policy that aimed at
consolidating the GDR. Decisions such as the 1975
increase in the price of Soviet raw materials to East
Germany indicated that the Honecker leadership could
not count on its patron to continually shield it from
the effects of more expensive vital resources. The
experience of early 1980 confirmed that the Federal
Government would look favorably upon the filling of
some East German economic gaps, even in the presence of
a harsh East-West climate. Yet the obvious quid pro

quo for such West German assistance, as SPD-FDP
governments publicly emphasized, could only have
consisted of eased GDR travel provisions, which both
Communist states viewed as a potential danger. Even
before the "Polish events" of 1980 and the October SED
currency measure, it had become clear that the choice
was made to avoid the latter risk. East Berlin
permitted neither an increase in East German travel
westward in urgent family cases nor agreed to a
lowering of the age for pensioner and youth travel to
the FRG, although both constituted preconditions for
envisioned economic projects.

A certain consistency could be detected in West
German responses to these setbacks. Given that the
founding premise of Brandt's Ostpolitik excluded Bonn's
unilateral attempt to alter the postwar arrangement of
frontiers in Europe and, by extension, Soviet primacy
in the GDR, Social Democratic-Free Democratic policy
renounced efforts to change East German internal
practices in ways that could be interpreted by Moscow
and East Berlin as programs to undermine or dismantle
the GDR political system. Although both Soviet and SED
announcements tended to favor the inner-German policies
conducted under Brandt and Schmidt over those of the
West German opposition, frequently ascribing periodic
"anti-Communist hysteria" in the Federal Republic to
the CDU/CSU,[109] both Communist leaderships were well
aware of the outline for social and political change in
the GDR contained in Egon Bahr's "change through
rapprochement" formula. Bonn's inner-German policy
was therefore confined to encouraging somewhat more
undramatic, long-range changes in GDR internal
conditions. In pursuance of such change, SPD-FDP
governments abstained from engaging in tit-for-tat
confrontation with the GDR over given East German
actions. Rather, the cumulative impact of inner-German
contacts, notably those of communication, travel, and a
certain amount of financial assistance, was considered
to hold the only possibility for a more liberal SED
policy.

Bonn therefore sought other means with which to
promote the form, if not the substance, of German unity
and Federal empathy for GDR inhabitants. The sustained
adherence to the principle of one German citizenship,
automatically bestowed on East Germans taking up
residence in the FRG, the West German judiciary's
support for the legality of escape contracts, Federal
consular and legal assistance for East Germans in third
states, the issuance of West German papers to GDR
inhabitants visiting the Federal Republic-- these steps
were adopted by the West German Government to lend
legal force to practical and humanitarian activities.

Yet the contradictions to be perceived in such a
policy are rooted in Chancellor Schmidt's remark that

"detente policy is only possible when both partners are stable."[110] As the October 1980 events confirmed, it is impossible to speak of an inner-German detente if the GDR's eastern neighbors are unstable, given the forward geopolitical position of the East German state. Furthermore, unchecked bilateral communication and personal contacts could not help but engender tensions in the GDR in the presence of a gap in FRG-GDR living standards, an impression continually conveyed by the West German "electronic media," and the failure of the SED to create a lasting and separate East German consciousness. SED insecurity, as evidenced in July-August 1976, January 1978, and April-June 1979, is therefore enhanced by both internal and external disturbing factors, with adverse impacts on both West German Deutschlandpolitik and East German liberalization. One can therefore recognize that if the dynamics of inner-German contacts are not sufficiently calculable or containable for East Berlin and Moscow, FRG-GDR "detente" becomes self-defeating.

The paradox in the two states' relationship thus lies in acknowledging that despite Bahr's formula, it is doubtful that too great an expansion of inner-German popular contacts would ultimately have been to Bonn's advantage. At worst, a Soviet military intervention to prevent destabilization of the GDR would have reversed the post-1973 cooperation policy; at best, SED measures to regain control over internal developments would have placed new restrictions on GDR inhabitants. Such a recognition illuminates the necessarily long-range focus of the Federal Republic's German policy and also renders understandable the somewhat more cautious policy conducted by Brandt's successor. Although the latter has been attributed to Schmidt's overriding preference for relations with the West,[111] it was also related to the genesis of a new phase when the SED leadership was compelled to adjust to a, in many ways, threatening West German opening to the GDR. This dictated considerable forbearance on the part of Bonn, with Schmidt serving as "caretaker" of Brandt's treaty-based policy toward East Germany.

A second unavoidable problem with the relationship in this period concerned the matter of ends. Pierre Hassner's reference to detente as a condition "within the framework of a competition whose goals are less and less tangible"[112] suitably describes post-1973 inner-German relations, particularly from Bonn's perspective. For it was difficult to foresee with precision the goals of future Deutschlandpolitik once the East-West German "business basis," including mutual representation, entry into the United Nations, and some "special" economic arrangements, had been laid alongside the traditionally differing conceptions of the two leaderships. Regardless of a general perception of increased flexibility of both governing elites, each was at pains to prevent encroachment on vital interests that had been protected in the past: Berlin, the matter of "international" recognition, and citizenship. Mutual breakthroughs were not to be expected here, although the disputes were not inevitably barriers to cooperation in other areas.

On the other hand, where viable links could be envisaged by West German leaders, as in the areas of transportation and communication, it proved impossible for Bonn to calculate in advance the exact limits of SED and Soviet tolerance for external influences on the GDR population. Further West German goals were adjusted in the aftermath of "test cases" and by the late 1970's it became clear that a "stabilization" of inner-German travel and of West German journalistic activities at a level somewhat less favorable for Bonn was determined by the two Communist allies to be optimal. The October 1980 currency action signalled that any future amelioration in travel would also depend on variables not subject to West German influence.

To the extent that FRG decisionmakers' expectations were lowered by these actions of the late 1970's, realistic policies shifted to considering the financing of individual East German projects to promote an atmosphere of "good neighborly relations" and All-German solicitude. The maintenance of a minimum threshold of cooperation in times of alliance confrontation, the last of which was greatly in evidence in 1979 and 1980, effectively became a goal in itself. SED inner-German policy remained defensive, as was seen in the 1979 journalist and 1980 traffic curbs, but displayed a receptivity to East-West German official contacts and agreements that were valued for their economic merit. At times East Berlin appeared almost as determined as Bonn to avoid a complete breakdown in the two states' relations.

Here some convergence of policy in 1980 gave some reason for hope. The traditional axiom of unremitting East German hostility to the Federal Republic in a confrontational East-West setting,[113] which would have been expected after the 1979 invasion of Afghanistan and the American response, did not possess predictive power in early 1980. Although an envisioned Schmidt-Honecker meeting was postponed early in the year, both German leaderships professed their desire to prevent an international spillover into proposed cooperation, confirmed their willingness for a later meeting of the two leaders, and signed a $282 million travel-facilitating pact in April. At this time, then, inner-German relations were hardly a faithful mirror of the superpower rivalry, although the West German decision to boycott the Moscow Olympics produced some repercussions in FRG-GDR athletic activities. The East-West German economic relationship clearly played a decisive role here, as GDR currency and energy needs dictated a more flexible approach to Bonn, needs which could not be met with Soviet assistance.

Taking into account all of the above considerations, can one establish that the overall picture of inner-German relations was one of early cooperation and expansion followed by a period of immobility and even stagnation in the late 1970's? The difficulty of separating the relationship into distinct developmental phases, noted earlier, precludes an unqualified answer to this question. Addressing the problem also presupposes that one can state with confidence the meaning of words such as "expansion" or "immobility" in the affairs of two states whose mutual relations have been so greatly circumscribed in the postwar period. Certainly in the all-important area of East-West German travel a general setback was experienced which the Federal Government could not and did not conceal by 1979: the 1973-1978 period, by contrast, had seen gradual increases. In addition, journalists became the targets of SED restrictive steps in 1979, while negotiations in a number of practical areas that were begun in 1973 and 1974 did not produce framework agreements in later years chiefly because of disagreement over the status of West Berlin.

Yet the single most important conclusion to be drawn from the 1973-1980 years is that visible failures in inner-German cooperation were not primarily the result of problems between the two leaderships that were in their essence bilateral, particularly in comparison to the years prior to the Basic Treaty. Of central importance here is the recognition that the status differences of the 1950's and 1960's that arose from East Berlin's demands for international recognition did not noticeably thwart practical accommodation. It should be recalled that frequent past attempts at inner-German dialogue or conflict resolution failed in part because Bonn could not or would not risk high-level consultation with the SED leadership. Among these efforts are to be counted Ulbricht's exploratory confederation proposals of the late 1950's and early 1960's, East and West German election plans of the early 1950's, and the East German linkage of reduced travel hindrances to the conclusion of FRG-GDR treaties in June 1968. Both the fear of thereby granting a recognition that East Berlin demanded as well as the East-West political climate inhibited the West German readiness for discussion.

As was stated before, competing East and West German conceptions on citizenship only impeded the attainment of an agreement in the area of legal assistance; the SED leadership did not seriously pursue its goal of "lasting recognition" in FRG-GDR talks but raised the demand to indicate the impossibility of GDR flexibility at times of East European instability or East-West conflict. The main sphere of Bonn's practical opposition to East Berlin's notion of nationhood was that of consular and legal activities, where the Federal Government tacitly obtained the right to continue past practices. Additionally, in the absence of unbridgeable East-West conflict in 1973-1974, inner-German relations survived the shocks of the 1973 travellers' payment increase and the Guillaume affair.

On the other hand, the difficulties stemming directly from the European alliance face-off and internal conditions in the Warsaw Pact states erected the most formidable barriers to East-West German detente. The conclusion of the Helsinki Agreement in August 1975 was of significance here for two reasons. Having acquired Western recognition of postwar border arrangements in Eastern Europe, the Soviet leadership was at this point under no duress to grant dramatic concessions to the NATO countries in general and Bonn in particular, in contrast to the earlier agreements on Berlin and the initiation of new inner-German contacts. Related to this political fact, "Basket Three" provisions for expanded communication and movement between East and West encouraged the activities of post-Helsinki "monitoring groups" in Warsaw Pact countries, with impacts in East Germany itself; the organization of an emigration group and the use of the Final Act by the creative intelligentsia increasingly surfaced in the year 1976. Interestingly, the escalation of inner-German border incidents in July-August 1976 followed by a few weeks worker disturbances in Poland over food price increases. The considerable interest of the Soviet press in these first events, conspicuous because of its usual sparing treatment of FRG-GDR relations, established beyond a doubt that the issue was far more than an inner-German quarrel. Clearly the palpable freezing of East-West German relations by the end of the year served notice on the Federal Government that if the Kremlin's acquisition of the Helsinki settlement prompted a more restrained use of the carrot, the Final Act's unsettling effect in Eastern Europe and the GDR demanded an application of the stick.

Furthermore, although it cannot be denied that the crucial problem of Berlin possessed an inner-German dimension, it was ultimately Bonn's differences with Moscow rather than East Berlin that produced negative consequences for the FRG-GDR relationship. The Kremlin, as one of the four occupation powers in Berlin, had no wish to relinquish its postwar rights in the city. For the FRG the nature of the Berlin dispute had changed slightly: the danger of an interruption of total physical access to West Berlin had declined somewhat as a result of the Quadripartite Agreement, although higher East German currency exchange requirements remained potential and real barriers. Bonn was obligated to maintain and promote its ties with the city, a policy opposed by the Soviet Government in line with its selective invocation of the 1971 agreement.[114] The West German Government's failure to scale down the Federal presence there which, as increasing Soviet statements made clear, the Kremlin saw as a violation of the Berlin settlement, impelled further the Soviet disposition to set stricter limits to inner-German undertakings.

Finally, it was a succession of extra-German developments that damaged a somewhat eased inner-German relationship in 1980. The pivotal impact of the Polish labor movement on the GDR leadership's October travel curbs was explained in earlier sections. Planned meetings between Erich Honecker and Helmut Schmidt were postponed in January and August at East and West German request, respectively, but neither could have taken place in the shadow of the Afghanistan invasion and then of the Polish events. While various news accounts asserted Honecker's displeasure at the second cancellation,[115] a more likely interpretation is that the West German Chancellor in postponing the meeting made allowance for the GDR leadership's need for time to regroup and readjust to the situation posed by East Germany's troubled eastern neighbor. The probability that such a meeting could have produced significant political results appears doubtful, the more so after the SED's October measures. Even so, the inner-German dialogue of early 1980 gave some evidence of the vitality of the new line of communication with East Berlin first established by Brandt as well as Bonn's importance in East German economic calculations.

---

[1]Melvin Croan, East Germany: The Soviet Connection (Beverly Hills/London: Sage Publications, 1976), p. 48; Frankfurter Allgemeine Zeitung, 25 August 1980.

[2]A December 1973 interview given by Erich Honecker for Soviet radio and television detailed the numerical levels of inner-German transportation, for example, implicitly notifying the Kremlin of the perceived dangers to the SED regime of new West German inroads permitted by Moscow's detente initiatives. Neues Deutschland, 10 December 1973.

[3]Approximations of the degree of popular identification with the East German state remain

problematical due to the necessarily indirect method employed in forming judgments. According to an Inner-German Ministry official, a statistical profile of West Germans questioned after returning from the GDR revealed 20% of East Germans "supporting" the SED leadership, 30% "indifferent," and 50% "opposed." A Spiegel poll concluded that 75% of young East Germans considered themselves German, as opposed to East German. Angela Stent, "The USSR and Germany," Problems of Communism 30 (September-October 1981): 18.; Der Spiegel 33 (1 October 1979): 105.

[4]Fred H. Eidlin, The Logic of Normalization (New York: Columbia University Press, 1980), p. 28; Harald Ludwig, "Die ideologische Gegensaetze zwischen Ostberlin und Prag," Deutschland Archiv 1 (1968): 691-697.

[5]Peter C. Ludz, "Continuity and Change since Ulbricht," in: Lyman H. Legters, ed., The German Democratic Republic: A Developed Socialist Society (Boulder, Colo.: Westview Press, 1978), p. 273.

[6]Ibid; Neues Deutschland, 20 June 1971.

[7]Anita M. Mallinckrodt, "An Aussenpolitik beteiligte Institutionen," in: DGFAP, Drei Jahrzehnte Aussenpolitik der DDR, p. 139.

[8]See Heinz Lippmann, Honecker and the New Politics of Europe (New York: MacMillan, 1972), pp. 109-131, 182-189.

[9]Neues Deutschland, 30/31 October 1985; Kurt Sontheimer and Wilhelm Bleek, The Government and Politics of East Germany (New York: St. Martin's Press, 1975), p. 74.

[10]Press accounts of the relations between the two Warsaw Pact allies depicted a Soviet leadership wary of East German undertakings with Bonn about which Moscow had been insufficiently informed, one prominent example being the December 1974 agreement. Bonner Rundschau, 24 March 1975; Muenchner Merkur, 19 June 1974. Moreover, the doubling of the price of Soviet oil deliveries to East Germany, which took effect on January 1, 1975, created additional strains for a resource-scarce East German economy. Wettig, Die Sowjetunion. p. 143.

[11]Melvin Croan also asserts that "there is good reason to assume that the Soviet ambassador prohibited certain inner-German contacts." DGFAP, Drei Jahrzehnte Aussenpolitik der DDR, p. 375.

[12]*New York Times*, 29 January 1978.

[13]Some expanded bilateral ties have also been effected institutionally. In addition to frequent "working discussions" between representatives of the GDR and Soviet foreign ministries, the "Joint Governmental Commission for Economic and Scientific-Technical Cooperation" concluded almost 100 agreements providing for research and production cooperation in 1977 alone. Numerous cultural and scientific agreements have also been achieved through a June 1976 "Plan for Cultural and Scientific Cooperation." DGFAP, *Drei Jahrzehnte Aussenpolitik*, p. 375.

[14]This apprehension was in evidence in particular during the June 1953 uprising. See Croan in *Drei Jahrzehnte Aussenpolitik der DDR*, pp. 351-353.

[15]The special designation of Soviet troops in the GDR as "Soviet Forces in Germany" was not modified after the GDR had been almost universally recognized as a state, and the very use of the term "Germany" by Soviet officials on certain occasions underscored the anomaly of the Soviet exercise of Four Power authority and the SED claim to full sovereignty. *Financial Times* (*London*), 29 March 1974. Croan, *Drei Jahrzehnte Aussenpolitik*, p. 348.

[16]*Frankfurter Allgemeine Zeitung*, 24 May 1976; Brandt, *Begegnungen und Einsichten*, p. 464; Griffith, *The Ostpolitik of the Federal Republic*, p. 164; Birnbaum, *East and West Germany*, p.4.

[17]The completion of a Soviet-West German agreement on bilateral arms consultations, signed during Brezhnev's November 1981 visit to Bonn, represented one instance of the Soviet desire to seek accommodation outside the purely economic realm. *Washington Post*, 26 November 1981.

[18]Gerhard Wettig, *Die praktische Anwendung des Berlin-Abkommens durch UdSSR und DDR (1972-1976)* (Koeln: Bundesinstitut fuer ostwissenschaftliche und internationale Studien, 1976), pp. 18-19.

[19]In addition to the building of the Environmental Federal Office, FRG leaders promoted such activities as conferences of Laender officials in the city and a number of meetings of CDU members of the Laender parliaments. Ibid., pp. 20-21.

[20]The 1964 Soviet-East German Friendship Treaty, for example, registered the Soviet position that West Berlin constituted "an independent political entity" in

contrast to the SED preference for upholding a "demilitarized free city" interpretation. Kupper, "Politische Beziehungen," in: DGFAP, Drei Jahrzehnte Aussenpolitik der DDR, p. 429.

[21]Neues Deutschland, 8 November 1973, 7/8 August 1976; "Chronik," Deutschland Archiv 9 (June 1976): 670.

[22]As Gerhard Wettig noted, "The GDR leadership at times demonstrated with very minor actions its claim to sovereign authority on the West Berlin access routes" with "demonstrative Soviet support." At other times, however, Soviet diplomats have delivered to Western officials an interpretation that Western access "is intimately connected with the recognition of a Soviet right to co-decision over West Berlin." Thus "the support of the GDR claim to sovereign authority was solely a tactical instrument." Gerhard Wettig, Die Sowjetunion, die DDR und die Deutschland Frage (Bonn: Bonn Aktuell GmbH, 1976), pp. 137-138.

[23]See Ilse Spittmann, "Heisse Tage im August," Deutschland Archiv 9 (September 1976): 898-899.

[24]Federal Republic of Germany, German Information Center, "Statements and Speeches," vol. 3, no. 2, (11 February 1980), p. 1.

[25]The fact that the Quadripartite Agreement stated that West Berlin was not governed by the FRG, whose representation of the city was based on an indirect Western bestowal of authority, underlined the weakness of the Federal position. Zehn Jahre Deutschlandpolitik, pp. 160-161.

[26]Frankfurter Allgemeine Zeitung, 16 October 1980.

[27]See, for example, CDU/CSU leader Helmut Kohl's January 1977 address before the Bundestag. Texte 4 (11 January 1976-27 February 1977): 388.

[28]Soviet opposition to the ensuing disruptive effects of Western influences probably received its sharpest expression in the Warsaw Pact leaderships' assault on the Helsinki Agreement's provisions for expanded communication, specifically television and radio broadcasts. See Gerhard Wettig, Broadcasting and Detente (London: C. Hurst and Co., 1976), pp. 1-55.

[29]New York Times, 23 September 1973.

[30]New York Times, 19 August 1973.

[31]Neues Deutschland, 1 November 1973.

[32]Ibid., 31 August 1973.

[33]Ibid., 1 November 1973. Neither _Pravda_ nor _Izvestia_ included this section of the interview in daily texts, although later Soviet statements called for the scaling down of the West German presence in West Berlin. Wettig, _Die praktische Anwendung_, pp. 18-19.

[34]_Neues Deutschland_, 5,8 November 1973.

[35]See Karl Wilhelm Fricke, "Zwischen Resignation und Selbstbehauptung," _Deutschland Archiv_ 9 (November 1976): 1135-1139; _New York Times_, 20, 27 January 1977.

[36]_Frankfurter Allgemeine Zeitung_, 17 November 1976; "Chronik," _Deutschland Archiv_ 9 (August 1977): 1007-1008.

[37]_Frankfurter Allgemeine Zeitung_, 14 March 1977.

[38]Ibid., 17 March 1977.

[39]"Die zweite Phase... wird gekennzeichnet durch den Versuch, durch viele einzelne Schritte einen Interessenausgleich herzustellen, ein Geflecht von Interessenausgleichen, das keine Seite ohne Nachteil fuer sich selbst zerreissen kann." _Der Spiegel_ 31 (31 January 1977): 22.

[40]_Frankfurter Allgemeine Zeitung_, 9 November 1973.

[41]_Frankfurter Allgemeine Zeitung_, 16 October 1980.

[42]"Man darf nichts tun, was die Buerger in den beiden deutschen Staaten und Berlin zusaetzlich in Bedraengnis bringt." Ibid.

[43]Ibid.

[44]"Es solle geprueft werden, wie dann die innerdeutsche Grosswetterlage ist." Ibid.

[45]According to one account, every third GDR resident possessed a television capable of receiving West German broadcasts, with the exception of the region surrounding Dresden. While over a half million individuals could view the regular VHF channels, UHF programs were only accessible to approximately 160,000 viewers. _Der Spiegel_ 32 (24 April 1978): 41. West German radio broadcasts are also well received in the GDR. Wettig, _Broadcasting and Detente_, p. 78.

[46]"die ja bei uns jeder nach Belieben ein- oder

ausschalten kann." Frankfurter Allgemeine Zeitung, 30 May 1973. East German parents were nevertheless advised by the authorities to exercise "patriotic" caution in exposing their children to external news programs and the West Berlin radio station RIAS was continuously jammed. Wettig, Broadcasting, p. 78.

[47]Croan, "New Country, Old Nationality," p. 148.

[48]"Die jetzt zu beobachtende Entwicklung in der DDR ruehrt an Grundprinzipien der Pressefreiheit, ueber die es zwischen Ost und West tiefgreifende Meinungsverschiedenheiten gibt. Wir koennen diesen ideologisch bedingten Konflikt nicht loesen. Auch Gegenmassnahmen... koennten daran nichts aendern. Und wir muessen aus politischen und aus humanitaeren Gruenden daran denken, dass die Arbeitsmoeglichkeiten unserer Journalisten nicht der einzige Faktor sind, der unsere Beziehungen zur DDR bestimmen kann. Die Bundesregierung ist gehalten, der Gesamtheit der Interessen der Bundesrepublik Deutschland gegenueber der DDR zu sehen und zu wahren." Zehn Jahre Deutschlandpolitik, p. 377.

[49]Wettig, Broadcasting, p. 23.

[50]Neues Deutschland, 23 December 1975.

[51]"Interview with Fritz Pleitgen," German Television Network ARD, Washington, D.C., 7 July 1983.

[52]It may, of course, be speculated that SED delays in granting working permission to a number of journalists in 1973 were connected to this troublesome question of the Berlin travel. Frankfurter Allgemeine Zeitung, 8 March 1973.

[53]Sueddeutsche Zeitung, 21/22 August 1976. The pastor's suicide amounted to a symbolic protest of SED policy toward GDR youth.

[54]Pleitgen replaced the expelled Lothar Loewe in early 1977 and continued to report from the GDR until mid-1982.

[55]"Interview with Fritz Pleitgen," 1 November 1983.

[56]Ibid.

[57]Ibid.

[58]"Interview with Fritz Pleitgen, 7 July 1983.

⁵⁹Ibid.

⁶⁰See Chapter 3.

⁶¹The imposition of "work norms" by Ulbricht in 1953 and the collectivization of agriculture in 1960-1961 served to imperil the SED position. Weber, Von der SBZ zur DDR, pp. 80-84. New York Times, 22, 23 April 1960.

⁶²New York Times, 29 October 1980.

⁶³New York Times, 23 March 1980.

⁶⁴In the words of General Secretary Brezhnev's November 12, 1968 speech at the Fifth Congress of the Polish United Workers' Party, "when external and internal forces hostile to socialism try to turn the development of a given socialist country in the direction of restoration of the capitalist system, when a threat arises to the cause of socialism in that country-- a threat to the security of the socialist commonwealth as a whole-- this is no longer merely a problem for that country's people, but a common problem, the concern of all socialist countries." Current Digest of the Soviet Press 20 (4 December 1968): 4.

⁶⁵See Andrew Gyorgy and Teresa Rakowska-Harmstone, ed., Communism in Eastern Europe (Bloomington, Ind.: Indiana University Press, 1979), pp. 95-96, 137.

⁶⁶Hans-Dieter Schulz, "Versuchsballons in Leipzig," Deutschland Archiv 12 (April 1979): 343; Der Spiegel 33 (19 March 1979): 19-20.

⁶⁷GDR currency needs reportedly motivated East German transportation negotiations with Guenter Gaus in late 1979 and early 1980. Frankfurter Allgemeine Zeitung, 2 February 1980.

⁶⁸Outside of the inner-German trade framework, however, considerable progress has been made in East German cooperation with the West German steel concern Krupp and chemical company Hoechst. On May 20, 1975, the two enterprises anounced agreements with the GDR providing for increased East German production and joint marketing in third countries, with the two pacts amounting to several million DM-West. New York Times, 21 May 1975.

⁶⁹The East German economy was also periodically plagued by bad weather, leading to crop failures, and labor shortages in certain sectors. Such developments

heightened the distribution problems exacerbated by the GDR's alliance export obligations that were all the more intensified after the 1980 Polish economic downturn. David Childs, The GDR: Moscow's German Ally (London: George Allen and Unwin, 1983), p. 92; Frankfurter Allgemeine Zeitung, 11 September 1981.

[70]Sueddeutsche Zeitung, 16 August 1976.

[71]The effect of Western inflation on the East German economic performance was acknowledged by Honecker in early 1977. New York Times, 19 May 1977.

[72]Fischer Weltalmanach, p. 927; Zehn Jahre Deutschlandpolitik, p.29; Frankfurter Allgemeine Zeitung, 16 October 1980; New York Times, 19 May 1977; Neues Deutschland emphasized that the "swing" level had been "restricted and not expanded." Neues Deutschland, 9 August 1976.

[73]See Chapter 3.

[74]Wilhelm Kewenig, "Die Bedeutung des Grundvertrags fuer das Verhaeltnis der beiden deutschen Staaten," Europa Archiv 2 (1973): 46.

[75]Siegfried Kupper, "Politische Beziehungen zur Bundesrepublik Deutschland, 1955-1977," in: DGFAP, Drei Jahrzehnte Aussenpolitik der DDR, p. 447; Michael W. Olzewski, "The Framework of Foreign Policy," in: Legters, ed., The German Democratic Republic, p. 188; Stent, "The USSR and Germany," p. 14.

[76]Neues Deutschland, 29 September 1978, 18 April 1979.

[77]In respone to the Gera speech, a West German cabinet statement announced the position that "a revision of Article 8 of the Basic Treaty does not come into question"; State Minister Guenter Huonker asserted that the Federal Government "holds to the hitherto existing practice" relating to the Missions. Frankfurter Allgemeine Zeitung, 16 October 1980, 20 October 1980.

[78]Bruns, Deutsch-Deutsche Beziehungen, p. 71.

[79]Aussenpolitische Korrespondenz 38 (1977): 298; Federal Republic of Germany, Deutscher Budestag; Woche im Bundestag 14 (1977): 27.

[80]One notable critic of West German legal provisos regarding citizenship was former Director Gaus, who in 1981 stated that the "anomaly" of the two states'

relations consisted of the fact that "we here have still not recognized the GDR internally." Der Spiegel 35 (2 November 1981): 24.

[81]See, for example, the January 1981 interview of Federal Constitutional Court Justice Martin Hirsch. Der Spiegel 35 (26 January 1981): 36.

[82]Frankfurter Allgemeine Zeitung, 27 August 1980.

[83]Ibid., 21 February 1977; New York Times, 5 November 1976, 5 December 1976.

[84]See Chapter 3 and Frankfurter Allgemeine Zeitung, 22 January 1975. The GDR leadership's willingness to allow the Austrian Government to legally assist and represent several thousand Austrians residing in the GDR hinged on the conclusion of the consular agreement.

[85]Neues Deutschland, 7 February 1975.

[86]Neues Deutschland, 3 January 1974.

[87]Damit hat die BRD die Verpflichtung unternommen, die Untastbarkeit der Grenze mit der DDR im Sinne der Grundnormen und Prinzipien des Voelkerrechts zu respektieren. Das innere Recht der BRD dagegen ist hier voellig gegenstandslos." Ibid.

[88]"Es genuegt zu sagen, dass sich die Bundesrichter letzten Endes bis zu der Forderung an die Regierung der BRD versteigen... die bestehende Ordnung des Schutzes der Grenze der DDR zu veraendern. Weiter geht es wirklich nicht."

[89]"Chronik," Deutschland Archiv 9 (August 1976): 896.

[90]An International Affairs (Moscow) article on the 1976 West German election campaign, for example, mentions the East German state only once in passing, despite the fact that relations with the GDR once more became a subject of public controversy in the FRG after the August incidents. A. Tyupaev and A. Urban, "FRG: Elections Ahead," International Affairs (Moscow) (September 1976): 68-74.

[91]Deutschland Archiv 9 (September 1976): 985-987.

[92]"Jedoch gibt es nichts Zufaelliges in den Grenzverletzungen von westdeutscher Seite aus. Sie stellen eine logische Folge der Versuche dar, die Grenze zwischen der BRD und der DDR entgegen den

vertraglichen Verpflichtungen als "Innerdeutsche
Grenze" auszugeben und gestuetzt auf diesen verlogenen
Vorwand, das Recht der DDR auf den Schutz der
Untastbarkeit ihres Territoriums in Zweifel zu ziehen."
Neues Deutschland, 11 August 1976.

[93]"Chronik," ibid., p. 1005.

[94]Reports surfaced in the Western media describing
the East German leadership's apprehensions over a
scarcity of goods in East German towns along the Polish
border because of an increase in purchases by Polish
citizens. New York Times, 27 June 1976.

[95]Ibid., 18 September 1976.

[96]BFIB, Informationen (Bonn: Bundesministerium
fuer innerdeutsche Beziehungen, September 1973), p. 5.

[97]Die Welt, 28 January 1974.

[98]Frankfurter Allgemeine Zeitung, 14 October 1978;
Neues Deutschland, 14/15 October 1978.

[99]Frankfurter Allgemeine Zeitung, 23 March 1979.

[100]Texte 3 (January-December 1975): 11. Like the
area of journalistic activity, however, this was not
apparently an issue on which the Federal Government
attempted to wrest concessions from East Berlin in
negotiations.

[101]Thus only 99 East Germans successfully escaped
over this border in 1979, compared with 368 in 1972 and
678 in 1969. Frankfurter Allgemeine Zeitung, 14
February 1973; New York Times, 20 July 1980.

[102]New York Times, 20 July 1980.

[103]Neues Deutschland, 27/28 March 1982.

[104]The vast majority of escapees reached the FRG
through third countries, particularly by way of the
less heavily fortified West German-Czechoslovakian
border. New York Times, 20 July 1980.

[105]Frankfurter Allgemeine Zeitung, 8 January 1975.

[106]Neues Deutschland, 1 August 1974.

[107]Ibid., 21 January 1976.

[108]Through their legal intervention, West German
officials consciously strove to nurture the All-German

ethic of the Basic Law.

[109]See Neues Deutschland, 23 December 1975, 11 August 1976. It is nevertheless reasonable to suppose that to the extent that a CDU/CSU government would have departed from the practices of Brandt's Ost- and Deutschlandpolitik, it would secretly have been preferred by SED leaders, who then could have pursued a more unburdened "Abgrenzung" policy.

[110]A "Chancellor's Office Study" released one month before the October 1976 election commented on the need for the Federal Government to educate public opinion on the impossibility of securing closer inner-German cooperation without East Berlin's assistance; it also observed that if such contacts "threatened the existence of the GDR," the East German population would suffer vital deprivations. Moreover, the study asserted that "trade sanctions will be carried on the backs of the people." Frankfurter Allgemeine Zeitung, 9 September 1976.

[111]Griffith, The Ostpolitik of the Federal Republic, p. 113.

[112]Pierre Hassner, "Europe: Old Conflicts, New Rules," Orbis 17 (Fall 1973): 897.

[113]This reflex action was reflected in both the SED ideological campaign after the building of the Berlin Wall and the 1968 travel hindrances in the presence of the "Prague Spring." See Weber, Von der SBZ zur DDR, pp. 160-165, and Chapter 1.

[114]The cited portion of the agreement thus read: "Berlin is not a constituent part of the Federal Republic and is not governed by it." Zehn Jahre Deutschlandpolitik, p. 160.

[115]New York Times, 4 November 1980; Der Spiegel 34 (17 November 1980): 156.

5
Inner-German Relations in the 1980's

The dominant influence of extra-German developments and the European alliance confrontation on the state of inner-German relations became, if anything, even more inescapable after 1980. In this context, two issues were undoubtedly of the greatest importance in determining for East and West German decisionmakers the outer possibilities of future German policy: negotiations over and eventual deployment of U.S. cruise and Pershing missiles in Europe and the fate of the Polish "Solidarity" movement. Since the above problems impinged on both Soviet and SED security interests in Europe, prospects for a West German securing of a "divisible" detente, a phenomenon of early 1980, faded markedly. No doubt could be left on this point after the Polish events in August and the ensuing East German travellers' payment increase in October.

THE CLOSE OF THE SCHMIDT YEARS

The December 1979 NATO "dual track decision, which foresaw negotiation over but possible future installation of the U.S. missiles, and the political crisis posed by "Solidarity," which led to the imposition of martial law under General Wojcieh Jaruzelski in December 1981, foreshadowed serious challenges to the durability of the inner-German relationship. Even in the shadow of the currency payment increase and an intense government-labor standoff in Poland, however, the Federal Government in July 1981 expressed interest in a Schmidt-Honecker meeting with "no preconditions" and an August exchange of letters between the two leaders revived anticipation of such an event. Moreover, Bonn's September release of Guenter Guillaume in a many-sided arrangement involving GDR and Soviet espionage agents, East German prisoners and emigrants, and a related West German payment to the GDR, reversed the SPD-FDP government's earlier disinclination to return the "Chancellor spy" and eased Leonid Brezhnev's November visit to Bonn. To a significant degree, then, the goal of inner-German and Soviet-West German "dialogue maintenance" was given renewed force through the treaty and consultative framework created in the 1970's. On the other hand, the Federal Government's announcement of "no preconditions" took account of the SED leadership's difficulty in reducing the minimum currency payments as long as internal developments in Poland could not be foreseen.

The December 1981 meeting between Helmut Schmidt and Erich Honecker in Werbellinsee, East Germany was on its second day overshadowed by the Polish Government's declaration of martial law, a development of grim irony in that Schmidt had reportedly cancelled an earlier meeting with Honecker out of a concern that the visit not be marred by the use of force in Poland.[1] Even without the politically damaging circumstances surrounding the visit, however, there would have been little hope that Schmidt could have achieved a crowning success that would have effectively neutralized oppostion criticism of his government's German policy. CDU/CSU attacks singled out the Federal Government's abandonment of contemplation of the use of sanctions against the GDR for the October 1980 currency action; opposition inner-German spokesman Peter Lorenz thus demanded a return to pre-1980 East-West German travel levels as a condition for further extension of the "swing."[2] The weakness of the Chancellor's political base had emerged to the foreground throughout 1981, manifested by internal disputes with the Free Democratic cabinet partners over fiscal policies and state subsidies, as well as rifts within Schmidt's own party over security policy. A budget-minded federal cabinet was less disposed to finance the envisioned natural gas pipeline and rail-electrification agreements with East Berlin, particularly after the connection between East German withdrawal of travel payment increases and Bonn's economic concessions was made more explicit by the Chancellor at Werbellinsee. This linkage was reflected in the fact that the "swing," which expired at the end of December 1981, was to be reduced to 600 million DM by 1985 in view of only minor East German concessions in the area of inner-German travel.[3]

The Polish Government's December 1981 action against "Solidarity," a decision fully approved by if not devised by Moscow, once more established that the Kremlin was not reluctant to create some domestic political discomfiture for the SPD-FDP "talking partner" when the security of the Warsaw Pact states was at issue. CSU Chairman Franz Josef Strauss contended that the successive unfolding of Brezhnev's visit to Bonn, Schmidt's travel to the GDR, and the military crackdown in Poland represented "a pre-arranged game" which was "a successful master stroke" for the Communist leaders. The introduction of martial law, while clearly not eliminating the long-term problems that gave rise to the birth of a broad-based labor movement, temporarily eased SED fears related to the sustained impact of Polish political dislocations on the GDR population, in addition to promoting some fissures in the Western alliance.

As internal conditions in Poland receded as the determining factor in East Berlin's approach to Bonn after the December 1981 "solution," the question of a possible INF deployment gained in importance for inner-German relations. This was true for the GDR both because of the SED's need to maintain Soviet confidence and because of the domestic impact of this controversial issue in East Germany. Aside from the fact of FRG and GDR alliance commitments, the ensuing debate once more focused attention on both German states' vulnerable geographic positions. A regeneration of All-German sentiment surfaced as well as a growing perception that each part of Germany had a special duty to prevent the sudden outbreak of a European nuclear conflict, the likelihood of which was judged to be enhanced by the division of Germany. This view was supported in particular by the increasingly successful West German Green Party and by the late East German regime critic Robert Havemann, a long-time advocate of German national unity. An October 1981 letter to General Secretary Brezhnev, which called for the neutralization and demilitarization of the two Germanys and was signed by over one hundred prominent East and West Germans, raised the German question anew in a public forum even while popular inner-German contacts languished after the October 1980 SED currency payment measure. In the presence of continuous West German television transmissions to the GDR and criticism of East German military preparations by members of the East German Evangelical churches, a GDR "peace protest" gained in importance on a scale even more noteworthy in view of the fact that considerable personal risk was entailed in its members' opposition to Warsaw Pact as well as NATO nuclear deployments.[4]

East German decisionmakers could not by any means ignore the All-German dimension of such extra-SED movements, given the incompatibility between assertions of "one German nation" and SED legitimacy. Nevertheless, the Honecker leadership adopted a differentiated approach to potential East German centers of dissent. SED officials supplied testimonials to the compatibility of socialism and Christianity, while re-affirming the party slogan "peace must be defended, peace must be armed" over the phrase "swords into plowshares" championed by the unofficial peace movement.[5] The East German Government's commemoration of the 500th anniversary of Martin Luther's birth gave form to an SED program of simultaneous coexistence with the Protestant churches, although church activists were still penalized in a number of ways,[6] and attempts to place the party within the mainstream of deeply-rooted German traditions. On the other hand, those participating in unauthorized peace demonstrations were increasingly subject to deportation by the year 1983; it was also reported that GDR spending for border fortifications in the 1982-1983 period increased by a percentage unequalled since 1976.[7]

CHANGEOVER IN BONN

In the midst of vigorous West German public debate over future deployment of the U.S. theater nuclear weapons, a CDU-FDP governing coalition assumed office in October 1982 under the Chancellorship of Helmut Kohl and received a popular mandate in March 1983. The conservative government's program for inner-German relations appeared ambiguous at the very outset. While reaffirming the validity of the Eastern treaties and the Basic Treaty, Kohl also declared that the Basic Law's preamble, containing the reunification imperative, would be the "central expression" of his government's German policy.[8] Although the new government strove to maintain contacts with East Berlin at the same official level, it soon became clear that CDU/CSU ministers were less hesitant to publicly advance All-German claims than had been their immediate predecessors. One notable example of this tendency was a January 1983 remark by Interior Minister Friedrich Zimmermann that questioned the permanence of the Oder and Neisse boundaries, a contention that drew extended rebukes in the Polish and East German media.[9] FRG-GDR relations then sank to a nadir in the spring of 1983 with the death by heart failure of three West German visitors to the GDR while under interrogation by East German customs authorities. Bonn's insistence on clarification of the circumstances surrounding these actions was soon followed by General Secretary Honecker's cancellation of a planned visit to West Germany.
    In an unexpected turn of events, however, what soon followed was the decisive inner-German stroke of 1983: the negotiation of a one billion DM credit for

the GDR prior to a July 1983 visit to East Germany by
Bavarian Minister-President Strauss. The anti-
communist Strauss' seeming volte face in facilitating
the loan, which was guaranteed by a consortium of West
German banks, verified anew several binding factors of
the relationship. First, whether or not the visit
represented a tactical action, it became clear that the
"floor" of inner-German contacts maintained under
Brandt and Schmidt would not be removed by Kohl. That
the credit could be bestowed a few months after
egregious East German actions to which the conservative
FRG parties had historically demanded stiffer responses
underscored this stable feature of the relationship all
the more. In authorizing Strauss' intermediary role in
the credit transaction, the Kohl Government in
principle recognized that GDR economic deprivations
would be "carried on the backs of the East German
population."

Second, the SED desire to reap economic benefits
through accommodation with Bonn, a priority reflected
in the December 1974 "swing" regulation and the cordial
relations of early 1980, dictated abandonment of the
"hostile image" (Feindbild) of the CDU/CSU and of
Strauss in particular formerly portrayed by the GDR
media. The East German credit balance in 1983, while
more favorable than that of East European clients of
the Soviet Union, had undergone significant
deterioration since 1980. In the year 1983 alone, the
East German leadership was required to pay $3.5 billion
in interest and repayment to Western banks, and
appreciation of the dollar in the first half of the
year added an additional $350-400 million burden.[10]
These financial obligations were accompanied by a
record GDR trade deficit with the FRG in the first
three quarters of 1983, although a substantial portion
of the West German deliveries represented GDR orders
"rolled over" from earlier years. In view of East
Berlin's own pressing necessities, one could understand
the SED leadership's readiness to acknowledge Strauss'
role in the credit arrangement in the official GDR
press as well as the General Secretary's call for more
East German "politeness" in the treatment of West
German visitors.[11]

NATO and Warsaw Pact objectives regarding the
deployment of and negotiation over intermediate range
missiles in Europe, on the other hand, intruded into
bilateral German affairs with the ambiguous effects
that have become such a permanent feature of the
relationship. East German protestations of solidarity
with the Soviet position naturally predominated in
post-1979 SED discussions of European security, but GDR
policy nevertheless conveyed a mixture of conciliation
as well as warnings in the case of a West German
decision to accept the 572 missiles. General Secretary

Honecker had already intimated that "good neighborliness cannot flourish in the shadow of American nuclear missiles" at Werbellinsee and East Berlin later communicated that a failure in the Soviet-American INF negotiations in Geneva would lead to a new "ice age" in the two German states' relations.[12] Yet such admonitions were balanced by East German detente probings which were in part geared to influencing West German public opinion. The most prominent of these recent efforts consisted of Honecker's September 5, 1983 letter to Helmut Kohl calling for an FRG-GDR "coalition of reason" in security policy and a West German restraining influence on Washington's deployment plans. In outlining the Federal Government's approach to military problems in a return letter, Kohl emphasized the importance of "maintaining German-German cooperation in the interests of human beings" regardless of East-West security differences and voiced the hope that the SED leadership would exercise a similar "restraining effect" on the Kremlin.[13] Both German governments were thus compelled to give credence to ideas of a "special German role" that was publicly defended as compatible with alliance commitments in the presence of probable deployment of the cruise and Pershing weapons.

Subsequent developments were to show that the change of government in Bonn was not to be followed by immobility in the realm of practical inner-German cooperation. Recent trade talks, to take one example, have indicated a "return to normalcy," as the Kohl Government agreed to restore the "swing" credit to its earlier level of 850 million DM in July 1985. Future prospects for FRG-GDR trade thus appear relatively promising. Although East Berlin has to some extent joined its COMECON partners in cutting back on imports from the West in the early 1980's, the GDR was able to surmount the difficulties of its 1982-1983 liquidity crunch and inner-German trade rebounded significantly in 1984, with an East German surplus of approximately 1 billion DM. Moreover, West German government speaker Friedhelm Ost viewed FRG-GDR trade in the first six months of 1985 as quite favorable from the Federal Government's perspective.[14]

Not surprisingly, West German promotion of the 1983 and 1984 credits was accompanied by East German concessions in the all-important area of travel. In these two years, the SED leadership successively exempted West German youths from compulsory payments for visiting the GDR and East Berlin, reduced such payments by pensioners from 25 to 15 DM per day, and permitted East German pensioners to increase their total visits to the FRG as well as to visit acquaintances. In addition, the end of 1982 saw the completion of a new section of the Berlin-Hamburg autobahn. Once

more, a West German government evaluated the FRG-GDR
"Grosswetterlage" in calculating its room for financial
generosity. This time, piecemeal GDR measures
succeeded in raising overall West German travel into
East Germany and through the GDR into third states to a
level that by 1984 was only 1.7 % less than that in
1979, the last full year before the October 1980 travel
payment increase. Bonn could view 1984 as a
particularly successful year for visits; all categories
of inner-German travel showed numerical improvements
over 1983 with the exception of East German visits to
the FRG in cases of family emergencies.[15] Events thus
testified to the Chernenko leadership's inclination to
permit East Berlin some latitude in regulating the
volume of traffic crossing the FRG-GDR border.

Other areas of negotiation in which framework
agreements are lacking have also not been devoid of
movement. Of special note is the possibility at the
time of this writing that the two German states will
soon sign a cultural agreement; it will be recalled
that disagreement over the question of ownership of art
objects from the Prussian Cultural Foundation had
precluded such an arrangement. Recently, however, East
Berlin's reported willingness to decouple this question
from the conclusion of an overall framework agreement
appears to have opened the way for a settlement. Both
environmental and science and technology discussions
reconvened in September 1983 and were as of September
1985 still in progress; an important step in resolving
the nettlesome problem of potash pollution in the
westward-flowing Werra River was taken with the signing
of an inner-German agreement in December 1984.

The Christian Democratic-Free Democratic
government, no less than earlier governments, thus
acted on the assumption that desired East German
practical concessions would only be forthcoming with a
sufficient level of West German financial compensation.
A tangible result of the one billion DM credit
transaction was a November 1983 East German
announcement of improvements in postal deliveries: the
new provisions foresaw a stepped-up time of delivery
for letters and packages, the opening of 400 additional
telephone networks for direct dialing into the GDR, and
an easing of mailing regulations. Bonn compensated the
GDR with annual payments of 200 million DM, compared to
the earlier figure of 85 million DM per year.[16]

The conservative government thus exhibited a
certain pragmatism in its approach to sensitive aspects
of the relationship that was often indistinguishable
from Social Democratic practices, the CDU/CSU's past
distaste for the East German regime notwithstanding.
This tendency could also be detected on one notable
occasion in the summer of 1984, when approximately 50
East Germans seeking emigration permits took up refuge

in the FRG Permanent Mission in East Berlin. The Federal Government eventually responded by closing the Mission in order to prevent any further attempts to force its hand, evincing the unmistakable desire to head off a collision with the SED leadership. Simultaneously, a meeting of the CSU in Banz, West Germany revealed that even the most conservative party in the government coalition subscribed to the thesis that conditions for 17 million East Germans should not be made worse in order to aid only 50.[17] Prudence was therefore the order of the day. Faced with the necessity to discourage such future escape efforts, Bonn readily entered negotiations with the much-celebrated East German lawyer Wolfgang Vogel to assure that several would-be emigrants could return to the GDR without facing prosecution.

Other items of contention such as the Elbe River boundary dispute and the issue of East German citizenship appeared less soluble. Inner-German Minister Heinrich Windelen's emphatic declaration that Bonn had "no mandate" to negotiate with the GDR on the boundary drawing in fact accorded with the Schmidt Government's pronouncements on the question.[18] With regard to citizenship, recent public statements have given evidence of an actual stiffening of the East German attitude. In contrast to Honecker's October 1980 insistence on West German "respecting" of a GDR citizenship, Neues Deutschland in January 1985 issued a call for the Federal Republic's elimination of the reunification imperative and explicit recognition of East German citizenship, a demand decisively rejected by the Chancellor's minister Wolfgang Schaeuble.[19]

Such a terminological shift in the East German position accented once more the incompatibility of FRG and GDR national doctrines. Moreover, one can speculate that Chancellor Kohl's inability (or un-willingness) to sufficiently disassociate himself from the expellee agenda for German borders[20] produced the SED leadership's recourse to its earlier maximal conditions. Nevertheless, Schaeuble's assertion that citizenship was not a matter for discussion echoed Honecker's earlier remark that it was "not fundamentally a matter for negotiation." Again, there have been few indications that the alternative East and West German conceptions have seriously affected practical cooperation.

THE EAST-WEST GERMAN "COMMUNITY OF RESPONSIBILITY"

As was noted earlier, events during the debate over INF deployment in 1983 and 1984 suggested an intertwining of the peace issue with an apparent surge of All-German sentiment in East and West Germany. This

identification of security questions with the common
fate of Germans was in fact to reemerge as a prominent
feature in East German policy, notably after President
Reagan's March 1983 announcement of the U.S. intention
to explore the development of an anti-ballistic missile
Strategic Defense Initiative (SDI). Public statements
by separate East German leaders in 1985 indicated East
Berlin's intention to monitor closely the level of
support for the project within the West German
Government, with possible ramifications for inner-
German cooperation.[21]

With regard to SDI, the SED leader's invocation of
German responsibility to resist this specific U.S.
initiative can be seen as East Berlin's dutiful support
for Soviet arms control priorities, given Moscow's
denunciation of the project as a widening of the
strategic competition. The public harmonization of
Kremlin and GDR positions on INF and SDI was therefore
hardly unexpected. However, there is a sense in which
Honecker's advocacy of a special FRG-GDR role is
representative of a recognition of the obvious
vulnerabilities of the two German states in the
military face-off between East and West. The
introduction of the cruise and Pershing missiles in the
FRG, an action following superpower repudiation of the
so-called "walk in the woods" medium-range missile
proposal that the Kohl Government apparently viewed
favorably,[22] has undoubtedly nourished such
forebodings. If West German wherewithal for
influencing U.S. arms negotiation policy was seen to be
quite limited, GDR suasion on its Soviet patron in the
interests of reducing inner-German fallout appeared
even more doubtful in view of the two Warsaw Pact
states' relative positions.

One might therefore best interpret the recent
surfacing of pan-German attitudes in the FRG and GDR as
essentially reactive in nature, a response to the
failure of U.S.-Soviet arms control talks to bear
tangible fruit rather than a concerted program for
overcoming Germany's division, which present conditions
make impossible.[23] West German disquiet over successive
NATO and Warsaw Pact missile deployments also has its
analogue at the governmental level, although the
considerations for Bonn decisionmakers are somewhat
more complicated. Past West German governments as well
as the present leadership have been conscious of the
propaganda value of recurrent Soviet arms control
initiatives, often directed at the West German public
through East Berlin, as well as their potential for
promoting US-FRG disharmony. Yet the Kohl Government's
firmer doctrinal commitment to the goal of German
reunification has not permitted it to be less cognizant
of the probable consequences of a European military
conflict for all Germans. Even in the absence of

outright military hostilities, the likelihood of severe
curbs on inner-German contacts and on practical
cooperation with other Warsaw Pact states would
increase markedly in the presence of an unchecked
European military buildup.

For East Berlin, on the other hand, the
"maintenance of peace" as a policy prescription can be
traced to several motivations. The General Secretary's
frequent emphasis on the necessity "that war never
again arise from German soil" has balanced the familiar
GDR broadsides against "the resurgence of militarism"
in the Federal Republic. In embroidering Soviet and
East German peace proposals, these expressions can also
be read as betraying genuine SED concerns over the
pressures encountered during times of rising East-West
tensions by the GDR, a much smaller state than West
Germany. The increase in East German emigration in
1984, characterized by the reported settlement of
40,000 East Germans in the West,[24] unfolded in the
presence of INF deployments in the Federal Republic.
Moreover, the problem of "inner-emigration" in the GDR,
manifested in inhabitants' frustration at being denied
permission to settle in the Federal Republic, can also
be expected to have destabilizing aspects. Rather than
enhancing "Abgrenzung" measures in the face of
U.S.-Soviet confrontation, a feature of Ulbricht's
inner-German policy, the Honecker leadership apparently
confronted internal tensions by loosening its exit
requirements after alliance measures that the GDR had
little power to affect.[25] Such a "pressure release"
analogy goes some distance in explaining the less than
liberal GDR decision to deport some of those active in
anti-military demonstrations. The domestic rationale
for the East German leadership's support for certain
arms control measures should therefore not be
minimized. Like Bonn, East Berlin cannot sanguinely
face the consequences of a deterioration of East-West
relations: continued high contributions for Warsaw Pact
military requirements, public disenchantment with
enhanced military training in the GDR, and periodic, if
isolated, protests of nuclear weapons. Maintenance of
the "Feindbild" image of the FRG is also arguably
rendered less effective through the ready access of GDR
inhabitants to West German television.

All of which suggests that the notion of an inner-
German "community of responsibility" possesses validity
to the extent that it describes both German
governments' stake in escaping the ill effects of each
side's military preparations. While FRG and GDR
interests are somewhat asymmetrical, both elites are
clearly wary of the domestic liabilities of the arms
race and the external constraints on East-West German
cooperation. Certainly a popular feeling of despair
following both the outcome of recent U.S.-Soviet

strategic and theater nuclear weapons talks and the general decline of detente is common to Germans in the two states today. Given the catastrophic aftermath of German militarism earlier in this century, the shared sense of obligation that war must be prevented would appear to be one of the most positive developments of the post-Basic Treaty era. Seen from the perspective of U.S. and Soviet interests, the immediate danger does not appear in the guise of the FRG and GDR poising themselves to conclude a surreptitious political arrangement. Rather, each alliance leader will necessarily exert itself to prevent the undermining of programs within "its" German area of interest, noting that the neighboring German state may be an influencing factor.

The practical recognition of the need to de-fuse East-West conflicts as an element of each German state's policy, however, should not obscure the impact of a second driving force behind the vitality of FRG-GDR relations: economic cooperation. If there were ever any doubts as to the importance of this feature of the relationship, they were removed with the signal inner-German event of 1984: a public Soviet-East German disagreement over the wisdom of close GDR economic contacts with the Federal Republic. The string of events preceding the September 1984 cancellation of Erich Honecker's planned visit to the FRG threw into sharp relief the latent differences of perspective between the two socialist allies with respect to East-West German undertakings.

To be sure, historians of the Kremlin-SED relationship could point to past policy disagreements on contentious issues, notably during Ulbricht's sustained actions against Brandt's detente initiatives. Yet never had these opposing designs received such public exposure as in the series of articles appearing in the official Soviet and East German media in late July and early August of 1984. Several entries in Neues Deutschland were characterized by commentary unambiguously defending the right and necessity of members of the socialist community to maintain "normal economic relations" with Western states; a supportive article by the Hungarian trade union newspaper "Nepszava" was also given front-page placement.[26] Moreover, recurrent Soviet pieces directly or indirectly criticizing inner-German travel and credit agreements were given selective treatment. In one case, Pravda's condemnation of the 1983 and 1984 arrangements was omitted from Neues Deutschland in favor of another Soviet entry affirming that "the future belongs to the policy of detente."[27]

That the dispute was cloaked in the customary dress of ideological discourse and the specific defense of inner-German contacts was left to the Hungarians did not diminish the significance of the Soviet-East German rift. In risking Moscow's displeasure, the Honecker leadership had given a bold signal that it intended to continue the pursuit of favorable financial transactions with its main Western trading partner. Seen in retrospect, the illness of Soviet General Secretary Chernenko and some apparent divisions within the Soviet leadership on the question of relations with the West[28] undeniably presented the SED with a unique opportunity to voice its preferences on the issue. Yet the GDR elite was also aware of the delicacy of the situation prior to Honecker's intended visit, a climate in some respects made more turbulent by Chancellor Kohl's appearance at the Silesian expellee rally.[29] Consequently, it appeared all the more remarkable that East Berlin would choose this moment to advance its separate interests in inner-German affairs through articles garnished with several "Eurocommunist" statements regarding the uniqueness of each national communist party.[30]

The entire incident served to confirm that the "community of responsibility" idea also encompasses an East German acknowledgment of the economic dividends of the GDR's "special relationship" with Bonn. The urgency of this consideration has arguably increased, in spite of recent GDR creditworthiness and a positive trade balance with the FRG. Here the necessity to import advanced Western technology in order to upgrade the quality of East German exports to meet international competition and satisfy Soviet import requirements is a top priority. Although East German output of such items as integrated circuits and semiconductors as well as installation of industrial robots have been impressive by COMECON standards,[31] Soviet insistence that the GDR produce higher quality products in bilateral trade paradoxically implies greater East German reliance on trade with the OECD states in selected areas. Compounding GDR difficulties is the reality that Soviet crude oil deliveries for the 1982-1985 period were cut by 10 % in 1982; the Soviets now may stop delivery to East Germany of all or a portion of the crude oil that prior to 1985 it received at 1966 prices or, alternatively, require that the GDR pay more for it.[32] While the GDR leadership has achieved considerable success in confronting this obstacle through greater industrial rationalization and conservation of energy resources, it is unlikely that the SED will be satisfied with a situation in which investment targets must be lowered or additional purchases of oil on world markets are required. In short, new developments in Soviet-East German economic relations do not foreshadow any impending major shift in GDR trade patterns toward the FRG but they do add a novel dimension to the security motive in encouraging

East Berlin's dealings with Bonn and should continue to
assure the present high level of trade.

THE FUTURE OF INNER-GERMAN RELATIONS

As is true with most inquiries into the political
activities of states, predicting the future course of
the FRG-GDR relationship is an extremely problematical
exercise. To begin with, the intimate connection
between the German question and the overall progression
of European and U.S.-Soviet developments illustrates
the degree to which independent variables will affect
the outcome. A good portion of any crystal ball-gazing
would necessarily center on the Soviet Union's crucial
interest in as well as influence over Germany's future.
Yet, as a comparison of the early 1970's and the 1980's
testifies, Moscow's stake in detente and perception of
Soviet security are subject to constant change.
Relations with the U.S., events outside of Europe and,
finally, the question of the stability of Communist
rule in the Warsaw Pact states contain their own
peculiar dynamics and implications for Soviet German
policy. Above all, it is difficult to precisely
foresee the direction that national movements in
Eastern Europe and the GDR will take in the future, nor
to exclude that the "Brezhnev Doctrine" will once more
receive military application, with devastating results
for inner-German relations.

It is not impossible, however, to identify and
weigh the critical determinants of future inner-German
policies and speculate on probable continuity in
addition to change. First, Bonn's essentially
supplicant status in seeking less harsh East German
domestic conditions draws attention to future Soviet
designs with regard to the GDR. Almost as important as
the direct security interests served by the Soviet
military presence in East Germany has been the
instrumental value of the GDR as a means to encourage
acceptable West German behavior in, for example,
military security areas. While "the East German card,"
to the extent that it was played, did not prove
successful in blocking INF deployment, there is little
reason to suppose that Soviet decisionmakers will
desist from playing to national sentiments in overtures
to Bonn. The West German intent to ameliorate the
negative effects of Germany's division, after all, made
possible favorable treaty arrangements with the FRG in
the early 1970's. A significant loosening of East
German political and economic links with the Soviet
Union and a simultaneous re-direction of GDR energies
toward West Germany would deprive Moscow of this
political lever and ultimately call into question the
reliability of East Germany as a military ally. In

this context, the September cancellation of Honecker's West German visit was less surprising for its materialization than for the prior room for maneuver permitted the SED leadership in attempting to maximize its own economic benefits.

Thus proposals for an East-West German political association advanced in earlier decades, such as GDR "confederation" soundings and the West German Globke Plan, are even less thinkable for the near future. The emergence of NATO and the Warsaw Pact as military and political facts and the geopolitical division of Europe through the 1980's continue to set FRG-GDR relations in a rather rigid cast. In spite of new possibilities for cooperation introduced by the SPD-FDP coalition, there are fairly narrow limits to the scope and intensity of inner-German rapprochement regardless of the state of East-West detente. Caution therefore continues to be the watchword. If one defines FRG-GDR intimacy in terms of the established categories of popular interaction--travel, media reporting--it is difficult to imagine a major increase in the current levels of activity, especially so long as the overall stability and internal welfare of Poland cannot be assured.

Due to the above constraints, it is quite likely that genuine future improvements in the bilateral relationship will be reflected in a high level of inter-governmental consultations. Given the evolution of a clear West German mandate for promoting the well-being of fellow Germans through cooperation with the SED regime, the Kohl Government has chosen not to devalue official mutual representation with East Berlin. Moreover, such contacts have a number of advantages from an East German perspective: they confine interaction to the two governing elites, hold out the prospect for further financial arrangements, and reinforce the image of the GDR as an equal negotiating partner of the FRG. Other likely forums for further dialogue exist and have in some cases already been explored, including regular contacts between Volkskammer and Bundestag deputies, discussions on European arms control, and increased contacts between churches in the two German states. Trade represents another promising area for institutionalized meetings in view of the economic benefits for both sides and the special tax and credit incentives offered by Bonn. However, it is to be expected that frequently envisioned projects such as joint marketing between West German firms and East German enterprises in third countries will still await SED consent to provide industrial and financial information for the undertakings.

Aside from the technical maintenance of current channels of communication, the FRG-GDR relationship should continue to give evidence of attempts by both to minimize deterioration in relations during periodic crises. Of the West German commitment to do so there can be little doubt, as a look at recent events plainly confirms. Statements by Franz Josef Strauss and government speaker Ost, for example, were distinguished by a marked reluctance to allow East German penetration of the West German Chancellory, President's office and intelligence services to derail inner-German undertakings.[33]

Since the "dual track" approach to relations with the FRG adopted by the Honecker leadership is subject to certain tensions, however, one cannot expect that the East German elite will show the same consistent enthusiasm for "damage limitation" as its West German partner. Whether the August 1984 dispute between Moscow and East Berlin symbolizes an evolutionary change in Soviet-East German relations is subject to interpretation; fragmentary information suggests that uncertainty in the Kremlin aided in bringing about an unprecedented assertion of East German interests which may not be repeated. Nevertheless, two observations lend support to the contention that the SED leadership had reappraised the value of the FRG-GDR relationship. First, East German participation in the "newspaper skirmish" followed the partial deployment of the new U.S. medium-range missiles that both Moscow and East Berlin had resolutely opposed and expended considerable political effort to prevent. Second, the Soviet and East German attitudes toward detente have undergone a role reversal from the 1970's. Whereas the GDR leadership had only grudgingly acceded to Soviet pressure to open discussions with Bonn in the early 1970's, the East Germans in 1984 moved to protect their enjoyment of benefits with the Federal Republic in opposition to open Soviet displeasure. Such impulses for GDR cooperation with Bonn can be expected to continue, not least because of the necessity for East Germnany to stay apace of technological advances to foster economic development. Moreover, the drive for "good neighborly relations" with the FRG will serve the purpose of assuaging a population sections of which are clearly unsettled by East German military preparations, even though Warsaw Pact membership will also demand frequent rhetoric denouncing "NATO war plans."

In some respects, then, it is an easier task to anticipate likely inner-German developments than to predict changes in the broader European or East-West political configuration. With regard to the former, there is little reason to expect that Bonn will agree to upgrade the Permanent Missions into embassies or to eliminate the All-German imperatives of the Basic Law, both of which are sought by East Berlin, just as the SED leadership will continue to formally reject the notion of "special inner-German relations."

It must be noted, of course, that recent actions and statements by members of the SPD have called into question somewhat the domestic political consensus regarding relations with the GDR. The signing of a joint SED-SPD proposal for the creation of a zone in Europe free of chemical weapons, in addition to the Social Democrats' participation in similar appeals with Poland and Czechoslovakia, accented FRG inter-party divisions. Inner-German Minister Windelen remarked that SPD adoption of a "shadow government" role would actually undermine Bonn's dealings with the SED regime.[34] Furthermore, numerous East German invitiations for visits by Social Democratic leaders have implied an SED preference for dealing with the SPD on a quasi-governmental level. These events have permitted the Social Democrats to cut a more distinct profile as the party of conciliation with the East, an impression which the SPD can sustain by emphasizing its role in the inception of broader FRG-GDR relations after 1972.

Although individual SPD politicians have exhibited an apparent willingness to meet the Honecker leadership in its demand for West German recognition of a separate GDR nationality, important hindrances to such a fundamental change in approach continue to exist regardless of the political party in power. For any West German government, concern for the long-term effect of full GDR recognition on the East German population as well as the necessity to prevent an erosion of FRG ties to West Berlin will loom large as policy objectives. It is significant that influential SPD members such as Guenter Gaus and Herbert Wehner have only suggested an exchange of inner-German embassies or recognition of a GDR citizenship after leaving Federal office or the Social Democratic changeover to an opposition status.[35] In addition, electoral and constituency calculations would argue against a modification of current practices by a CDU/CSU government. However, SED attempts to encourage the formation of a separate national identity will not cease. This East German program, of course, will contain elements of both "Abgrenzung," particularly in fortification of the inner-German border and military education, and the positing of a GDR state tradition in harmony with the German cultural legacy, as was strikingly depicted in the 1983 Luther commemoration.

Another constant in the FRG-GDR relationship concerns the Federal Government's perception of the utility of economic cooperation with its East German partner. In line with earlier and currently existing practice, it is probable that the Federal Government will in the future abstain from outright financial pressure in an effort to modify GDR internal or external policies. This is not to say that West German leaders will view trade transactions as unrelated to other SED activities, particularly in the area of travel; the linkage of the "swing" to a reduction of West German travellers' payments was for Helmut Schmidt unavoidable by December 1981. Rather, Bonn will necessarily take account of the effect of economic deprivations on the East German populace and a GDR leadership troubled by a volatile Polish neighbor, by a larger and more prosperous German state to the west, and by a Soviet patron whose political support is a prerequisite for continued existence.

On this last point, the political latitude conceded to East Berlin in its dealings with Bonn under new Soviet General Secretary Mikhail Gorbachev has given rise to some positive expectations after his accession to office in March 1985. GDR travel concessions to Bonn and the restoration of the full amount of the "swing" credit in July 1985 were important instances of "exclusive" inner-German undertakings that the Soviet media had attacked in the summer of 1984. Moreover, General Secretary Honecker hinted at a further loosening of travel regulations for family contacts.[36] Soviet policy under Gorbachev has thus displayed some continuity with that of his two predecessors, under whom inner-German financial arrangements were allowed to unfold even while East-West relations experienced repeated strains. The litmus test of near-term Kremiln intentions, however, may be provided by the issue of a Honecker visit to the FRG, an event twice postponed since Kohl's term in office.

The broader milieu of the relationship is less easily predicted due to the often sudden impact of external pressures on East and West Germany. One can venture few confident forecasts other than to note that the two states' relations will continue to be hostage to foreign developments and programs for the most part beyond their influence. The scenario of a Soviet leadership, either because of engagements elsewhere or the sheer economic costs, adopting a "Finlandization" strategy toward Eastern Europe would seemingly hold out new opportunities for West German "Deutschlandpolitik." Yet it would be difficult to imagine that ensuing domestic experimentation in the GDR would be especially dramatic, given the importance of East Germany in Soviet security calculations and its proximity to the FRG. An alternative, and less inviting, case might be provided by new upheavals in Eastern Europe or the GDR leading to an even stronger Soviet military presence and the contraction of East-West political and economic contacts. Kremlin pressures on the GDR elite to severely cut back on inner-German popular contacts dating from Brandt's chancellorship would no doubt be irresistible after such a development.

In spite of the objective limits to inner-German relations imposed by the division of Europe into rival military alliances and social systems, the crafting of an FRG-GDR "business basis" which has thus far largely transcended party lines in the Federal Republic must be seen as a stabilizing influence on European politics. Due to the improbability of any near-term elimination of Soviet or American military power in Europe, the two German states will share a relationship in which the near and ultimate goals are often ill-defined. Although the division of Germany will continue to pose special problems, the current impossibility of reunification has occasioned a West German understanding that the "second best" outcome can only be predicated on a commitment to participate with the SED leadership at an agreed-upon level of representation and thus at a standard threshold of confidence. The GDR elite has in its often positive responses to FRG overtures perceived distinguishable but substantial interests as well, with an eye to the consequences for both domestic and alliance harmony. Whether the safeguarding of European security and the fulfillment of the German "we-feeling" can ultimately be accommodated remains to be decided.

---

[1]Die Welt, 23 August 1980.

[2]Frankfurter Allgemeine Zeitung, 9 October 1981.

[3]Die Welt, 21 June 1982. GDR authorities had only agreed to ease East German pensioners' travel to the FRG for first communions, confirmations, and birthdays of 60, 65, 70, and 75.

[4]Press reports disclosed the arrest by GDR authorities of East German inhabitants staging anti-missile protests before the American and Soviet embassies in East Berlin. Frankfurter Allgemeine Zeitung, 5 November 1983.

[5]Washington Post, 5 January 1983; Frankfurter Allgemeine Zeitung, 7 November 1983.

[6]A bishop of the East German Evangelical Church, for example, charged that active Christians were refused positions in economic and scientific endeavors and deterred from activity in the schools. Die Welt, 19 September 1983, 11 November 1983.

[7]Ibid., 25 November 1983.

[8]Frankfurter Allgemeine Zeitung, 4 October 1982.

[9]Neues Deutschland, 1 February 1983.

[10]Die Welt, 3/4 September 1983.

[11]Wall Street Journal, 16 September 1983.

[12]Washington Post, 13 December 1983; Neues Deutschland, 10 October 1983.

[13]Die Welt, 21 October 1983.

[14]Frankfurter Allgemeine Zeitung, 2 September 1985.

[15]"Innerdeutsche Reiseverkehr, Deutschland Archiv 18 (March 1985): 237-238.

[16]Die Welt, 17 November 1983.

[17]Der Spiegel (2, 9 July 1984)

[18]It should be noted, however, that several members of the opposition SPD have exhibited some willingness to accede to the SED leadership's position that the line should be drawn in the middle of the river. Die Welt, 28 March 1985.

[19]Die Welt, 22 June 1985; Washington Post, 3 February 1985.

[20]The Chancellor's attendance at the Silesian expellee rally in Hannover prompted criticisms in the Polish and GDR media in addition to embroiling Kohl in a noisy domestic debate. Doubts about his commitment to continued observance of the Eastern and Basic Treaties were not dispelled through alteration of the rally's banner to read "Silesia Remains Our Future in a Europe of Free Peoples." Sueddeutsche Zeitung, 31 January 1985.

[21]Frankfurter Allegemeine Zeitung, 22 June 1985.

[22]Washington Post, 22 July 1983; Sueddeutsche Zeitung, 23/24 July 1983.

[23]This reactive element has been particularly prominent in the program of the West German Green Party. See Josef Joffe, "The Greening of Germany." New Republic (14 February 1983), pp. 18-22.

[24]New York Times, 23 August 1985.

[25]Ronald Asmus notes that East Berlin's own charges of aggressive NATO and West German designs and

increased threats to the peace have often done little to assuage popular anxieties. Ronald Asmus, "Is There a Peace Movement in the GDR?" Orbis 27 (Summer 1983): 305.

[26]Neues Deutschland, 30 July 1984.

[27]Ibid., 4 August 1984.

[28]Washington Post, 11 August 1984.

[29]See footnote 20, this chapter.

[30]See, for example, the August issue of the GDR journal Horizont, p. 10.

[31]See The Economist (January 19, 1985): 71.

[32]John M. Kramer, "Soviet-CEMA Energy Ties," Problems of Communism 34 (July-August 1985), p. 42.

[33]Die Welt, 2 September 1985; Frankfurter Allgemeine Zeitung, 2 September 1985.

[34]The Economist 297 (5 October 1985): 45-46; Washington Post, 27 November 1985.

[35]Die Welt, 2 March 1983; Die Zeit, 30 January 1981.

[36]The Economist 297 (15 October 1985): 45.

Appendix

Table 1

Trade between the FRG and GDR (in millions of DM)

Year	FRG Payments to GDR	FRG Deliveries	Total
1952	119.0	153.5	272.5
1953	294.7	261.4	556.1
1954	434.4	450.4	884.8
1955	583.5	576.4	1159.9
1956	656.7	671.5	1328.2
1957	844.7	838.3	1683.0
1958	879.8	872.8	1752.6
1959	935.4	1062.6	1998.0
1960	1007.3	1030.3	2037.6
1961	917.3	911.0	1828.3
1962	898.9	901.5	1800.4
1963	1028.7	907.2	1935.9
1964	1111.9	1192.8	2304.7
1965	1249.0	1224.9	2473.9
1966	1323.7	1680.8	3004.5
1967	1254.8	1490.6	2745.4
1968	1450.5	1458.5	2909.0
1969	1656.1	2077.8	3734.0
1970	2064.2	2483.9	4548.1
1971	2583.5	2652.3	5235.8
1972	2394.8	2959.8	5354.6
1973	2688.1	2938.2	5626.3
1974	3256.2	3662.0	6918.2
1975	3390.9	4028.2	7419.1
1976	3938.4	4469.9	8408.3
1977	4071.0	4663.0	8733.0
1978	4066.0	4754.0	8821.0
1979	4792.0	5093.0	9885.0
1980	5855.0	5875.0	11730.0
1981	6350.0	6129.0	12479.0
1982	6988.0	7080.0	14068.0
1983	7562.0	7681.0	15243.0
1984	8241.0	7251.0	15492.0

(Source: Bundesministerium fuer innerdeutsche Beziehungen, Zehn Jahre Deutschlandpolitik; Fischer Weltalmanach/1982; Deutschland Archiv (May 1984, April 1985).

Table 2

Travel between the FRG and the GDR since 1953 (in millions)

| Year | Travel into the | |
	FRG	GDR*
1953	1.516	1.388
1954	2.555	2.534
1955	2.270	2.186
1956	2.432	2.259
1957	2.720	2.696
1958	.690	.695
1959	.876	.867
1960	.807	.761
1961	.675	--
1962	.027	--
1963	.050	--
1964	.664	--
1965	1.219	--
1966	1.055	--
1967	1.072	1.424
1968	1.047	1.261
1969	1.042	1.107
1970	1.048	1.254
1971	1.045	1.267
1972	1.079	1.540
1973	1.298	2.279
1974	1.354	1.919
1975	1.370	3.124
1976	1.371	3.121
1977	1.364	2.988
1978	1.433	3.177
1979	1.412	2.923
1980	1.595	2.746
1981	1.601	2.088
1982	1.600	2.218
1983	1.463	3.020
1984	1.550	3.560

(Source: Federal Ministry for Inner-German Relations, "Statistics on Inner-German Travel," and Facts and Figures; Deutschland Archiv, 1983, 1984).

*No statistics on West German travel into the GDR are available for the years 1961-1966, and the above figures do not include the Berlin travel.

Table 3

Inner-German Athletic Events*

Year	No. of Events
1957	1,530
1958	396
1959	624
1960	683
1961	738
1962-65	--
1966	82
1967	88
1968	46
1969	57
1970	19
1971	18
1972	13
1973	12
1974	40
1975	63
1976	64
1977	71
1978	75
1979	75
1980	77
1981	72
1982	80
1983	80
1984	75

*The above figures represent only those sporting events financially supported by the German Federation of Sports (DSB) but are the sole available statistics for these years. In addition, the interruption of inner-German athletics after the building of the Berlin Wall eliminated such officially sponsored events from August 1961 through 1965, in spite of some "illegal sports activities" held in the GDR.

(Source: Wilfried Lemke, Sport und Politik; Deutschland Archiv 17 (April 1984); Frankfurter Allgemeine Zeitung, 31 January 1981.)

Selected Bibliography

Books

Barzel, Rainer. Es ist noch nicht zu spaet. Muenchen: Droemer Knaur, 1976.

Bender, Peter. Die Ostpolitik Willy Brandts. Reinbeck bei Hamburg: Rowohlt, 1972.

Birnbaum, Karl E. East and West Germany: A Modus Vivendi. Westmead, Farnborough, Hants, England: Saxon House, 1973.

Biskup, Reinhold. Deutschlands offene Handelsgrenze. Berlin: Verlag Ullstein GmbH, 1976.

Bleek, Wilhelm, and Sontheimer, Kurt. The Government and Politics of East Germany. New York: St. Martin's Press, 1975.

Brandt, Willy. Begegnungen und Einsichten: Die Jahre 1960-1975. Hamburg: Hoffmann und Campe, 1976.

Bruns, Wilhelm. Deutsch-deutsche Beziehungen: Praemissen, Probleme, Perspektiven. Opladen: Leske Verlag, 1979.

Catudal, Honore M., Jr. A Balance Sheet of the Quadripartite Agreement on Berlin. Berlin: Berlin Verlag, 1978.

Childs, David. The GDR: Moscow's German Ally. London: George Allen and Unwin, 1983.

Dean, Robert W. West German Trade with the East: The Political Dimension. New York: Praeger, 1974.

Dieckmann, Johannes. In Deutschlands Entscheidungsvoller Zeit: Reden und Aufsaetze. Berlin: Kongress-Verlag, 1958.

Eidlin, Fred H. The Logic of Normalization. New York: Columbia University Press, 1980.

Gieseler, Karlheinz, and Mans, Ferdinand. Sport als Mittel der Politik. Mainz: Institut fuer staatsbuergerliche Bildung in Rheinland-Pfalz, 1966.

Griffith, William E., The Ostpolitik of the Federal Republic of Germany. Cambridge: MIT Press, 1978.

Grotewohl, Otto. Im Kampf um die einige Deutsche Demokratische Republik. Berlin: Dietz Verlag, 1954.

Gyorgy, Andrew, and Rakowska-Harmstone, Teresa, ed. Communism in Eastern Europe. Bloomington, Indiana: Indiana University Press, 1979.

Hacker, Jens. Der Rechtsstatus Deutschlands aus der Sicht der DDR. Koeln: Verlag Wissenschaft und Politik, 1974.

Hanrieder, Wolfram. The Stable Crisis: Two Decades of German Foreign Policy. New York: Harper and Row, 1970.

Hartmann, Frederick H. Germany between East and West. Englewood Cliffs, N.J.: Prentice-Hall, 1965.

Hassner, Pierre. Change and Security in Europe, Part I: The Background. London: Institute for Strategic Studies, 1968.

Holbik, Karel, and Myers, Henry. Postwar Trade in Divided Germany. Baltimore: Johns Hopkins Press, 1964.

Ihmels, Karl. Sport und Spaltung in der Politik der SED. Koeln: Verlag Wissenschaft und Politik, 1965.

Lemke, Wilfried. Sport und Politik. Ahrensburg bei Hamburg: Verlag Ingrid Czwalina, 1971.

Lippmann, Heinz. Honecker and the New Politics of Europe. New York: MacMillan, 1972.

Loewenthal, Richard. Vom kalten Krieg zur Ostpolitik. Stuttgart: Seewald Verlag, 1974.

Ludz, Peter Christian, ed. DDR Handbuch. Koeln: Verlag Wissenschaft und Politik, 1979.

Maunz, Theodor. Deutsches Staatsrecht. Muenchen: Beck, 1955.

Meyer, Michel. Des hommes contre des marks. Donoel: Stock, 1976.

Niclauss, Karlheinz. Kontroverse Deutschlandpolitik. Frankfurt: Alfred Metzner Verlag, 1977.

Pieck, Wilhelm. Reden und Aufsaetze. 4 vols. Berlin: Dietz Verlag, 1954.

Ress, Georg. Die Rechtslage Deutschland nach dem Grundlagenvertrag vom 21 Dezember 1972. Berlin: Springer Verlag, 1978.

Rumpf, Helmut. Land ohne Souveraenitaet. Karlsruhe: Verlag C.F. Muller, 1973.

Scheuner, Ulrich. Die Entwicklung des voelkerrechtlichen Stellung Deutschlands seit 1945. Friedenswarte, 1951.

Schierbaum, Hansjuergen. Intra-German Relations. Munich: Tuduv, 1980.

Ulam, Adam. Expansion and Coexistence. New York: Praeger, 1974.

Ulbricht, Walter. Die Entwicklung des deutschen volksdemokratischen Staates. Berlin: Dietz Verlag, 1958.

----------------. Die gegenwaertige Lage und die neuen Aufgaben der Sozialistischen Einheitspartei Deutschlands. Berlin: Dietz Verlag, 1952.

Weber, Hermann. Von der SBZ zur DDR, 1945-1968. Hannover: Verlag fuer Literatur und Zeitgeschehen, 1968.

Wettig, Gerhard. Broadcasting and Detente. London: C. Hurst and Co., 1976.

----------------. Die praktische Anwendung des Berlin-Abkommens durch UdSSR und DDR (1972-1976). Koeln: Bundesinstitut fuer ostwissenschaftliche und internationale Studien, 1976.

----------------. Die Sowjetunion, die DDR und die Deutschlandfrage. Bonn: Bonn Aktuell GmbH, 1976.

Whetten, Lawrence L. Germany East and West: Conflicts, Collaboration, and Confrontation. New York: New York University Press, 1980.

Articles and Periodicals

Andelman, David A. "The Road to Madrid." Foreign Policy, Nr. 39 (Summer 1980): 159-172.

Asmus, Ronald. "Is There a Peace Movement in the GDR?" Orbis 27 (Summer 1983): 305.

"Brezhnev discusses Czechoslovakia at Polish Congress." Current Digest of the Soviet Press 20 (4 December 1968): 3-5.

Brzezinski, Zbigniew. "The Future of Yalta." Foreign Affairs 63 (Winter 1984-85): 294-295.

Croan, Melvin. "East Germany: The Soviet Connection." The Washington Papers 4 (1976).

------------. "Entwicklung der Politischen Beziehungen zur Sowjetunion seit 1955." In Drei Jahrzehnte Aussenpolitik der DDR, pp. 347-379. Edited by Hans-Adolf Jacobsen, Gert Leptin, Ulrich Scheuner, and Eberhard Schulz. Muenchen, Wien: R. Oldenbourg Verlag, 1980.

------------. "New Country, Old Nationality." Foreign Policy, Nr. 37 (Winter 1979-1980): 142-160.

DePorte, A.W. "The Uses of Perspective." In The Atlantic Alliance and Its Critics, pp. 29-59. New York: Praeger, 1983.

The Economist 272 (14 July 1979); 289 (8 October 1983); 294 (19 January 1985); 297 (1-15 October 1985)

"Entwurf Vertrag ueber die Grundlagen der Beziehungen zwischen der Deutschen Demokratischen Republik und der Bundesrepublik Deutschland." Quick, 25 October 1972, pp. 12-13.

Fricke, Karl Wilhelm. "Zwischen Resignation und Selbstbehauptung." Deutschland Archiv 9 (November 1976): 1135-1139.

Gotto, Klaus. "Adenauers Deutschland- und Ostpolitik, 1954-1963." In Untersuchungen und Dokumente zur Ostpolitik und Biographie, pp. 67-78. Edited by Rudolf Morsey and Konrad Repgen. Mainz: Matthias-Grunewald Verlag, 1974.

Griffith, William E. "Bonn and Washington: Fron Detente to Crisis?" Orbis 26 (Spring 1982): 117-133.

Hassner, Pierre. "Europe: Old Conflicts, New Rules." Orbis 17 (Fall 1973): 895-911.

Helwig, Gisela. "Vertrauen wagen." Deutschland Archiv 16 (July 1983): 673-674.

Holzman, Franklyn D., and Levgold, Robert. "The Economics and Politics of East-West Relations." In World Politics and International Economics, pp. 275-320. Edited by C. Fred Bergsten and Lawrence B. Krause. Washington, D.C.: Brookings, 1975.

"Innerdeutsche Reiseverkehr." Deutschland Archiv 18 (March 1985): 237-238.

Joffe, Josef. "The Greening of Germany." New Republic (14 February 1983): 18-22.

Kewenig, Wilhelm. "Die Bedeutung des Grundvertrages fuer das Verhaeltnis der beiden deutschen Staaten." Europa Archiv 28 (25 January 1973): 37-46.

Knecht, Willi. "Beginn des deutschen Sportverkehrs." Deutschland Archiv 7 (June 1974): 568-571.

-------------. "Unveraenderte Stagnation im deutsch-deutschen Sportverkehr." Deutschland Archiv 11 (March 1978): 231-234.

Kramer, John M. "Soviet-CEMA Energy Ties." Problems of Communism 34 (July-August 1985): 32-47.

Kroeger, Herbert. "Adenauer's 'Identitaetstheorie' und die voelkerrechtliche Stellung der DDR." In Bundesministerium fuer Gesamtdeutsche Fragen, Dokumente zur Deutschlandpolitik 3 (1967): 693-703.

Kuppe, Johannes. "Phasen der Aussenpolitik der DDR." In Jacobsen, ed., Drei Jahrzehnte Aussenpolitik der DDR, pp. 173-200.

Kupper, Siegfried. "Politische Beziehungen zur Bundesrepublik Deutschland." In Jacobsen, ed., Drei Jahrzehnte Aussenpolitik der DDR, pp. 403-452.

Lambrecht, Horst. "Entwicklung der Wirtschaftsbeziehungen zur Bundesrepublik Deutschland." In Drei Jahrzehnte Aussenpolitik der DDR, pp. 453-472.

----------------. "Die Entwicklung des Interzonenhandels von seinen Anfaengen bis zur Gegenwart." In Deutsches Institut fuer Wirtschaftsforschung, Sonderhefte Nr. 72. Berlin: Duncker and Humboldt, 1965.

Ludwig, Harald. "Die ideologische Gegensaetze zwischen Ostberlin und Prag." Deutschland Archiv 1 (1968): 691-697.

Ludz, Peter Christian. "Continuity and Change since Ulbricht." In The German Democratic Republic: A Developed Socialist Society, pp. 255-281. Edited by Lyman H. Legters. Boulder, Colo.: Westview Press, 1978.

Mahnke, Hans Heinrich. "Rechtsprobleme des Grundlagenvertrages." Deutschland Archiv 7 (February 1974): 130-139.

--------------------. "Der Vertrag ueber die Grundlagen der Beziehungen zwischen der Bundesrepublik und der DDR." Deutschland Archiv 6 (November 1973): 1163-1180.

Malinckrodt, Anita M. "An Aussenpolitik beteiligte Institutionen." In Drei Jahrzehnte Aussenpolitik der DDR, pp. 134-149.

McAdams, A. James. "Surviving the Missiles: The GDR and the Future of Inner-German Relations." Orbis 27 (Summer 1983): 347-370.

Morawitz, Rudolf. "Der innerdeutsche Handel und die EWG nach dem Grundvertrag." Europa Archiv 28 (25 May 1973): 353-362.

Olzewski, Michael W. "The Framework of Foreign Policy." In Legters, ed., The German Democratic Republic, pp. 179-198.

Ress, Georg. "Summary: The Legal Status of Germany after the Conclusion of the Treaty on the Basis of Relations between the Two German States of 1972." In The Federal Republic of Germany and the German Democratic Republic in International Relations, vol. I, pp. 447-462. Edited by Jens A. Brueckner and Guenther Doeker. Dobbs Ferry, N.Y.: Oceana, 1979.

Schulz, Eberhard. "Die sowjetische Deutschlandpolitik." In Osteuropa Handbuch: Sowjetunion, Teil: Aussenpolitik II, pp. 258-280. Edited by Dietrich Geyer. Koeln: Bohlau Verlag, 1976.

Schulz, Hans-Dieter. "Scheinbar ohne Swing und Zwang." Deutschland Archiv 14 (September 1981): 1017-1021.

——————————————————. "Versuchsballons in Leipzig." Deutschland Archiv 12 (April 1979): 343.

——————————————————. "Weniger Besuche--mehr Devisen." Deutschland Archiv 6 (December 1973): 1241-1248.

Schwarz, Hans-Peter. "Brauchen wir ein neues deutschlandpolitisches Konzept?" Europa Archiv 32 (10 June 1977): 327-338.

Sosnovskaya, T. ""Soviet-Union-FRG: Possibilities and Prospects." International Affairs (Moscow) (February 1974): 47-52.

Der Spiegel 17-39 (17 March 1965-9 July 1984).

Spittmann, Ilse. "Heisse Tage im August." Deutschland Archiv 9 (September 1976): 898-899.

Stent, Angela. "The USSR and Germany." Problems of Communism 30 (September-October 1981): 1-24.

Tyupaev, A., and Urban, A. "FRG: Elections Ahead." International Affairs (Moscow) (September 1976): 68-74.

Well, Guenther van. "Die Teilnahme Berlins am internationalen Geschehen: ein drigender Punkt auf der Ost-West Tagesordnung." Europa Archiv 31 (21 October 1976): 647-657.

Winterfeld, Achim von. "Potsdamer Abkommen, Grundgesetz und Wiedervereiningung Deutschlands." Europa Archiv 11 (5 October 1956): 9203-9212.

<u>Die</u> <u>Zeit</u>, 17 November 1972.

----------, 30 January 1981.

----------, 31 December 1982.

<u>Documentary</u> <u>Material</u> <u>and</u> <u>Government</u> <u>Publications</u>

        Author's note: The predominant sources for government documents utilized in this study were the FRG Ministry for Inner-German Relation's documentation <u>Zehn</u> <u>Jahre</u> <u>Deutschlandpolitik</u>, <u>1969-1979</u> (Bonn, 1980) as well as the Ministry's 31-volume publication <u>Dokumente</u> <u>zur</u> <u>Deutschlandpolitik</u> (1955-1966), Frankfurt: Alfred Metzner Verlag, 1963-1981. Extensive use was also made of the chronologies of events contained in the <u>Deutschland</u> <u>Archiv</u> "Chronik" from 1974 through 1985. In addition to the above, the following materials proved to be of value in the study:

"Anordnung ueber die Erteilung von Interzonenpaessen und Aufenthaltsgenehmigungen." <u>Gesetzblatt</u> <u>der</u> <u>Deutschen</u> <u>Demokratischen</u> <u>Republik</u> (9 June 1952): 447.

"Bekanntmachung ueber die Ratifikation des Vertrages ueber Freundschaft, Zusammenarbeit und gegenseitigen Beistand." <u>Gesetzblatt</u> <u>der</u> <u>Deutschen</u> <u>Demokratischen</u> <u>Republik</u>, Teil I (13 June 1955): 381-391.

"Bericht ueber die aussenpolitische Lage vom Bundesminister des Auswaertigen, Dr. Heinrich von Brentano, vor dem Deutschen Bundestag am 28 Juli 1956." In Auswaertiges Amt, <u>Die</u> <u>auswaertige</u> <u>Politik</u> <u>der</u> <u>Bundesrepublik</u> Deutschland, pp. 321-322. Koeln: Verlag Wissenschaft und Politik, 1972.

"Beschluss zur Wahl des Ersten Sekretaers." <u>Dokumente</u> <u>der</u> <u>Sozialistischen</u> <u>Einheitspartei</u> <u>Deutschlands</u> 13 (1974): 158.

<u>Bundesanzeiger</u>, 11 October 1949, 6 May 1950, 25 November 1958.

Bundeskanzler Schmidt: Regierungserklaerung zur Lage
    der Nation." Texte zur Deutschlandpolitik 3
    (January-December 1975): 9-24.

"Bundesminister Franke: Rede vor dem Deutschen
    Bundestag." Texte zur Deutschlandpolitik 4:
    98-105.

Bundesminister Genscher: Rede vor der
    Generalversammlung der Vereinten Nationen." Texte
    zur Deutschlandpolitik 3 (24 September 1975):
    424-435.

Bundesministerium fuer innerdeutsche Beziehungen.
    "Angaben zum Reiseverkehr zwischen der
    Bundesrepublik Deutschland und der DDR seit 1953."

------------."Statistiken in innerdeutschen
    Postverkehr." (10 June 1983).

Bundesverfassungsgericht. "Urteil des
    Bundesverfassungsgerichts vom 31. Juli 1973."
    Seminarmaterial des Gesamtdeutschen Institut (date
    not given).

------------. "Urteil vom 13. Juni 1952." Sammlung
    der Entscheidungen des Bundesverfassungsgerichts 1
    (1952): 341.

Conference on Security and Cooperation in Europe: Final
    Act. Ottawa: Information Canada, 1975.

"DDR Staatsrat Erklaerung." Texte zur
    Deutschlandpolitik 2 (1968): 246-247.

"Declaration by the Allied High Commissioner Denying
    the Sovereignty of the 'East German Regime.'" In
    U.S., Congress, Senate, Documents on Germany,
    1944-1970. 92nd Congress, 1st sess., 1971, p.
    243.

Deutsche Bundesbank. "Monthly Reports of the Deutsche
    Bundesbank." (February 1983).

Deutsche Reichsbahn im Vereinigten Wirtschaftsgebiet.
    "Besprechung ueber den Interzonenverkehr am 3.9.49
    in Offenbach." Offenbach, 3 September 1949.

Deutscher Bundestag, Sammelblatt 18 (9 June 1967): 849.

----------. Verhandlungen des Deutschen Bundestages
    81, 7 Wahlperiode, 14 Sitzung, 1972/1973; 82, 7
    Wahlperiode, 31 Sitzung, 1973; 111, 112, 8
    Wahlperiode, 166 Sitzung, 1979.

----------. Woche im Bundestag 14 (1977): 27.

----------. Presse- und Informationszentrum. Deutschlandpolitik: Oeffentliche Anhoerungen des Ausschusses fuer innerdeutsche Beziehungen 1977. Bonn: Druckhaus Bayreuth, 1977.

Dokumentation der Bayerischen Staatsregierung zur Pruefung der Verfassungsmaessigkeit des Grundvertrags durch das Bundesverfassungsgericht. Muenchen: Bayerische Staatskanzlei, 1973.

"Draft Election Law of the East German Volkskammer, January 9, 1952." In U.S. Senate Committee on Foreign Relations. Documents on Germany, 1944-1961. 87th Congress, 1st sess., 1961, pp. 102-111.

"Elfte Durchfuehrungsbestimmung zum Zollgesetz Genehmigungsverfahren fuer die Aus- und Einfuhr von Gegenstaenden in grenzueberschreitenden Reiseverkehr." Gesetzblatt der DDR (30 December 1968): 1057-1062.

"Erklaerung der Bundesregierung und Entschliessung des Deutschen Bundestags ueber die Nichtanerkennung der 'Souveraenitaet' der Sowjetzonenregierung, 7 April 1954." In Auswaertiges Amt, Die auswaertige Politik, pp. 253-254.

"Erklaerung der Bundesregieriung vor dem Bundestag zur Bildung der Deutschen Demokratischen Republik und zur Lage Berlins vom 21 October 1949." Dokumente des geteilten Deutschland, pp. 202-205. Edited by Ingo von Muench. Stuttgart: Alfred Kroener Verlag, 1968.

"Erklaerung des Bundeskanzlers Dr. Konrad Adenauer, 16 October 1951." In Auswaertiges Amt, Die auswaertige Politik, pp. 183-185.

"Erleichterungen im Personen- und Gueterverkehr zwischen der Bundesrepublik Deutschland und der DDR." Deutschland Archiv 12 (December 1979): 1243.

Europa Yearbook. London: Europa Publications Ltd., 1982.

Federal Republic of Germany. German Information Center. "Statements and Speeches." vol. 3, Nr. 2 (11 February 1980).

----------. Press and Information Office. The Bulletin 20, Nr. 38 (14 November 1972).

----------. Press and Information Office. "The Week in Germany." vol. 11, Nr. 26 (10 July 1981).

Der Fischer Weltalmanach--Zahlen, Akten, Fakten, Hintergruenden. Frankfurt: Fischer Verlag, 1981.

Franklin, Noble, ed. Documents on International Affairs, 1955. London: Oxford University Press, 1958.

"Friedensnote der Bundesregierung." In Auswaertiges Amt, Die auswaertige Politik, pp. 559-563.

"Gesetz ueber das gerichtliche Verfahren in Zivil-, Familien- und Arbeitsrechtssachen-- Zivilprozessordnung." Gesetzblatt der DDR, Teil I (11 July 1975): 533-564.

"Gesetz ueber die innerdeutsche Rechts- und Amtshilfe in Strafsachen." Bundesgesetzblatt, Teil I (7 May 1953): 161-164.

"Hermann Axen zur nationalen Fragen." Deutschland Archiv 7 (February 1974): 192-212.

"Hermann Axen: Zwei Staaten--Zwei Nationen. Deutsche Frage existiert nicht mehr." Deutschland Archiv 6 (April 1973): 414-417.

Intergovernmental Conference on the Common Market and Euratom. Treaty establishing the European Economic Community and Connected Documents. (date not given).

International Olympic Committee. "Extracts fron the Minutes of the 50th Session of the International Olympic Committee." In Bulletin du Comite International Olympique. (15 November 1965).

"Interview der 'New York Times' mit Erich Honecker." Deutschland Archiv 6 (January 1973): 90-98.

"Interview des Ersten Sekretaers des Zentralkomitees der SED, Erich Honecker, vom 6 Juni 1972." Dokumente zur Aussenpolitik der DDR 20: 989-990.

"Interview des Leiters der Politischen Abteilung des Auswaertigen Amtes." In Auswaertiges Amt, Die auswaertige Politik, pp. 314-315.

"Interview des Staatssekretaers beim Ministerrat der Deutschen Demokratischen Republik vom 13 September 1972." Dokumente zur Aussenpolitik der DDR 20 (1975): 869-873.

"Interview mit Ewald Moldt, Stellvertreter des Ministers fuer Auswaertige Angelegenheiten." Aussenpolitische Korrespondenz 16 (18 October 1972): 320-322.

"Interview mit Erich Honecker zu den Parteiwahlen 1973-74." Deutschland Archiv 6 (December 1973): 1322-1339.

"Interview von Aussenminister Otto Winzer." Aussenpolitische Korrespondenz 16 (28 June 1972): 205-206.

"Ministerpraesident Dr. Filbinger: Rede vor dem Bundesrat." Texte zur Deutschlandpolitik 12 : 119-124.

Nationale Front des Demokratischen Deutschland. Programmatische Dokumente der Nationalen Front des Demokratischen Deutschland. Berlin: Dietz Verlag, 1967.

"Der neue Freundschafts- und Beistandsvertrag zwischen UdSSR und DDR." Deutschland Archiv 8 (November 1975): 1204-1206.

"Note der DDR-Regierung." Deutschland Archiv 8 (March 1975): 332-333.

Panorama DDR. "Attack on the GDR's Representation at Bonn." Dresden: Verlag Zeit im Bild, 1972.

Peaslee, Amos J., ed. Constitutions of Nations. 4 vols. The Hague: Martinius Nijhoff, 1968.

Presse- und Informationsamt der Bundesregierung. Bundeskanzler Brandt: Reden und Interviews. Melsungen: A. Bernecker, 1971.

---------. Dokumente zur Entspannungspolitik der Bundesregierung. Hamburg: Hanseatische Druckanstalt GmbH, 1981.

---------. Erfurt: March 19, 1970: A Documentation. Opladen: Dr. Middelhauve GmbH, 1971.

----------. Kassel, May 21, 1970: A Documentation. Opladen: Dr. Middelhauve, 1971.

----------. "Pressemitteilung, 10 Oktober 1980." Nr. 259/80.

"Rechtsverwahrung des Deutschen Bundestages vom 13 Juni 1955 zur Warschauer Deklaration." In Muench, ed., Dokumente, pp. 496-497.

"Rede des Ministers fuer Auswaertige Angelegenheiten der DDR, Otto Winzer, auf der 6. Tagung der Volkskammer am 16 Oktober 1972." Dokumente zur Aussenpolitik der DDR 20 (1971): 869-875.

"Report on the Tripartite Conference of Berlin (Potsdam Conference)." Official Gazette of the Control Council for Germany (1946), Suppl Nr. 1, pp. 13ff. In Brueckner and Doeker, ed., The Federal Republic of Germany and the German Democratic Republic, I: 47.

Sieben, Richard, ed. Interzonenhandel. Frankfurt am Main: Verlag fuer Wissenschaft und Verwaltung, 1965.

Siegler, Heinrich von, ed. Dokumentation zur Deutschlandfrage 3-5 (1966-1970).

Sozialistische Einheitspartei Deutschlands, Beschluesse und Dokumente des III Parteitages der SED. Berlin: Dietz Verlag, 1950.

----------. Beschluss des V. Parteitages der SED. Berlin: Dietz Verlag, 1958.

Staatliche Zentralverwaltung fuer Statistik der DDR. Statistisches Jahrbuch der DDR. Berlin: Staatsverlag der DDR, 1977.

----------. Statistisches Taschenbuch der DDR. Berlin: Staatsverlag der DDR, 1977.

"Statement by the Soviet Government on the Relations between the Soviet Union and the German Democratic Republic, Berlin, March 26, 1954." In Brueckner and Doeker, ed., The Federal Republic of Germany and the German Democratic Republic, I: 160.

"Statement by the United States Secretary of State, Dean Acheson, on the Illegality of the East German Government." In Documents on Germany under Occupation, p. 424. Edited by Beate Ruhm von Oppen. London: Oxford University Press, 1955.

Statistisches Bundesamt Wiesbaden. Warenverkehr mit der Deutschen Demokratischen Republik und Berlin (Ost) 1981. Stuttgart: W. Kohlhammer GmbH, 1981.

"Die 13. Tagung des Zentralkomitees der SED." Deutschland Archiv 8 (January 1975): 93-94.

United Nations, General Assembly, 28th Session, 18 September 1973. Resolutions adopted by the General Assembly during its Twenty-Eighth Session (A/3050).

----------. UN Yearbook of International Trade Statistics. New York: United Nations, 1967.

United States. Department of State. General Agreement on Tariffs and Trade: Torquay Protocol and Schedules. vol. 1. Washington, D.C.: Government Printing Office, 1951.

"Urteil des Obersten Gerichts vom 31 Oktober 1951." Neue Justiz 6 (May 1952): 223.

"Urteil vom 28.6.1951." Juristenzeitung 6 (5 November 1951): 696.

"Vereinbarung ueber den Swing." Deutschland Archiv 8 (January 1975): 82-83.

"Verfassung der Deutschen Demokratischen Republik." Deutschland Archiv 7 (November 1974): 1188-1224.

"Vermerk ueber die Besprechung betr. Interzonen-Omnibusverkehr zwischen dem Vereinigten Wirtschaftsgebiet und der sowjetischen Besatzungszone am 4.10.1949 in Helmstedt." Offenbach/M., 5 October 1949.

"Verordnung ueber den Geschenkspaket- und paeckchenverkehr auf dem Postwege mit Westdeutschland, Westberlin, und dem Ausland." Gesetzblatt der DDR (20 August 1954): 727-729.

"Vertrag zwischen der Deutschen Reichsbahn und dem Deutschen Reisebuero GmbH, Berlin, Verwaltungssitz Frankfurt am Main." Berlin, 8 July 1954, pp. 40-44.

"Wortlaut der neuen Verfassung der DDR." Deutschland Archiv 1 (February 1968): 166-181.

"Zeittafel." <u>Europa Archiv</u> 21 (1966): Z177-Z179; 23 (1968): Z44-Z45, Z121-Z123; 26 (1971): Z45-Z47.

Zentralkomitees der Sozialistischen Einheitspartei Deutschlands. <u>Dokumente der Sozialistischen Einheitspartei Deutschlands</u>. Berlin: Dietz Verlag, 1956.

Newspapers

This study made comprehensive use of a variety of newspapers. For specific dates, the reader is referred back to chapter footnotes; listed below are the newspapers researched and the time period covered.

<u>Berliner Morgenpost</u>, 17 August 1967, 4-6 March 1969, 12 September 1969.

<u>Bonner Rundschau</u>, 24 March 1975.

<u>Financial Times</u> (London), 29 March 1974.

<u>Frankfurter Allgemeine Zeitung</u>, 3 September 1951-2 September 1985.

<u>Frankfurter Rundschau</u>, 23 January 1964, 14, 23 September 1972, 26, 27, 30 July 1976.

<u>Koelner Staatanzeiger</u>, 29 July 1976.

<u>Muenchner Merkur</u>, 19 June 1974.

<u>Neues Deutschland</u>, 30 December 1956-4 August 1984.

<u>New York Times</u>, 2 June 1952-23 August 1985.

<u>Sueddeutsche Zeitung</u>, 14/15 August 1961-31 January 1985.

<u>Der Tagesspiegel</u> (<u>Berlin</u>), 16 January 1963, 24 February 1974.

<u>Times</u> (London), 1 October 1964, 10 October 1977, 14 November 1977.

<u>Wall Street Journal</u>, 7 December 1982, 16 September 1983.

256

<u>Washington</u> <u>Post</u>, 17 February 1981-27 November 1985.

<u>Die</u> <u>Welt</u>, 12 May 1949, 3 February 1961-2 September
    1985.

Interview

Pleitgen, Fritz. German Television Network ARD,
    Washington, D.C. Interview, 7 July 1983, 1
    November 1983.

Index